Winfried Gödert, Jessica Hubrich, Matthias Nagelschmidt
Semantic Knowledge Representation for Information Retrieval

Winfried Gödert, Jessica Hubrich,
Matthias Nagelschmidt

Semantic Knowledge Representation for Information Retrieval

DE GRUYTER
SAUR

This work has been published with the financial support of the Cologne University of Applied Sciences.

Fachhochschule Köln
Cologne University of Applied Sciences

ISBN 978-3-11-030477-0
e-ISBN 978-3-11-032970-4

Library of Congress Cataloging-in-Publication Data
A CIP catalog record for this book has been applied for at the Library of Congress.

Bibliographic information published by the Deutsche Nationalbibliothek
The Deutsche Nationalbibliothek lists this publication in the Deutsche Nationalbibliografie; detailed bibliographic data are available in the Internet http://dnb.dnb.de.

Typesetting: Michael Peschke, Berlin
Cover image: bentaboe/iStock/Thinkstock
Printing: Hubert & Co. GmbH & Co. KG, Göttingen
♾ Printed on acid-free paper
Printed in Germany

www.degruyter.com

MIX
Papier aus verantwortungsvollen Quellen
FSC® C016439

Preface

An information seeker – in our context usually referred to as user or end user of search interfaces of collections of information resources like online libraries, domain-specific databases, or the World Wide Web – thinks of something he or she wants to find in a collection. "Something" may be of a very specific or of a very vague kind. Search operations are always designed with the intention to reconcile as far as possible these individual conceptualizations of a person's search interests with the represented conceptualizations of stored indexing data. The retrieval success highly depends on a suitable correspondence between these two components. Information seekers commonly express their search interests in words that they think are grasping best the intended meaning and thus promise best-possible retrieval results. The used words either comply with semantically controlled terms of an indexing language or constitute free-text tokens. They reflect conceptual ideas whose meaning does not manifest itself in isolated concepts as it includes a time-dependent context and semantic relations to other concepts. Although recent trends explore semantic relations with statistical and linguistic methods, there are reasons for cognitively analyzing the context as well, to represent it adequately and thereby to provide additional support for automated processes. This is particularly true for information systems that are designed to facilitate knowledge exploration and searching in semantic context by inference or reasoning processes.

Historically, there are at least two essential approaches for representing semantic connections between entities of artificial languages: on the one hand indexing languages that are used for representing the content of information resources, on the other hand knowledge representation systems that are used for machine-based knowledge exploration. Combining both approaches might significantly improve the efficiency of subject-oriented search processes.

Within the framework of document indexing, extensive methods have been developed for representing concepts as elements of controlled indexing languages and using them as tools for retrieval processes. Indexing languages represent common knowledge – or more precisely, extracts of common or specialist knowledge – in a standardized manner and provide terminological building blocks for subject indexing. As connectors between specific knowledge and corresponding information spaces, they significantly improve thematic access to documents described in form of bibliographic data in a way other systems cannot cope with. Modeled conceptual structures reflect familiar knowledge contexts that are primarily processed for cognitive interpretation. They point to connections information seekers are possibly not aware of but that might nevertheless have a positive impact on the success of the search process if proposed to them. Frequently, the resources of interest are indexed by headings that are not the first wordings the seeker thinks of, and only by offering such headings as additional vocabulary to the seeker positive retrieval results are obtained. Traditionally, such relationships are not regarded as tools for machine-supported analysis. Therefore, they are not sufficiently formalized for automatic reasoning processes. Usually, attributes or properties justifying a particular relation between two concepts are not stated explicitly. Relational structures commonly make use of a rather small set of relationships that is not expressive and does not allow making precise, differentiated statements about semantic connections. Until now, mainly theoretical proposals give valuable hints for creating an adequate inventory of specified relation types; there are only very few attempts for practical realization.

In the context of artificial intelligence, systems for knowledge representation have been developed that focus on formal considerations and techniques for modeling knowledge, neglecting issues of indexing and retrieval of documents. They primarily aim at enabling machine processing and especially at drawing inferences on the formalized knowledge level. Expert or diagnostic systems give respective examples. Document indexing and retrieval are considered in the context of special applications, if at all. In general, existing indexing languages are not included; tools for knowledge representation are rather newly created or recreated.

The conception of a Semantic Web marks a new step of development. It is proposed that distributed data resources should be technically combined, and it is envisioned that appropriate ontological representing and linking of distributed resources could generate an additional semantic value from which thematic search processes could enormously benefit. As a matter of fact, some retrieval tests could already adduce the empirical evidence that ontology-based search processes lead to a higher performance than keyword-based searches. However, it is not clear yet how subject indexing and document retrieval can benefit from these visionary and technological impulses and how appropriate strategies for realization could look like. These questions are far from being trivial. This is reflected by the fact that the focus has shifted from Semantic Web to Linked Data applications. These intend to achieve added semantic value by merely connecting existing data reservoirs, making them technically interoperable. Combining cognitive and mechanical interpretation of semantic data for improving retrieval efficiency and retrieval results lies outside the interest of such projects. Yet, a semantic space that is cognitively and at the same time machine-interpretable and that brings together different existing and newly created resources for the benefit of knowledge acquisition and information retrieval is the most challenging idea connected with the Semantic Web. In such a space, information seekers could formulate their cognitive interests and automated tools would subsequently provide additional support that would lead to an improved search success.

When designing improved search environments, it is important to ensure that content-descriptive terms of different systems are exchangeable, that semantic entities are interoperable. Suitable models of semantic interoperability would support both, switching between different indexing languages as well as combining entities of more than one indexing language to execute thematic queries. In case valid conclusions on the conceptual level were reached, it would be essential considering not only mechanical interoperability and string matching but also the semantic content of entities and the relational structure of the respective indexing languages.

The final stage may be characterized as ontology-based indexing and retrieval with respect to semantic interoperability in heterogeneous environments. Combining the methodological approaches to the semantic representation standards of the Semantic Web provides the opportunity to separate from proprietary application contexts. Already developed knowledge structures can be used for or shared with other applications in the sense of a content-oriented semantic interoperability.

The main character of this book can be described as twofold. First, it gives a state-of-the-art report with regard to the mentioned issues. It presents a framework for interconnecting the described two strands of development and shows how they can benefit from each other. In particular, it is discussed how document retrieval and search results can be improved based on an expanded set of differentiated semantic relation types that allow for drawing machine inferences along the relational structure. Secondly, it contains proposals to which extent existing indexing languages can be used and what requirements have to be met to develop them further towards knowledge representations being able to fulfill both the conceptual interpretations of their elements and to support formal inferences for the design of advanced retrieval environments.

This part of the book is based on two projects that were conducted at the *Cologne University of Applied Sciences* during the years 2006 to 2011: *CrissCross* and *Reseda*. The *CrissCross* project was financially supported by the *Deutsche Forschungsgemeinschaft* (*German Research Foundation*) and was executed in cooperation with the *German National Library*. It aimed at creating a multilingual, thesaurus-based and user-friendly research vocabulary that facilitates research in heterogeneously indexed collections. To achieve this aim the subject headings of the German subject headings authority file *Schlagwortnormdatei (SWD)* were mapped to notations of the *Dewey Decimal Classification*, i.e., its German version (*DDC Deutsch*). Within its framework, the *German National Library* also linked *SWD* headings to their equivalents in the *Library of Congress Subject Headings*

(LCSH) and the French indexing vocabulary *Rameau*, thus contributing to the *MACS* project. The results of the project became part of the Linked Data service of the *German National Library*.

The experiences and expertise gained in the *CrissCross* project were utilized within the second project, *Reseda - Representational models for semantic data*. This project was made possible by the financial support of the *Cologne University of Applied Sciences*. Its focus was on designing, developing and improving models and frameworks for the representation of semantic information in knowledge organization systems. The project's aim was to explore strategies for precisely specifying the semantic content and characteristics of concepts and the semantic relations between these concepts in indexing languages and other knowledge organization systems, thereby augmenting the semantic richness and expressivity of these vocabularies for machine support within retrieval scenarios. Many results of this project form the basis of this book.

Initial and target point of all considerations presented in this book are processes of information retrieval for subject content, viz. automatic and cognitive strategies to explore knowledge or to facilitate access to information.

An introductory chapter gives a description of the problems and objectives for solutions, technical details of the subsequent discussion are thus not anticipated. From the perspective of the authors, the selected sample environment has a special aptitude for this objective. For the subsequent discussion, however, it is not of substantive importance. The focus of the considerations are always general problems and solutions. All of the examples of the book are designed to support abstract considerations or to illustrate general methods. None of the displayed methods is designed for a specific example of the sample environment alone.

After this introduction, the text is divided in three parts, each describing a stage for the development of a concept that we call an "ontology-based model for indexing and retrieval". The first part reports state-of-the-art essentials of knowledge organization, indexing principles, and paradigms of information retrieval. Essential characteristics of semantic technologies for knowledge representation are introduced in Chapter 3. The basic features of web-specific representation languages for semantic content are sketched as far as they are of special interest for our context. Besides *XML*, *RDF*, and *OWL*, application-specific representation languages are described. Chapter 4 discusses different levels of semantic expressivity in search processes and how the resulting requirements can be supported by combining features of indexing results and retrieval environments. Limitations indexing languages face in view of multilingual and heterogeneous information spaces are also outlined.

Part B presents in its first chapter various approaches for handling heterogeneity in indexing and retrieval, including citation pearl growing, multilingual indexing languages, and vocabulary linking. Design and outcomes of several projects are presented. It is questioned whether these approaches can be seen as possible solutions for a heterogeneity treatment that human beings can interpret and that at the same time are promoting machine supported inferences. The latter aspect gives rise for continuing the discussion in Chapter 6 by a more detailed analysis of the problems that must be taken into concern if heterogeneity should be solved be methods of semantic interoperability. It is clarified how semantic interoperability should be understood for indexing and retrieval purposes and how to combine this understanding with a model for conceptual knowledge representation by entities and improved relational structures. Conditions under which entities of different indexing languages can be viewed as semantically interoperable are derived as requirements for the following discussion.

The third part presents in 4 chapters the components of our understanding of a model for ontology-based indexing and retrieval by combining the established methods of indexing and retrieval with the strength of formal knowledge representation. In more detail, the primarily cognitively interpretable terms and the established relations between them are embedded into a formal framework of semantic models, typed relations and inference procedures to develop enhanced procedures of search and find scenarios. Within this frame, refining and restructuring their relational inventories is indispensible. Based on first examples, we show the potential of specified, logically valid semantic data being interpretable both for cognitive and machine-supported information retrieval processes. We devote special attention to the crucial task of enriching and restructuring existing indexing languages viz. refining the relational inventory by means of abstraction and generalization.

The presentation concludes with a short discussion of some open questions and suggestions for further research.

Although the chapters are based on each other in content, it was the aim to make each chapter as self-explanatory as possible. In doing so, duplication and cross-references could not always be avoided. Sometimes the re-treatment of a question under a changed point of view was required. The chosen cross-disciplinary approach made it necessary in some places to use an own terminology. The particularly important terminological definitions have been compiled in a systematic glossary in the appendix.

Many colleagues have substantially supported our work and contributed to our findings especially by patient and continuous discussions. At first, we would like to mention the members of the Cologne staff of both projects *CrissCross* and *Reseda*: *Anne Betz, Felix Boteram, Jan-Helge Jacobs, Tina Mengel, Katrin Müller* and *Michael Panzer (neé Preuss)*. We would like to thank them all; our work would not have been successful without their help. A special thanks to *Jens Wille* who set up a Web search environment for our experiments with typed relations and thus allows performing the first tests as well as verifying our statements. We also got benefit from many persons we cannot mention all by name, especially the members of our project partner institutions and other colleagues interested in our work. We wish to thank them, too.

Winfried Gödert

Jessica Hubrich

Matthias Nagelschmidt

Table of Contents

Part B **Status quo – Handling Heterogeneity in Indexing and Retrieval**

Part C **Vision – Ontology-based Indexing and Retrieval**

Part D **Appendices**

1 Introduction: Envisioning Semantic Information Spaces

Indexing languages, interoperability, information retrieval, semantic technologies – is it really worth examining the particular interaction of these rather differing subjects, as we do in this book? In this preliminary chapter we try to give a first answer why we think it is. Therefore we will pick up the idea of a *semantic information space* again, which was already mentioned in the preface and make it more concrete by envisioning some examples. We will take a first naive look at search situations and the impact of semantic knowledge representation, yet without considering the conceptual or technical background. Thus in this first look, information retrieval systems, indexing languages and semantic technologies are treated as a black box, which ideally provides a search environment that can be somehow characterized as a semantic information space.

Examples in this book are heterogeneous and (amongst some others) taken from the domains of chemistry, physics and biology, particularly ornithology. Although neither the authors nor the subjects of this book are affiliated to these disciplines, we will nevertheless occasionally revert to them, as they are clearly outside of our own profession and can be seen insofar as a "neutral" domain, which seems to provide a lower risk of misunderstanding than examples from the less accurate fields of humanities or social sciences would probably provide. However, there are of course no special skills in natural sciences needed to read and understand the examples and to follow the argumentation. All examples are trivial enough to be understood even without any substantial chemical, physical or zoological knowledge.

When speaking of an "information space", one could quite generally think of two extremes: either a collection of information resources that are widely homogenous in form and content and centralized in one storage or a heterogeneous collection, distributed over several repositories and organized independently from each other – the first extreme is e.g. embodied by traditional library collections, while the most prominent example for the latter is the *World Wide Web*. In the following, both extremes and every possible specification between them shall be understood as information spaces.

We begin our consideration with a relatively simple organized information space. Figure 1.1 shows a situation that is remindful of a bibliographic database. The document store contains a number of bibliographic records, which are representing two monographs written by the German chemist and Nobel Prize laureate *Otto Hahn* and one book of correspondence from the physicist *Lise Meitner* to *Otto Hahn*. To represent the authorship of *Otto Hahn* and *Lise Meitner* for each document consistently, a name authority file is used, which contains personal name authority records of both scientists that can be linked to the stored documents. In doing so, one can easily search the information space e.g. for all documents written by *Otto Hahn* – this search operation is often referred to as a collocation search.

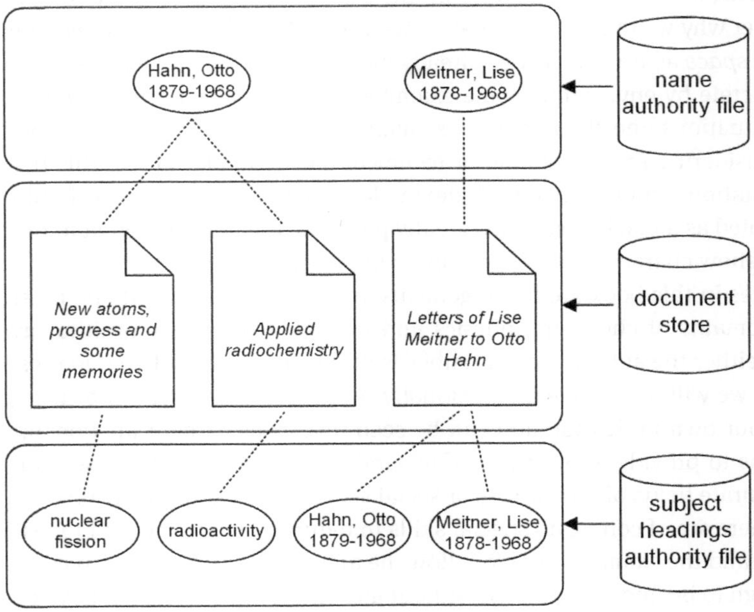

Fig. 1.1: Authority files in information spaces.

Another search operation can be described as a subject search. That would be a search e.g. for all documents about "radioactivity". To carry out subject searches, the information space must somehow provide the information of what each document is "about" – in the indexing context we also speak of the *aboutness* of a document (cf. Ingwersen 1992, 50–54). In bibliographic databases this aboutness is traditionally represented by one or more subject headings or thesaurus descriptors. In order to provide a consistent representation, the subject headings can be organized in a subject headings authority file, so that each subject heading has its own authority record that can be linked to the appropriate document records (cf. Fig. 1.1).

There is nothing special to the situation described so far and everybody who has ever used an online catalog of a library should be familiar with it, as it corresponds to the way bibliographic data has been organized for a long time and still continues to be organized by documentary institutions and especially libraries. However, knowledge representation is beginning beyond this situation.

In Figure 1.2 the authority files are replaced by a network-like structure. The now grey shaded elements of Figure 1.1 seem to become more complex, as they are somehow embedded in a meaningful context – later on in this book, we will address these elements precisely and speak more abstractly of *entities* of a *knowledge representation.* What we are characterizing here rather vague as a "meaningful context" raises these entities from the keyword-based level in Figure 1.1 to a conceptual level in Figure 1.2. We will examine this important step in the following chapters and confine ourselves here to the determination that these concepts primarily can be used for indexing the stored documents and thereby fulfill the same basic descriptor function as simple keywords, but that they also open up a broader context, as they are connected to other, somehow related concepts. In the following, this situation will be referred to as a *knowledge structure.*

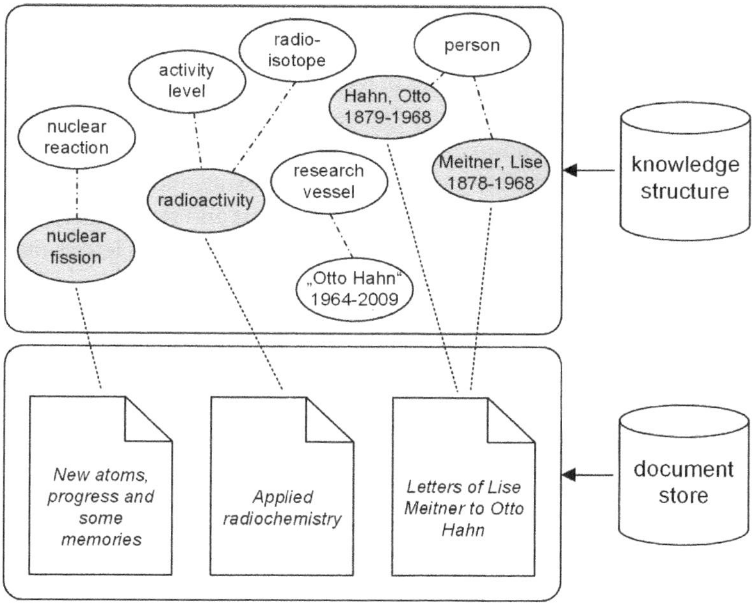

Fig. 1.2: Knowledge structures in information spaces.

Searching the information space in Figure 1.2 with a descriptor "radioactivity" leads not only to the indexed monograph of *Otto Hahn* "Applied radiochemistry", but also to the related descriptors "activity level" and "radioisotope". It becomes apparent that an information seeker, who is interested in "radioactivity", could also be interested in certain levels of radioactivity or in concrete radioactive isotopes. The same seems to apply to "nuclear fission" and "nuclear reaction" – it isn't unlikely that an information seeker with an interest in nuclear fission may also be interested in other nuclear reactions. Beyond that, the knowledge structure of Figure 1.2 also establishes a relationship between *Otto Hahn* and the rather abstract concept "person" explicit, as well as between *Otto Hahn's* research colleague *Lise Meitner* and "person". As a human there's no difficulty in the cognitive interpretation of these relations – we can easily see that *Otto Hahn* and *Lise Meitner* are persons, even if we never heard their names before. By using semantic technologies, this knowledge can be made machine-readable, so that it would be able to infer (Glossary C3.2) that *Otto Hahn* is a person due to the fact that the concept "Hahn, Otto" is related to the concept "person" in a specific way. Likewise the risk of confusing the person *Otto Hahn* with the homonymous research vessel, which was launched in 1964 and named after the famous scientist, could be avoided.

At this point we have already mentioned many aspects and reached to the core issues of this book. In the following, we will take a closer look at searches in information spaces and the underlying information retrieval processes and therefore give a first impression of the usefulness of relations like the above described. We will also look at the interdependency between indexing and information retrieval processes, introduce *Knowledge Organization Systems* (KOSs) as types of knowledge structures that are designed to support indexing and retrieval and finally concern questions like how it could be made explicit and recognizable for a KOS that a document "Letters of *Lise Meitner* to *Otto Hahn*" is about letters that *Lise Meitner* wrote to *Otto Hahn* and not vice versa.

Based on this, we will provide a more systematic discussion of the specific types of relations and their functionality within and between knowledge structures – later on we will speak of them as *intra-* and *intersystem relations*. Yet, before that, some preliminary considerations will be provided, in order to facilitate a better understanding of the mentioned issues.

Accordingly, we will address the functionality of *intersystem relations*, i.e., those relations that are bridging two knowledge structures and therefore make them somehow interoperable. In this context, we will focus on the problems of heterogeneity that may arise e.g. from the use of different knowledge structures for indexing purposes. This is denoted in Figure 1.3, where single concepts of our introduced example knowledge structure are linked to other, really existing structures, namely the *Library of Congress Subject Headings (LCSH)*, the *International Nuclear Information System / Energy Technology Data Exchange (INIS/ETDE)*, and the *YAGO* project.

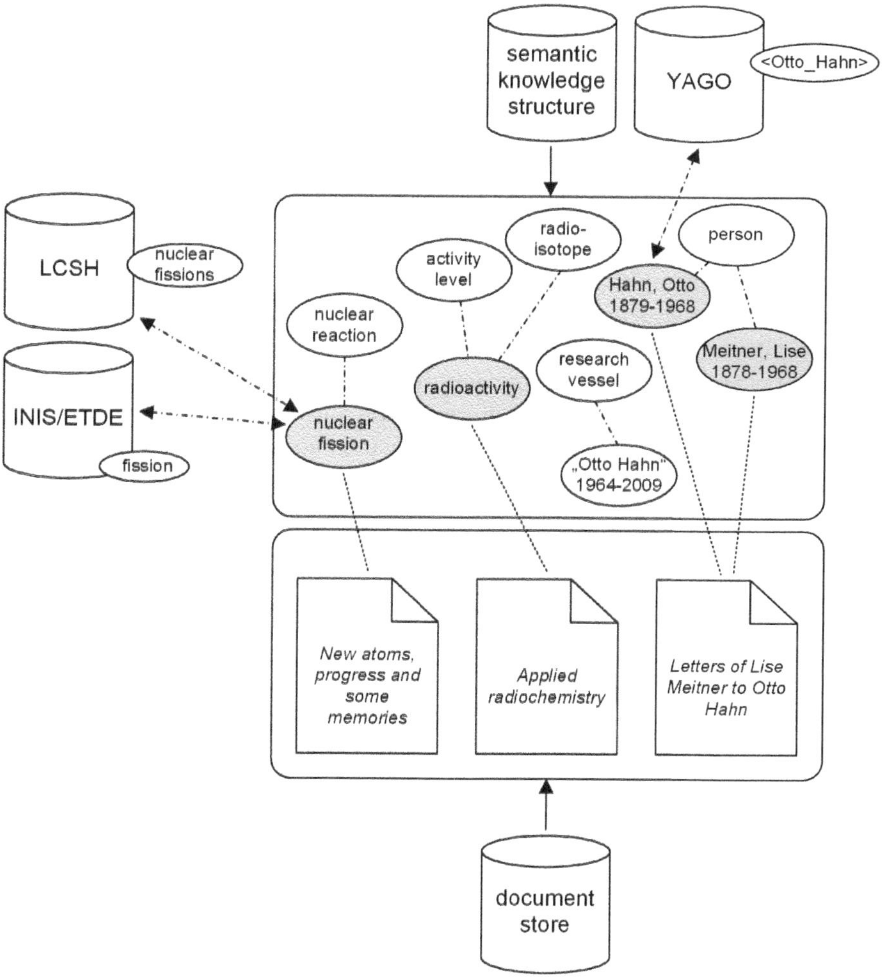

Fig. 1.3: Interoperability in information spaces.

These three structures, which were arbitrary selected for this example, are quite different in their organization, coverage and purpose. The *LCSH* can be characterized as an authority file, *INIS/ETDE* is a thesaurus that has been developed and used by the *International Atomic Energy Agency (IAEA)*[1], and *YAGO* is an ontology mainly built up with vocabulary from the *Wikipedia*[2]. Since we haven't

1 http://www.iaea.org/inis/products-services/thesaurus
2 http://www.mpi-inf.mpg.de/yago-naga/yago

introduced the thesaurus and the ontology as two essential types of knowledge representation yet, we won't stress the differences between these structures here and now. Instead, we simply assert that concepts of one structure can also be part of another structure, as denoted in Figure 1.3, were the concept "nuclear fission" also seems to appear as "fission" in *INIS/ETDE* and as "nuclear fissions" in the *LCSH*, while "Hahn, Otto" also appears as "Otto_Hahn" in *YAGO*.

What we don't know is, in which particular contexts these concepts are embedded in and if the meaning of these concepts really corresponds to the meaning in our example structure. This would be important to know, if we wanted to integrate these structures in a search about, e.g., "nuclear fission" in order to find more documents from other information spaces. Later on, we will summarize a number of vocabulary linking projects that have approached these questions.

Beyond that, we will raise the more general question of how the meaning of knowledge structure relations can be made machine-readable by using semantic technologies. This question holds the most important potential for the envisioning of a "semantic" information space. Several web-based representation languages have been continuously developed by the *World Wide Web Consortium (W3C)* to make the notion of a *Semantic Web* increasingly real. We will provide a close discussion of this potential on the basis of encoding examples for annotating semantic information to a given structure.

Taking all mentioned aspects into account, the idea of an information space arises, which could be described with the simplified view of Figure 1.4. Our document store is now accessible through a semantic knowledge structure. The elements of this structure can be used as descriptors for indexing purposes, but furthermore the meaning of each relationship between the structure's elements is made machine-readable via semantic technologies. Thus a KOS application would be able to understand e.g. the kind of relationship between "nuclear reaction" and "nuclear fission" (of course the latter is a special type of the former – consequently all searches about "nuclear reaction" would automatically include "nuclear fission").

Furthermore, highly specific searches could be conducted, e.g., "Every person born in 1879, who received letters from Lise Meitner" – one can easily see that in Figure 1.4 this would match to "Otto Hahn". By using semantic annotation techniques we cannot only make the simple fact machine-readable that *Otto Hahn* is a person, but also add some relevant attributes as e.g. the years of birth and death to our knowledge structure. The information that *Otto Hahn* received letters from *Lise Meitner* (and not vice versa) would be provided by an expressive indexing of the linked document "Letters of Lise Meitner to Otto Hahn".

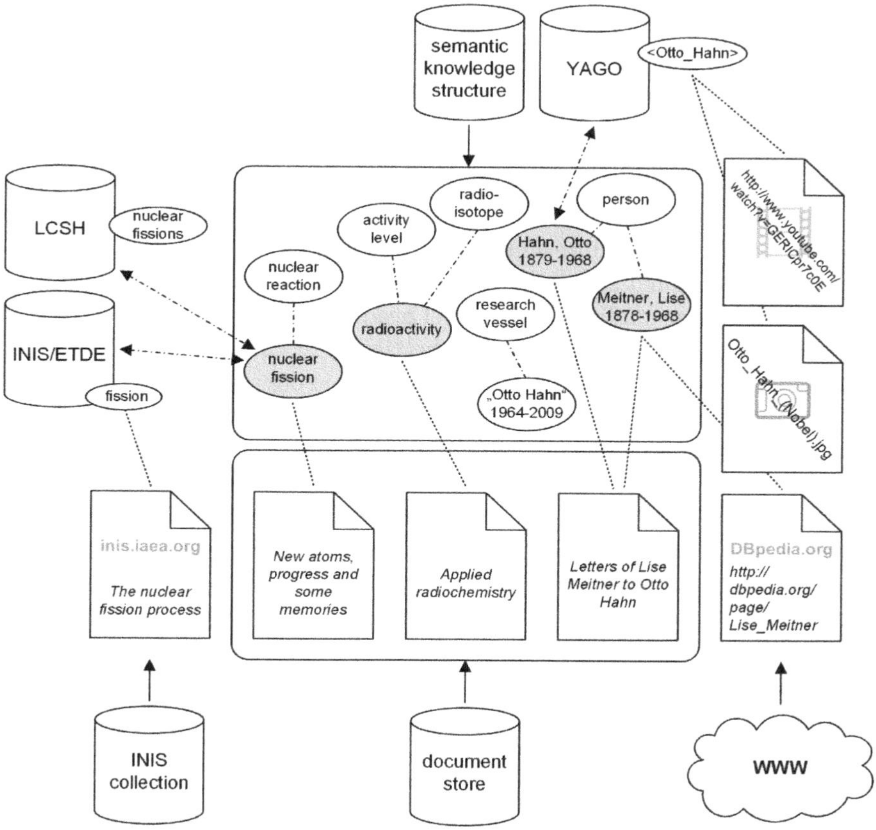

Fig. 1.4: Semantics and linked data in information spaces.

As the element "Otto Hahn" of our knowledge structure is interoperable, we can considerably expand the information space by "moving" into another knowledge structure, e.g. the *YAGO* ontology, where we find direct linkages to a video file and a photograph of *Otto Hahn*. Our own knowledge structure could provide linkages to web resources likewise, as demonstrated on the element "Lise Meitner", which is linked to a *DBpedia* site about *Lise Meitner* (cf. Fig. 1.4).

Projects like *DBpedia*[3] are promoting the idea of linked open data, that is a growing network of semantic annotated web resources, which are addressable through individual identifiers (URIs) (cf. Bizer et al. 2009). Nevertheless, we don't see the linked open data initiative as an adequate approach of knowledge rep-

3 The *DBpedia* project pursues the goal of extracting data from the *Wikipedia* and making it available on the *WWW* in a meaningful structure. Cf. http://dbpedia.org

resentation, but merely as a network of data reservoirs that can be addressed by knowledge representation. Applied to our example of an information space, the linked open data concept could be interpreted as a "middle layer" between knowledge representation and concrete information resources on the web.

Our semantic information space could also be amended by more conventional data reservoirs, such as library catalogs or other bibliographic databases. By providing interoperability between the element "nuclear fission" in our example knowledge structure and the descriptor "fission" in the *INIS/ETDE* thesaurus, a search could also be extended to the *INIS* bibliographic collection of the *IAEA*. The same applies to the subject heading "nuclear fissions" within the *LCSH*, which allows us to include e.g. the Library of Congress catalog or other *LCSH* indexed and web accessible library catalogs in our search.

The interaction of information retrieval and expressive indexing methods, semantic technologies and interoperability as outlined in Figure 1.4 is, of course, a visionary one, while the number of realized projects that revert at least to some of the here introduced functionalities is quite small. One relevant example is the *DOPE* project ("Drug Ontology Project for Elsevier"), an information system providing access to multiple information sources of the life sciences domain (Stuckenschmidt et al. 2004). The goal of *DOPE* is to allow an explorative searching over various, heterogeneous information spaces via one single interface. Therefore *DOPE* uses the semantic web standard *RDF*, which we will get to know later on in this book, and generates *RDF*-based representations of selected metadata and keywords, which were extracted from the considered information spaces. Consequently, *RDF* representations are well suited for accessing distributed stored resources. In addition, adequate knowledge structures, which are embedded in the *DOPE* environment to support search processes, are encoded in *RDF*, too. The crucial advantages of using the *RDF* standard in *DOPE* are lying in the potential of using semantic annotations (as described above in our example about *Otto Hahn* and *Lise Meitner*), as well as in handling heterogeneity between the individual knowledge structures and information spaces by making them at least technically interoperable (cf. ibid.).

A *DOPE* prototype was built, addressing large collections of about five million abstracts and 500,000 full-text articles from the databases *Medline* and *ScienceDirect*[4] that were indexed with descriptor vocabulary of the *Emtree thesaurus*, an extensive knowledge structure, containing more than 56,000 descriptors[5] (cf. ibid.). Stuckenschmidt et al. conducted a small user study of this prototype and received predominantly positive feedback, which indicated the practical rel-

4 http://www.ncbi.nlm.nih.gov/pudmed and http://www.sciencedirect.com
5 http://www.elsevier.com/bibligraphic-database/emtree

evance of integrated, semantically enhanced information systems like *DOPE* (cf. ibid., 38–39).

Having named an example that approximates our conceptions of a semantic information space, it seems appropriate to draw a clear borderline between these conceptions and the role of knowledge representation in the field of artificial intelligence, which must not be confused with the use cases described in this book.

While we understand knowledge representation as the subsumption of methods and techniques to represent the aboutness of information resources, we must distinguish this from the understanding of knowledge representation in the sense of a formalized knowledge base, as it is used e.g. in so-called *expert systems* or decision support systems[6]. Those systems are not designed for providing access to information resources, but to derive assertions from their particular knowledge bases. One example for such an assertional system is the *Cyc* project resp. its open source variation *OpenCyc*[7]. The goal of *Cyc* is to build an extensive knowledge base that contains a store of formalized general knowledge suitable for various reasoning and problem-solving tasks in various domains (cf. Matuszek et al. 2006, 44). In the following, we will illustrate the functionality of *OpenCyc* representative for many other formalized knowledge bases by using a simple example to make the fundamental differences between formalized knowledge representation and knowledge representation in document-oriented information spaces transparent.

Let "fissionable materials" be a given information need – if one would communicate this information need to an information space as denoted in Figure 1.4, the result would be a set of various documents from different sources that have ideally one thing in common: an aboutness somehow related to the subject of fissionable materials. Communicating this information need to a knowledge base like *OpenCyc*, the result would not be a set of documents, but one or more somehow derived assertions about fissionable materials. What kind of assertions one can expect, depends mainly on what kind of knowledge is stored.

6 We have tackled this distinction already in Chapter 1.

7 http://www.cyc.com/platform/opencyc

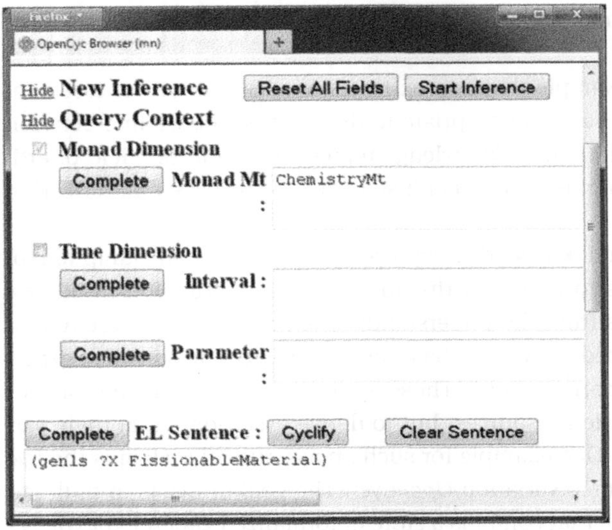

Fig. 1.5: Querying in *OpenCyc*.

The screenshot in Figure 1.5 shows an example for querying in *OpenCyc*. The user is going to submit his information need about fissionable materials to the system, with the intention to receive some useful assertions about this subject. Therefore he must consider some syntactical rules while formulating his question – *OpenCyc* would not understand a natural language question like "what do you know about fissionable materials?", so he describes the information need in a formalized way, corresponding to the syntactical requirements of *OpenCyc's* language "*CycL*" (cf. ibid.). This could lead to a statement like:

```
(genls ?X Fissionable Material)
```

Without going into the details of the *CycL* language, it is said that the above statement would deliver assertions by deriving them from the generic relationships modeled in the knowledge base from the object FissionableMaterial to other objects (this is effected by the genls statement) and loading them into a variable ?X. The Parameter "ChemistryMt" tells *OpenCyc* that this question shall be answered using a particular part of the *OpenCyc* knowledge base that stores formalized knowledge about chemistry.

The screenshot in Figure 1.6 shows the results. Again, we won't analyze this screenshot in detail, but would like to just mention the fact that the result is a different one than we would expect in a document-oriented information space, as it doesn't consist of documents but of a number of statements about fissionable materials, derived from the particular part of the *OpenCyc* knowledge base containing chemical knowledge. By clicking on the "explain" link in front of the every statement, we can follow the assertion process in a new window, shown in Figure 1.7 using the example of the "(IsotopeFn Plutonium 241)" statement of Figure 1.6.

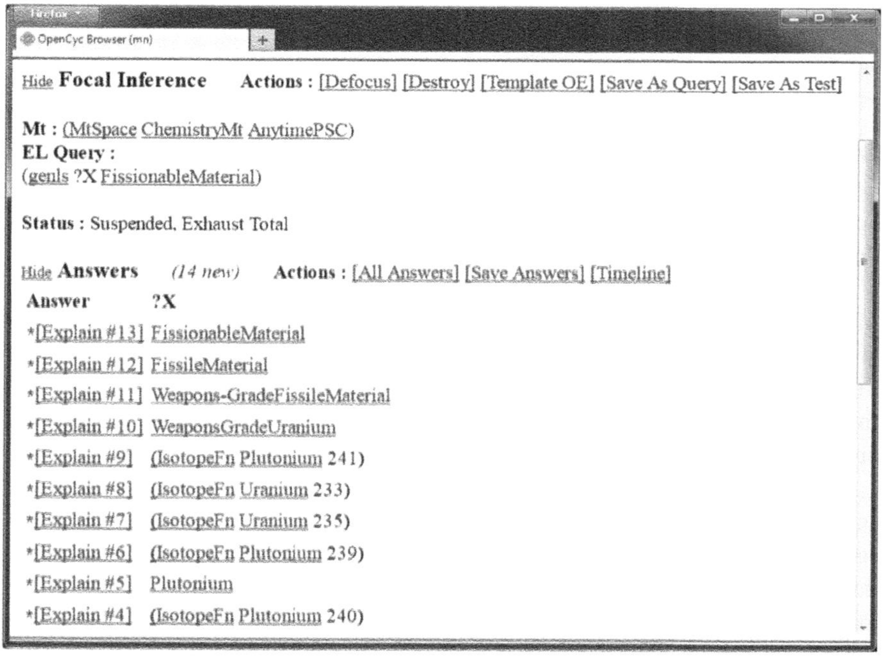

Fig. 1.6: Result set in *OpenCyc*.

In Figure 1.7 we see just under "Justifications" that the element plutonium with a mass number of 241 (in *OpenCyc* written as "(IsotopeFn Plutonium 241)") is related via genls to "FissionableMaterial". Thus *OpenCyc* infers from this statement that the element plutonium with the mass number of 241 (or – as the result in Figure 1.6 shows – with the mass numbers 233, 235, 239, or 240, or without a specific mass number) holds the characteristics of fissionable material.

Please note that in a document-oriented information system we would not receive such information within the knowledge representation. Through these systems we could only find access to specific information resources, which may contain this information in a textual, visual, or audio form. The understanding of this fundamental difference seems important to us to prevent wrong exceptions about the role of knowledge representation in this book.

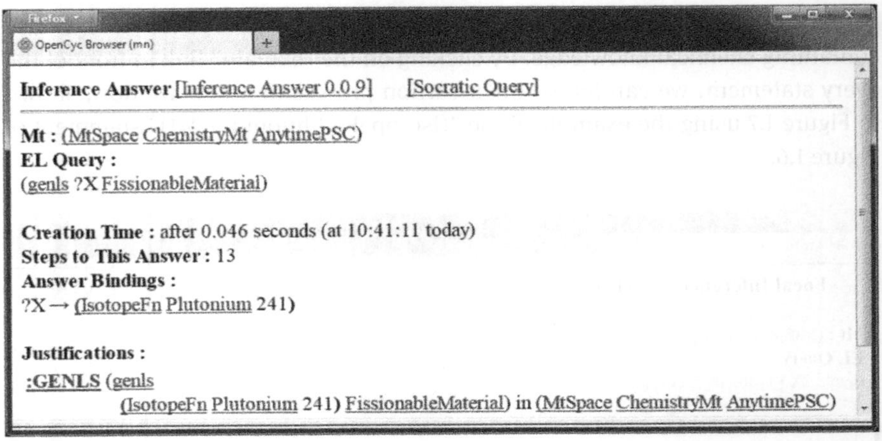

Fig. 1.7: Explanation in *OpenCyc*.

After finishing this excursion to formalized knowledge representation, we may get back to document-oriented knowledge representation and the envisioned information space in Figure 1.4. It remains to say that the single modules of which this vision could be realized and which are introduced in the following chapters, are rather different in age, sophistication, and popularity.

Some ideas about expressive indexing methods have their origins in library science and can be dated back far into the last century. In contrast, the vision of a semantic web and the spectrum of appropriate semantic technologies have been developed in the recent past and drew not only the interest of informatics, but of many different research communities. Eventually, the considerations about providing interoperability in different environments with heterogeneous indexing data emerged at least partially from our own project experiences. The innovative potential of our semantic information space now lies in the combination of these different ideas and approaches. In the following we will try to sharpen this potential.

Part A

Propaedeutics – Organizing, Representing, and Exploring Knowledge

2 Indexing and Knowledge Organization

In this chapter we will provide an introduction in the organization of knowledge for indexing purposes. We will define indexing languages as a KOS application for indexing purposes and take a closer look on the abstract modeling principles of a KOS intended for indexing. Beyond that, we will give a brief overview of *ISO 25964*, as an example of a prominent standard for the design and development of KOSs and of the *Functional Requirements for Subject Authority Data (FRSAD)*, as an example of a KOS modeling framework.

2.1 Knowledge Organization Systems as Indexing Languages

To begin with, two definitions from the previous chapter are worth to be repeated. We have stated that we understand knowledge representation as the subsumption of methods and techniques to represent the aboutness of information resources – or, as expressed from now on: the *topics* (Glossary A4) which an information resource is about. We have also said that a KOS is a type of knowledge structure, being designed to support indexing and retrieval processes. As knowledge structures, and therefore KOSs, consist of nothing else but knowledge representations, a KOS can be identified as an instrument for indexing and retrieving information resources. Thus, making information search- and findable is a key motivation for the design and application of a KOS (Dextre Clarke 2011). In the following, we will address this process of making information search- and findable – referred to as indexing – and its interdependency with KOSs more detailed.

According to *ISO 5963* (1985), indexing is the process of identifying and describing the subject content (i.e. the topics) of a document (i.e. an information resource). We have illustrated this process in the previous chapter by a number of simple examples, in which concepts taken from a knowledge structure (resp. a KOS) were used as descriptors representing the topics of information resources. Therefore the KOS itself can be seen as an *indexing language*, as it provides a collection of descriptors for indexing purposes – when we speak about an indexing language in the following, we're thinking of a KOS that is used for indexing. In this context, the type of KOS makes the difference of how descriptors are represented (e.g. in natural or artificial language) and how they are provided and assigned to an information resource in an indexing process (e.g. free or rule-based).

Hodge (2000) gives a fundamental typification of KOSs, when he states that KOSs "include classification and categorization schemes that organize materials at a general level, subject headings that provide more detailed access" as well as "authority files that control variant versions of key information such as geographic names and personal names" and "highly structured vocabularies, such as thesauri [...] semantic networks and ontologies". Other presentations, e.g. in (Stock 2010), are also referring to this listing of KOS types. In the following, we will set aside from discussing these well-known KOS types in detail and reference to basic KOS-related literature, e.g., (Hodge 2000), or (Stock & Stock 2013, 635–706). Instead, we will focus on the use of KOSs as indexing anguages on a rather abstract level. We will introduce specific building and structural elements by which the modeling of an indexing language can be generally described and we will look at the outcomes of an indexing process, the so-called *indexates*. (Glossary D1) For the sake of definition, we will also introduce some new technical terms as an extension of the established indexing terminology. Parts of this new terminology has already been used within the *FRSAD* modeling framework.

2.1.1 Building Elements: Entities and Terms

Indexing languages represent restricted knowledge domains that are built of *entities* (Glossary C1) and *terms* (Glossary A2). Here, an entity is to be understood as a representation of a *concept* (Glossary A1) in an indexing language. In turn, a concept is to be understood as a representation of abstract, real-life or fictive things, or aspects of things.

A term is to be understood as a representation of an entity within an indexing language. Terms are linguistic representations and consist of sequences of strings in natural or artificial language.

These definitions are directly derived from the idea of a *semiotic triangle*, which was most prominently proposed by Odgen and Richards (1923). We leave the indexing-related context aside for a moment by replacing our idea of topics as the aboutness of information resources with an idea of things in the world. It is important to understand that these things are in existence, whether they become topic of an information resource or not. Things in the world are independent from their possible occurrence in any information resources. When cognitively reflecting the existence of these things, we are inventing units of thoughts, which we use as mental references to the things in the world. The result of those mental references are concepts – and concepts, as we remember from the above text, represent things or aspects of things. Finally, we need a way of manifesting and communicating our mental concepts. This is done by representing them linguistically with words of a specific language.

Figure 2.1 outlines the considerations we have made so far. It is divided in an area *world*, an area *indexing language* and an area *information resources*. The area world contains various things, being represented by concepts. Those concepts are formed by a process of cognitive examination, and linguistically represented by words. Transferred to the area of *indexing language*, we can say that an indexing language is based upon the examination of concepts of a restricted knowledge domain, the formation of entities representing those concepts, and the collection of terms as linguistic representations of the entities.

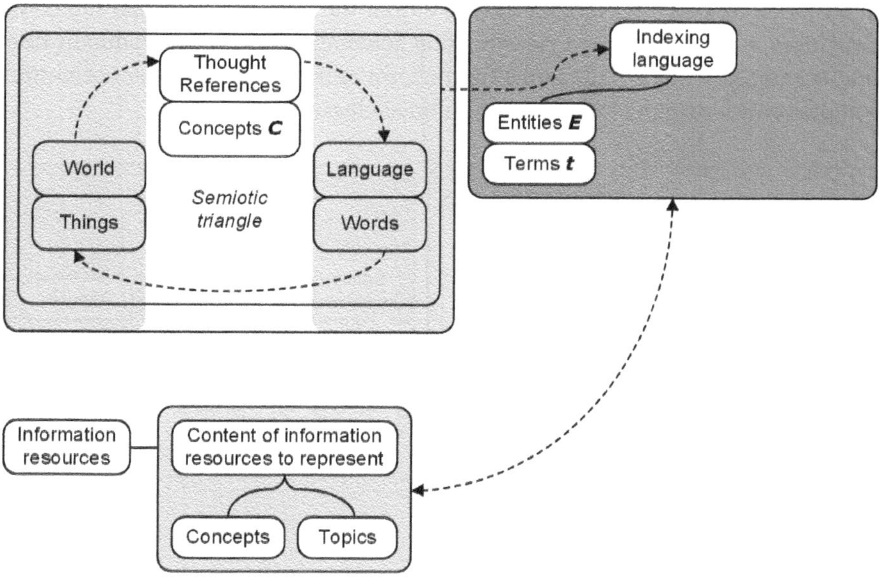

Fig. 2.1: Indexing languages reference framework.

Taking a closer look at the first building element of indexing languages, the entities, we realize that they may differ significantly in terms of their complexity. We speak of a *simple entity* (Glossary C1.1), if it represents exactly one concept and is represented by a term that consists of exactly one string. The second form of entities are the *complex entities* (Glossary C1.2), entities that can be characterized by a form of complexity either in their denomination or their conceptual components. Two types can be distinguished. We speak of *terminologically complex entities* (Glossary C1.2.1), if represented by a term that consists of more than one string. Finally, we speak of a *semantically or conceptually complex entity* (Glossary C1.2.2), if it represents a complex concept with a multifaceted character. Semantic complexity is often associated with the terminological complexity. However, it is actually quite difficult to define the cases to which this really applies. To what extent the terminological complexity of entities reflect their semantic complexity depends on the characteristics of the indexing language. In German, for example, compounding is a ubiquitous strategy of word formation where simple strings represent concepts of different semantic complexity. This is reflected in German verbal indexing languages, which often make use of compound terms representing terminologically simple entities that nevertheless can provide a high degree of semantic complexity. Indexing languages make use of those semantically complex entities when they are expected to be frequently needed as descriptors in an indexing process. Another example from the field of non-verbal indexing languages are pre-combined classification schemes. Here, it is a common rule that terminologically simple terms (in the form of notations) represent semantic complex entities (in the form of pre-combined classes).

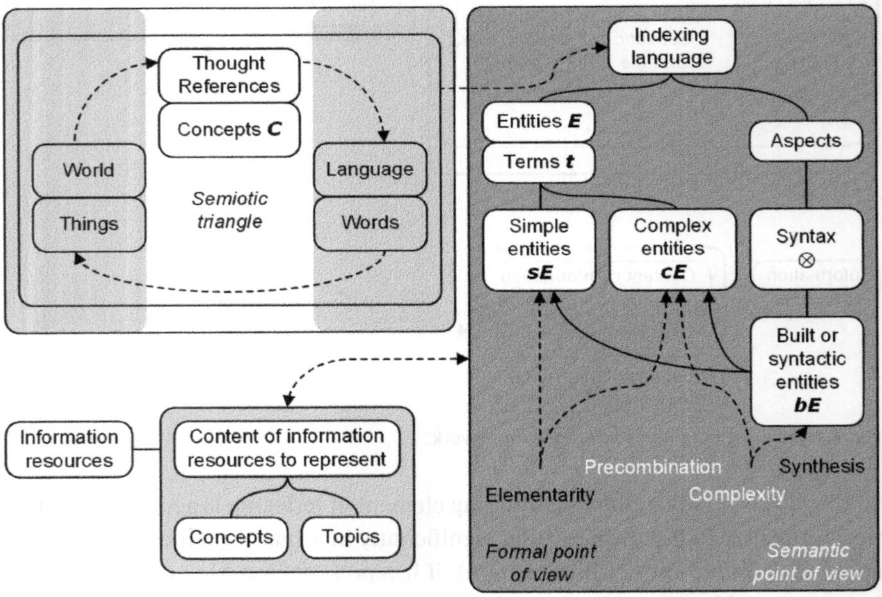

Fig. 2.2: Indexing languages reference framework with building elements.

Pre-combined indexing languages, whether verbal or non-verbal, commonly allow to represent a complex concept with one entity, we speak of them as *pre-combined entities* (Glossary C1.5). In cases where the indexing language provides no adequate entity for a given concept, the alternative lies in connecting several entities, each of them representing one or more aspects of the concept, to one *built or syntactic entity* that matches the concept as a whole and that may be seen as part of the indexing language. Commonly, the *DDC* or the *UDC* are cited as best-known examples for this method. *Built entities* (Glossary C1.5.1) consist of more than one conceptual component without making them explicit. *Syntactic entities* (Glossary

C1.5.2) consist more than one conceptual component with making them explicit by formal or syntactical devices. In an indexing process, this procedure supports post-coordination for searching, as the indexing language is already set up and entities have to be coordinated afterwards to represent a given topic adequately.

In Figure 2.2 the indexing language section is supplemented by a differentiation between simple, complex and built entities. As denoted in Figure 2.2 synthesizing of entities can be done by considering a given syntax with rules about valid entity combinations and sequences.

Let us now focus on the second building element of indexing languages, the *terms* (Glossary A2). As already defined above, a term consists of one or more strings that linguistically represent an entity. Thus, a term can be understood as a semantic reflection of the represented entity. In an indexing process a term is assigned to an information resource, and later on is displayed to information seekers in an information retrieval process (we will give attention to this in Chapter 4).

In many cases an entity can be semantically reflected not just by one term, but by several terms. In an indexing language, these terms are set semantically equal to each other and are therefore treated as *synonyms*. From these sets of synonyms, one term is defined as the main representation of the entity, the so-called *preferred term*, as it is preferentially assigned as a descriptor to an information resource in an indexing process. Accordingly, the other synonymous terms are called "non-preferred terms" and therefore are not assigned in an indexing process. Non-preferred terms ought to be additional entry points and guiding the information seeker to the particular preferred term and finally to the indexed information resources (ISO 5963, 1985).

However, which term should be and which should not be integrated in a set of synonyms is not always clear. In the not rare cases where this decision is rather difficult, we speak of *near synonyms*. In case of near synonyms two terms represent different or at least partly different aspects of one entity.

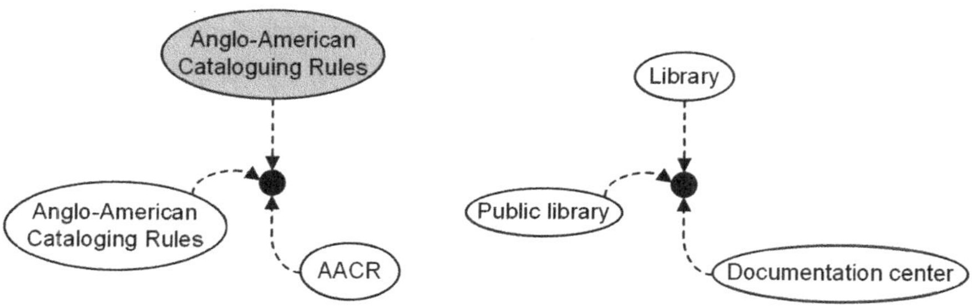

Fig. 2.3: Synonymous and near synonymous terms.

Figure 2.3 shows two simple examples. Let the two black knots be two entities and the labeled knots be terms representing the entities at which they are pointing. The entity on the left is represented by the terms “Anglo-American Cataloguing Rules”, “Anglo-American Cataloging Rules”, and “AACR”, while the right entity is represented by the terms “library”, “public library” and “documentation center”. The three terms representing the entity on the left are reflecting exactly the same semantics of their entity, as “AACR” is a well established acronym for “Anglo-American Cataloguing Rules”, which is in turn just an alternative spelling of “Anglo-American Cataloging Rules”. The grey shaded knot, labeled with “Anglo-American Cataloguing Rules” represents the preferred term from this set of synonyms.

The three terms on the right are clearly not reflecting the same semantics – a library is not the same as a public library or a documentation center. Nevertheless, it can be stated that they are somehow near synonyms as they are sharing at least some semantic aspects of their referential entity. As indexing languages only differentiate between synonymy and non-synonymy but usually don’t consider any cases of near synonymy, one has to decide whether to set these terms synonymous or not. This modeling decision makes synonyms and near synonyms formally indistinguishable so that their differences are only cognitively recognizable. Consequently, the semantics that are exclusively inherent in near synonyms become only apparent for those information seekers who search the KOS independently from its indexing language application.

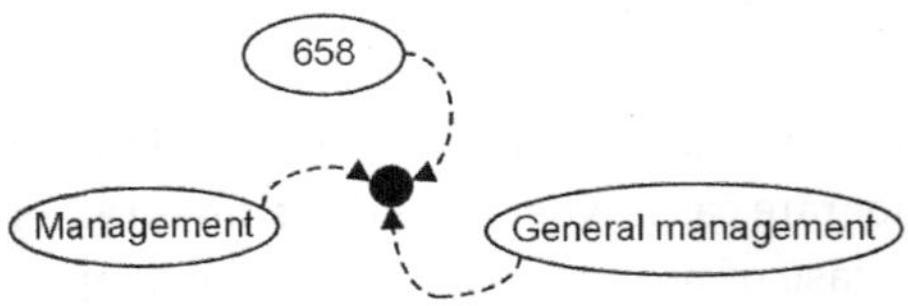

Fig. 2.4: Verbal and non-verbal terms.

As we differentiate between verbal and non-verbal indexing languages, this differentiation can also be applied to *indexing language terms* (Glossary C2). Figure 2.4 shows an example of two verbal terms, “general management” (from the subject heading scheme *LCSH*) and “management” (from the *ASIST Thesaurus*) and one non-verbal term “658” (the notation of the “general management” class in the *DDC* classification scheme).

Besides the different kinds of linguistic representation, it should also be noted that the relation between “general management” and “management” remains unclear. One could interpret this as another case of near synonymy, as both terms seem to reflect an entity representing management. On the other hand, it may be questioned whether the term “management” is actually more general than the term "general management", as "general management" seems to be somehow semantically included in "management". This would lead us to a hierarchical structure between these two terms. Whatever the decision might be with respect to this concrete modeling problem, it already denotes the importance of an indexing language's structure. In the following, we will take a closer look on how indexing languages are structured and what kinds of relationships between entities and/or terms determine this structure.

2.1.2 Structural Elements: Intrasystem Relations

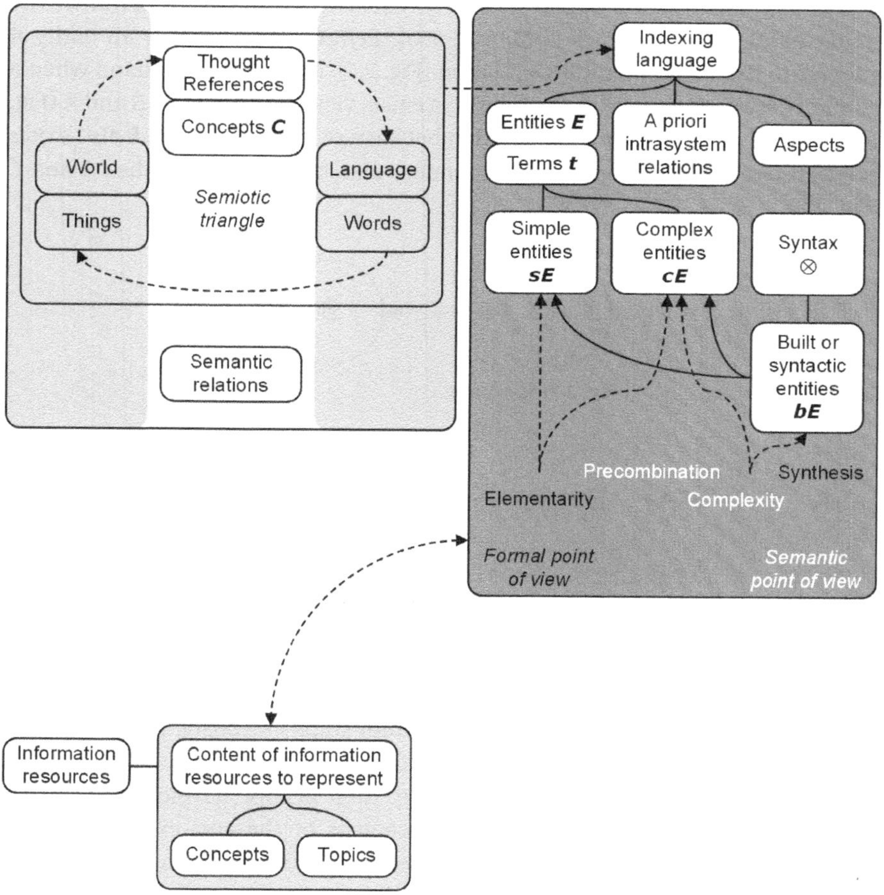

Fig. 2.5: Indexing languages reference framework with building and structural elements.

Until now, we referred to concepts, entities and terms as being independent from each other. In fact, they are conceptually interrelated, as we have already shown by our examples in Chapter 1. Those conceptual or *semantic relations* (Glossary A3) between concepts or between entities or terms of an indexing language can be seen as *a priori* given structural elements by which a given concept, entity or term is embedded in its particular semantic environment. Regarding to indexing languages we will refer to them as *intrasystem relations* (Glossary C3), since they are defined and implemented into the system *before* it is applied to an indexing or retrieval process and valid only within one self-contained system. In Figure 2.5 these considerations are added to our framework.

Semantic relations in KOSs resp. in indexing languages are usually characterized by three formal properties, namely reflexivity, symmetry, and transitivity (Jouis 2002), (Stock & Stock 2013, 548–550). *Reflexivity* states how an entity *A* adheres to itself with regard to a relation (Fig. 2.6). *Symmetry* is on hand when a relation between two entities *A* and *B* also exists vice versa between *B* and *A* (Fig. 2.7). *Transitivity* is given when a relation between two entities *A* and *B* also exists between two entities *B* and *C*, and therefore also between the entities *A* and *C* (Fig. 2.8).

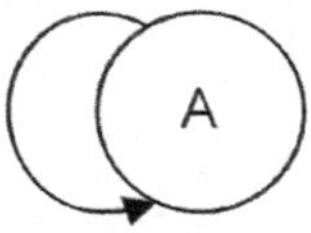

Fig. 2.6: Reflexivity.

Fig. 2.7: Symmetry.

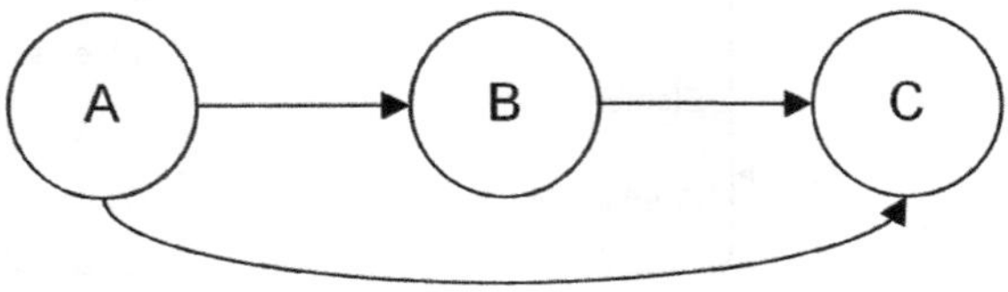

Fig. 2.8: Transitivity.

Jouis (2002, 127) introduces these formal properties as a contribution to compare conceptual representations against the relationships established between concepts and therefore proof the validity of modeled representations.

However, it should be noted that due to their historic development, indexing languages such as subject heading schemes or thesauri exhibit a rather incomplete relational structure. The used set of relations is commonly limited to unspecified equivalent, hierarchical and associative relations.

Equivalent Intrasystem Relations

Equivalent intrasystem relations are connecting all terms that represent the same entity and therefore hold between the preferred term and all non-preferred terms within a set of synonyms (Fig. 2.9)[8]. This relation type does not properly apply to symmetry, since a relation starting from a non-preferred term and pointing to a preferred term can obviously not have the same meaning as a relation that starts from a preferred term and points to a non-preferred term.

A non-preferred term "Anglo-American Cataloging Rules" can be related to a preferred term "Anglo-American Cataloguing Rules" (the grey shaded knot in Fig. 2.9), while this preferred term cannot be related in the same way to another non-preferred term "AACR". Hence, equivalent intrasystem relations are not only asymmetric, but also intransitive.

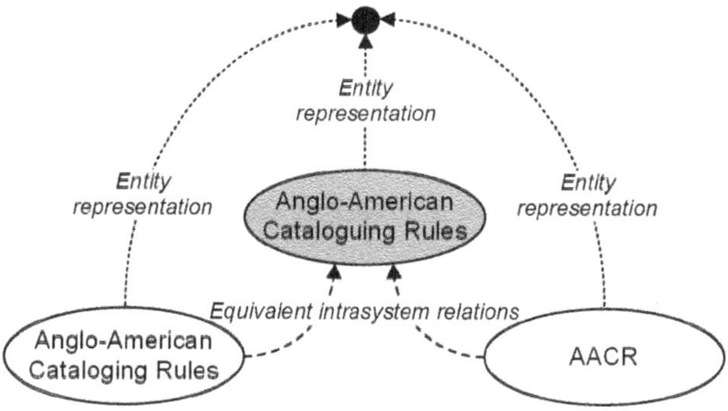

Fig. 2.9: Equivalent intrasystem relations.

Hierarchical Intrasystem Relations

In contrast to equivalent intrasystem relations, *hierarchical intrasystem relations* commonly connect entities and therefore express levels of sub- and superordination between them. Hierarchical intrasystem relations are asymmetric and often associated with transitivity, which allows deriving valid statements about the relation between not directly linked entities (Fig. 2.10).

8 If arguing in the context of only one indexing language it may seem not necessary to speak of equivalence as an intrasystem relationship. This terminological agreement will become beneficial later on, when speaking of relationships between different indexing languages as intersystem relationships.

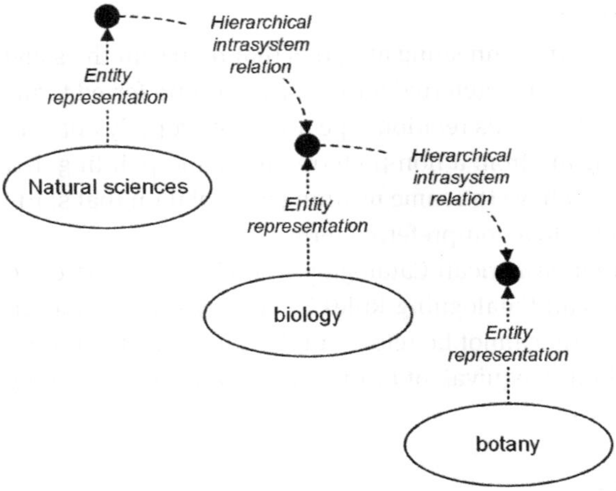

Fig. 2.10: Hierarchical intrasystem relations.

If "natural sciences" is hierarchically related to "biology", and "biology" is hierarchically related to "botany", then "natural science" is also hierarchically related to "botany". Being able to draw such inferences paves the way for processes of automatic retrieval – we will focus on such processes in Part C of this book. Yet, transitivity only applies if the corresponding hierarchical relations share the same semantic characteristics and relate entities with comparable characteristics.

```
025.472-025.479 * General subject cataloging and indexing schemes
in specific languages

000      Computer science, information & general works
020      Library & information sciences
025      Operations of libraries, archives,
               information centers
025.4          Subject analysis and control
025.47               Subject indexing [formerly
                     025.48] and cataloging
025.472-025.479      General subject cataloging and
                     indexing schemes in specific languages
```

The above example, which is taken from the *DDC*, shows that structural elements of hierarchy in existing indexing languages by no means always lead to transitivity. One can easily see that the hierarchical relation between the *DDC* classes *computer science, information & general works*, and *library & information sciences* is not the same as between *library & information sciences*, and *operations of libraries, archives, information centers.*

Hierarchical intrasystem relations may also lead to polyhierarchical structures (Fig. 2.11). This is on hand when an entity has more than one superordinate entity. Polyhierarchical indexing languages meet with the multidimensionality of some entities and allow the different aspects to be made explicit. Sometimes the aspects for creating hierarchies are changing from one level to another. However, transitivity requires hierarchies to be modeled according to one specific aspect, while changing aspects are leading to intransitive structures.

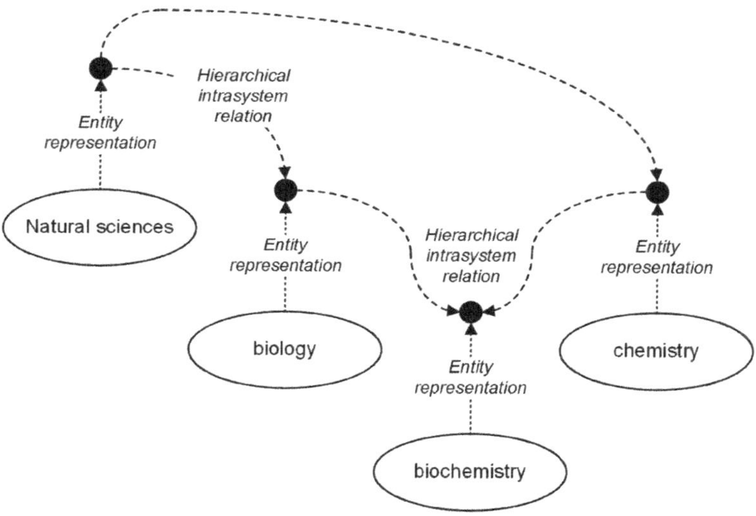

Fig. 2.11: Polyhierarchical intrasystem relations.

An indexing language dealing e.g. with furniture, might integrate an entity referring to "dining tables made of glass". A polyhierarchical indexing language could place this entity in a hierarchical relation to an entity referring to "dining tables" as well as to an entity referring to "glass tables", both being modeled as subordinate to an entity describing "tables" in general. Information seekers can follow both relation paths to find information resources associated with the entity. In contrast, a mono-hierarchical indexing language defines the entity "dining tables made of glass" as subordinate either to the entity "dining tables" or to the entity "glass tables", providing just one explicit path for information seekers.

Three subtypes of hierarchical relations in KOSs resp. in indexing languages can be differentiated: generic, partitive and instance relationships (ISO 25964-1 2011, 58–62). The *generic relationship* represents the link between a class or category and its members or species. In ISO 25964-1 (2011, 59), this hierarchical relation type is illustrated by a simple example concerning the entities "birds" and "parrots". As some members of the entity "birds" are known as "parrots" and in turn all "parrots" are by definition and irrespective of context are regarded as "birds", the hierarchical relation between these two entities is of generic character.

The *partitive* (i.e. *whole-part*) *relationship* refers to situations in which a part of an entity belongs uniquely to a particular possessing whole. ISO 25964-1 (2011, 60) gives four ideal cases for this situation, namely systems and organs of the body (e.g. veins and arteries are parts of the blood vessels are parts of the cardiovascular system), geographic locations (e.g. Toronto is part of Ontario is part of Canada), disciplines and fields of discourses (e.g. botany is part of biology is part of natural sciences), and finally hierarchical social structures (e.g. divisions are part of corps are part of armies). Most other cases of partitive relationships are deemed to be not eligible for a hierarchical relation, because a part could belong to more than one whole (e.g. a wheel could be part of a bicycle or part of a motor car) (ibid.).

Instance relationships relate general entities to individual instances of that entity, for example, the entity "mountain regions" to their instances "Alps", "Himalayas", etc. "Alps" and "Himalayas" are subordinate to "mountain regions" in a hierarchy without being a specific kind or part of "mountain regions", but individual instances.

Associative Intrasystem Relations

Associative intrasystem relations include all non-hierarchical relations between entities. Associatively related entities either have a strong overlapping meaning or represent completely different concepts that are somehow semantically related. Being intrasystem relations, *associative relationships* are symmetric, since the relation holds between two entities *A* and *B* and likewise between *B* and *A*. Yet, the underlying semantics that are reflected by this relation type are often directional and asymmetric.

Figure 2.12 shows an example of two semantically associated entities that are related via a symmetric associative intrasystem relation. Nevertheless, the relation between the hen and its egg is of course asymmetric, as the hen produces the egg but not vice versa.

Due to their unspecific character, associative intrasystem relations are not suitable for the support of any automatic retrieval processes. Their value lies at best in guiding the information seeker through the structure of an indexing language and supporting the cognitive reflection of the represented concepts.

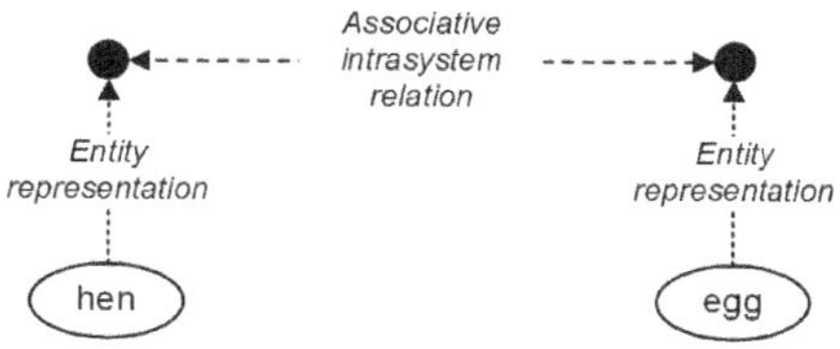

Fig. 2.12: Associative intrasystem relations.

2.1.3 Result Elements: Indexates

Having introduced the building and structural elements of indexing languages, we will now focus on the result elements that emerge from an indexing process. As we already pointed out, an indexing process means the assignment of a term as a descriptor to an information resource. From now on we speak of *indexates* (Glossary D1) when we refer to those assigned terms. Indexates are representations of topics of information resources modeled by means of an indexing language. Thus, the generation of indexates can be interpreted as the result elements of an indexing language application.

Basically, we distinguish between two types of indexates. An *elementary indexate* (Glossary D1.1) constists of a term that refers to exactly one entity. A *built indexate* (Glossary D1.2) consists of two or more terms, each of them referring to their specific entities. Figure 2.13 shows our reference framework again, now augmented by an area *result elements*.

Built indexates are constructed by combining individual building elements of an indexing language to one single terminological unit that provides a new level of representational specificity. Obviously, those combinations are not made arbitrarily, but under consideration of specific rules for synthesis. These rules define in which cases and how built indexates can be created during an indexing process. Essential modeling and application questions in this context are:

- Which topics of information resources should be represented through built indexates at all?
- How could a built indexate be formed?
- What kind of relations exist between the combined individual building elements of a built indexate?
- How could these relations be made visible?
- Should these relations be visible at all?

In the following, we focus on the second of the above mentioned questions, i.e., how a built indexate could be formed, and therefore briefly introduce three different types of built indexates concerning their terminological representation: compound, composed, and syntactic indexates.

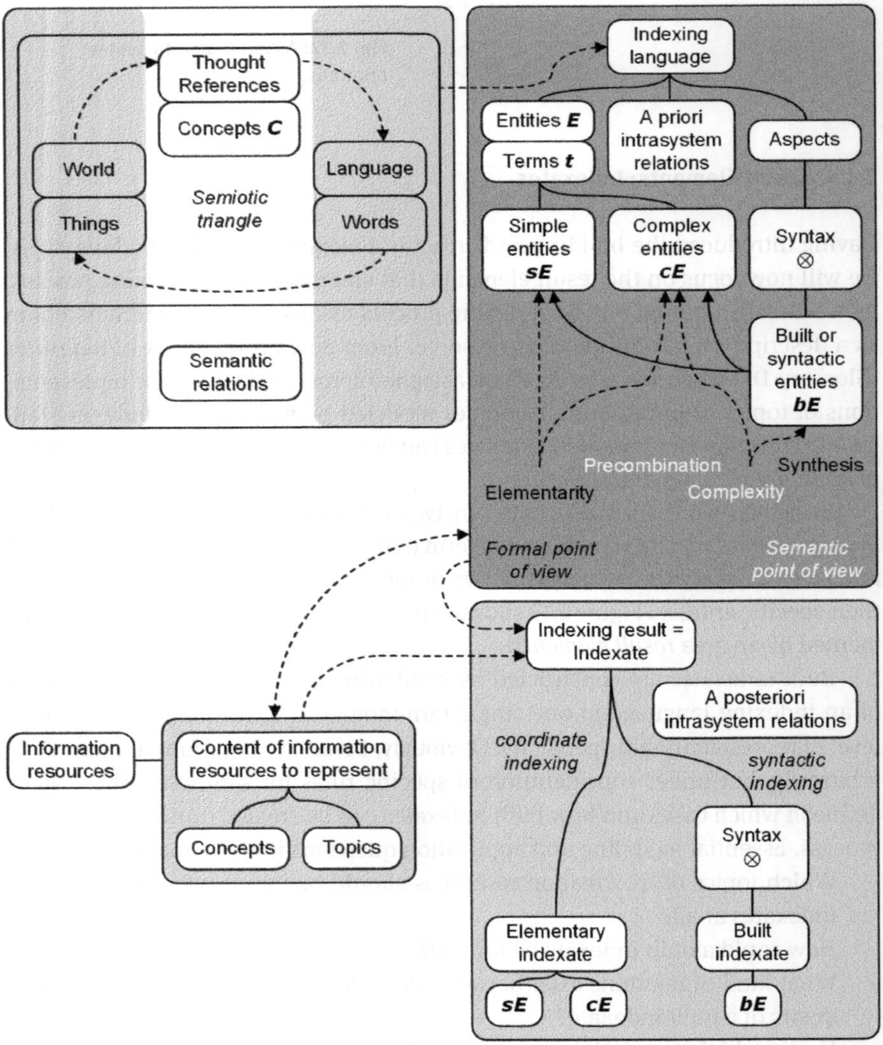

Fig. 2.13: Indexing languages reference framework with building, structural and result elements.

Compound indexates (Glossary D1.2.1) are built indexates, represented by simple terms. The topic of an information resource is represented by a subsumption of several entities of an indexing language in one terminological unit. Decomposing this unit can be rather difficult, as its parts do not necessarily exactly match with the terms that represent the entities of the underlying indexing language (Reiner 2008a), (Reiner 2008b).

Creating a compound indexate can be simplistically described as follows: The entities of the indexing language should be combined in meaningful, context-dependent order, following a specific *citation order*. This order begins with the entity that represents the main, leading topic of the information resource. This topic is further specified with recourse to additional entities that represent aspects or facets of the topic. Understanding the meaning of the built indexate requires knowledge of the underlying rules for synthesis and the ability to recognize the individual building elements. Due to the lack of machine-understandable application of synthesis rules that would allow an automatic decomposition of compound entities, automatic processing is confined to identify the leading entity but not the following terminological parts of the built indexate.

Composed indexates (Glossary D1.2.2) are built indexates, represented by complex terms. Composed indexates are intellectually and automatically recognizable in all their parts, as they exactly match the terms representing the entities of the indexing language. The arrangement of the building elements may follow a specific citation order which may set semantically more closely related elements next to each other in order to make the indexate intellectually more easily interpretable. Otherwise the display of building elements could also follow a random and therefore does not indicate how the elements are related to each other. As a matter of fact, in many cases it is immediately recognizable, which elements represent a leading topic, and which are referring to specific aspects of a topic. This leaves room for several possible interpretations and increases the cognitive effort to understand the meaning of the composed indexate correctly.

Syntactic indexates (Glossary D1.2.3) are built indexates, represented by complex terms that are combined by using syntactic operators. Syntactic indexates are clearly the most expressive representations of topics of information resources and leave little room for alternative interpretations. Thus, information seekers can more easily identify their intended meaning. Syntactic indexates, which contain the same building elements and/or the same number of building elements do not necessarily represent the same topic, as their meaning is also affected by the syntactic operators that are connecting two elements with each other. Taking Figure 2.12 as an example, one could built a syntactic indexate by selecting the terms “hen” and “egg” and connecting them with a syntactic operator indicating that the “hen” is the producer of the “egg” – this would obviously represent a different topic than a syntactic indexate, which contains the terms “hen” and “egg” and connecting them e.g. with an operator indicating that the "egg" is the germ cell of the "hen". We will address this issue again in Chapter 4 from a retrieval perspective.

2.2 Standards and Frameworks

In the previous sections we introduced building, structural and result elements of KOSs, which are used as indexing languages. In the following, we will illustrate these rather abstract considerations by two concrete modeling solutions, namely one international standard for thesauri and one modeling framework for subject authority data. At first, we will take a look on the modeling solution for thesauri, which are one of the most standardized types of KOSs in indexing applications (Dextre Clarke 2011, 3164). Therefore we will outline the first part of the *ISO 25964* (2011), giving recommendations for the development and maintenance of thesauri. Subsequently, we will briefly introduce the *Functional Requirements for Subject Authority Data (FRSAD)* (Zeng et al. 2011) as an example for a subject data oriented modeling approach, focusing on controlled vocabularies in subject indexing applications.

2.2.1 ISO 25964: Thesauri and Interoperability with other Vocabularies

The *ISO 25964* is a thesauri-related standard, succeeding the outdated standards *ISO 2788* (1974) and *ISO 5964* (1985), and complementing national standards like the *ANSI/NISO Z39.19* (2005) or the *BS 8723-2* (2005). *Dextre Clarke* states that the underlying set of principles between these different families of standards is constant and that they are simply evolving in step with the context in which they are applied (2011, 3172). Main differences would lie in scope and presentation, as each of these standards covers some aspects that the other does not, and organizes the content differently (ibid.). Inconsistencies were hard to find and the coexistence of these national and international standards would therefore cause no harm and could be even interpreted as a benefit, as the coexistence allows working groups all over the world to learn from each other (ibid., 3173).

However, due to its international focus, *ISO 25964* can somehow be seen as a generic framework for the development and maintenance of thesauri in indexing and information retrieval applications. It claims to be applicable to vocabularies used for retrieving information from all types of information resources, irrespective of the media used, including information spaces such as knowledge bases and portals, bibliographic databases, text, museum or multimedia collections, and the items within them (ISO 25964 2011, 1). Beyond that, it considers monolingual as well as multilingual thesauri, and provides a data model and format for thesaurus data exchange (ibid.).

ISO 25964 starts with defining an overall objective of thesauri, namely to function as a guide for the indexer and the information seeker to choose the same term for the same concept. This refers to our considerations about the building elements of indexing languages in Section 2.1.1, and the “preferred term” element in particular. The second overall objective is seen in presenting preferred terms in such a way that users will easily identify those terms they need for describing a given topic, whether to index or to retrieve information resources that are about this topic. According to *ISO 25964*, this is achieved by establishing semantic relationships for presenting the terms in a structured display (ibid., 15). This objective is obviously based on the structural elements of indexing languages, as we introduced them in Section 2.1.2. In *ISO 25964*, the interplay between building elements (i.e. entities and terms) and structural elements (i.e. semantic relationships) is manifested in a modeling artifact by using *UML* (Unified Modeling Language) and can therefore be interpreted as an approach of reference modeling for thesauri (ibid., 103–115). This model artifact is complemented by a tabular presentation of the modeling elements and an *XML* schema definition for im- and export of thesaurus data. As no proof of concept or evaluation has been documented within the standard, one can hardly derive statements about the practical relevance of this modeling approach.

2.2.2 Functional Requirements for Subject Authority Data (FRSAD)

The *Functional Requirements for Subject Authority Data (FRSAD)* (Zeng et al. 2011) are a theoretical framework, focused on KOSs that are used as indexing languages for subject indexing. In contrast to the previously introduced *ISO 25964*, it does not give any concrete reference model for designing a KOS, but focuses more on the process of applying a given KOS in an indexing environment and in particular on the result elements (i.e. indexates), and on how they represent information resources. Therefore, the *FRSAD* framework is embedded in the well-known *Functional Requirements for Bibliographic Records (FRBR)* (IFLA Study Group on the functional requirements for bibliographic records [IFLA] 1998) and achieves to build a conceptual model for addressing the so-called “Group 3” entities within the *FRBR* framework (i.e. *object*, *concept*, *event*, and *place*) as they relate to topics of information resources.

Other relevant goals of *FRSAD* are to provide a clearly defined, structured framework for relating existing indexing language vocabulary and indexates to the needs of information seekers and the assistance in an assessment of the potential for international sharing and use of indexing language vocabulary both within the library sector and beyond (Zeng et al. 2011, 6).

In its essentials, *FRSAD* is compatible with acknowledged representation models for the Semantic Web, e.g., the *Simple Knowledge Organization System (SKOS)*, or the *Web Ontology Language (OWL)*, which we will introduce in Chapter 3. As it is manifested by an entity-relationship-model, it does not only consider entities of indexing languages in subject indexing applications, but also their in between relations.

Without going to much into the details of *FRSAD*, it can be characterized by two key aspects. First, *FRSAD* introduces two types of building elements: *thema* and *nomen*. *Thema* is defined as an "entity used as a subject of a work" (Zeng et al. 2011, 12) and therefore corresponds to the conception which is called *topic*. It subsumes all entities modeled in indexing languages and used as result elements (i.e. indexates) in subject indexing. *Nomen* describes all signs or sequences of signs that represent these *themas* (ibid.) and therefore corresponds to the building element *term*, as introduced in Section 2.1.1. The *FRSAD* framework assumes a "has appellation / is appellation of" relation between *thema* (i.e. topic) and *nomen* (i.e. term). It is stated that this relation is – due to the ambiguity of natural language – a potential many-to-many relation: "a *thema* has one or more *nomens* and there may be a *nomen* referring to more than one *thema*" (ibid. 15).

Secondly, *FRSAD* confirms one of the relationships in the *FRBR* framework. The "has a subject / is subject of" relationship describes the connection between entities modeled in indexing languages on the one hand and so-called *works* (i.e. information resources) on the other hand. This relationship refers to the topic of an information resource and is modeled with a many-to-many cardinality, based on the underlying assumption that one information resource can have many topics and one topic can be associated to many information resources.

3 Semantic Technologies for Knowledge Representation

In the previous chapter we discussed the organization of knowledge in terms of indexing and indexing language application from a rather general perspective of KOS modeling. In this chapter, we will focus on the question how knowledge can be actually represented. Therefore, we will present semantic technologies as one prominent technical enabler for knowledge representation and describe the range of modeling possibilities provided by web-based representation languages (i.e. *RDF/RDFS* and *OWL*) as well as application-oriented languages (i.e. *XTM* and *SKOS*).

3.1 Web-based Representation Languages

Web-based representation languages emerged through the upcoming vision of a "Semantic Web", which is promoted and developed at the *World Wide Web Consortium (W3C)* (Berners-Lee, Handler & Lassila 2001). The Semantic Web is to be understood as a yet visionary interaction of several basic technologies and markup languages, providing machine-readable annotations for the information that is distributed over the web. Web-accessible information can be contained in various resources, like websites or single text, audio or video resources, or even referencing not machine-readable resources of material or immaterial kind. As the main driver of this technical and conceptual progress, the *W3C* passes recommendations for further development of semantic technologies and markup languages. The Semantic Web stack, shown in Figure 3.1, is a prominent concept of the interaction of these technologies.

The bottom layer provides a consistent encoding in the Unicode character set and a distinct referencing of the various resources by allocating individual *Uniform Resource Identifiers (URIs)*. Building on that, the *Extensible Markup Language (XML)* achieves a neutral and logic structuring of the web resources. The *Resource Description Framework (RDF)* is used to represent the existing relations between the resources, while the *Web Ontology Language (OWL)* goes even beyond that by allowing for a differentiated knowledge representation based on logical axioms.

Compared to former versions of the Semantic Web stack, the visualization in Figure 3.1 includes further components, e.g. the *Rule Interchange Format (RIF)* by which the underlying *OWL* description logic can be translated into several formal languages or the *RDF*-specific query language *SPARQL*. These components are integrated in a unifying logic. Flanked by adequate cryptographical methods, a trustful access to valid knowledge shall become possible. The application areas of these semantic technologies are numerous and not exhausting in the web, but are providing significant progress beyond that, e.g. in the field of information or expert systems.

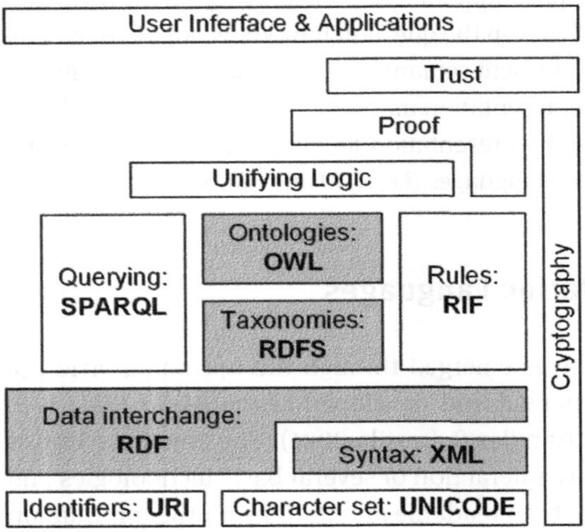

Fig. 3.1: Semantic Web stack (modified from W3C 2007).

In the following, we give a brief overview of the languages *XML*, *RDF/RDFS*, and *OWL* (i.e. the grey shaded elements of Fig. 3.1). Therefore, we are focusing on minimal examples from the chemistry domain. Although this domain is not particularly related to semantic technologies, nevertheless it provides a vivid demonstration of the basic principles of structuring and modeling of domain-specific knowledge. For a widespread introduction in Semantic Web technologies we recommend Antoniou and van Harmelen (2008).

3.1.1 XML

XML emerged as a subset of the extensive *Standard Generalized Markup Language (SGML)*. It is no markup language in the narrower sense, but a universal instrument for defining markup languages (Bray et al. 2008). *XML* can also be used for the specification of common interchange formats, e.g., as an interface in the client-server communication. Geroimenko (2003) provides a glossary about the various *XML* technologies. In the context of knowledge representation we are focusing on logical structuring of text documents via *XML*. Therefore structural information is added to each component of a text by using specific *XML* elements.

A well formed *XML* document consists of a sequence of *XML* elements, which may be nested into another, whereas every element must have a start tag and an end tag:

```
<chemistry>
<chemicalElement>
iron
</chemicalElement>
</chemistry>
```

In this simple example *chemistry* is the so-called "root"-tag, which includes all other elements. The elements can be attributed to add further information by writing specific attributes in the start tag:

```
<chemistry>
<chemicalElement aggregateState="solid">
iron
</chemicalElement>
</chemistry>
```

The structure of an *XML* document can be divided into a header, a declaration section, and a document instance section. The header contains information about the *XML* syntax and the used encoding standard.

```
<?xml version="1.0" encoding="utf-8"?>
```

Specific constraints and syntactical requirements are set up in the declaration section by using *Document Type Definitions (DTDs)* or *XML Schemata*. The *W3C* recommends the use of *XML Schemata*, which should substitute *XML-DTDs* in medium term. For the sake of simplicity, we only give a brief example for a *DTD*. The use of *DTDs* allows the implementation of basic constraints by a simple description of the valid document structure.

```
<!DOCTYPE chemistry [
<!ELEMENT chemistry (chemicalElement+)>
<!ELEMENT chemicalElement (#PCDATA)>
<!ATTLIST chemicalElement aggregateState (solid|liquid|gas)
#REQUIRED
Name CDATA #REQUIRED>
]>
```

In this example, two valid *XML* elements *chemistry* and *chemicalElement* are defined. To define the nested order of these elements, they can be marked up as parental and child elements. In the given example the parental element *chemistry* is amended by the child element *chemicalElement* in round brackets. Thus the "+" character functions as a quantifier and makes evident that the bracketed child element is allowed to appear one or more times in its parental element – other valid quantifiers are "?" (appears zero times or once) and "*" (appears zero or more times).

The attributes and their valid values for each element can also be defined. The above example defines two attributes *aggregateState* and *Name* for the element *chemicalElement*. Beyond that, for the attribute *aggregateState* the three valid values *solid*, *liquid*, and *gas* are predetermined, meaning that other attribute value for *aggregateState* will be accepted.

The range of valid values for the *Name*-attribute is defined by *CDATA*, meaning any character string. For a detailed documentation cf. Bray et al. (2008). An *XML-Schema* documentation can be found at Shudi, Sperberg-McQueen, and Thompson (2012). Finally, the document instance section contains the actual document text. This leads to the following structure for a valid *XML* document:

```
<?xml version="1.0" encoding="utf-8"?>
<!DOCTYPE chemistry [
<!ELEMENT chemistry (chemicalElement+)>
<!ELEMENT chemicalElement (#PCDATA)>
<!ATTLIST chemicalElement
aggregateState (solid|liquid|gas) #REQUIRED
Name CDATA #REQUIRED>
]>

<!-- document instances -->
<chemistry>
<chemicalElement aggregateState="solid">
iron
</chemicalElement>
</chemistry>
```

The growing extent of an *XML* document leads to an increasing certainty of name conflicts. A name conflict appears, when different *XML* elements are equally named so that they are not distinct anymore:

```
<chemicalElement>
<Name>radon</Name>
<Discovered>
<Date>1900</Date>
<Name>Friedrich Ernst Dorn</Name>
</Discovered>
</chemicalElement>
```

In the above example the *XML* element *Name* appears twice. Once as a child element of *chemicalElement*, representing the name of the element radon, and a second time as a child element of *Discovered*, representing the researcher's name, who discovered the element radon. This ambiguity causes a name conflict, in which one cannot distinct between the meaning of Name as an appellation of a chemical element and as a person's name.

In *XML*, the avoidance of such name conflicts is managed by the declaration of "namespaces" (Bray, Hollander, Layman, Tobin & Thompson 2009). A namespace provides a specific vocabulary, in which every name has a distinct meaning. By adding the information about the namespace source, a name in an *XML* document can be disambiguated.

Like every resource in the WWW, namespaces are referenced via URIs. URIs are referencing addressable resources and consist of a schema and a colon-separated following part, for eample, "http://www.example.org", "file:///C:/Users/User1/prog.m", or "mailto:user@example.org" (cf. Connolly 2006 for a widespread documentation of web naming and addressing).

To solve the name conflict from the previous example, an *XML* namespace is embedded in the root element:

```
<chemicalElement xmlns:chem="http://www.example.org">
<chem:Name>radon</chem:Name>
<Discovered>
<Date>1900</Date>
<Name>Friedrich Ernst Dorn</Name>
</Discovered>
</chemicalElement>
```

The namespace "http://www.example.org" is introduced as an attribute xmlns of the root element and uses the prefix *chem* for further referencing the URI in the document instances. To add this namespace information to an *XML* name, the *XML* name is initiated by the previous defined prefix. It has to be mentioned that the namespace URI doesn't need to reference an actual web resource, because it provides no real linkage, but just a distinct, formal appellation for each particular namespace.

In this section, the very basic principles of *XML* data structuring were shown. Building on that principles, the ontology languages *RDF* and *OWL* will be introduced in the following.

3.1.2 RDF/RDFS

While *XML* is limited to the structuring of resources, *RDF* offers the opportunity of describing the relations between resources and thereby making statements about resources (Beckett 2004). *RDF* can graphically be described as a set of nodes, which are connected with each other by directed edges. The statements are expressed in triples with subject, predicate, and object. Figure 3.2 is illustrating this principle by a simple example of two triples.

The two triples in Figure 3.2 are sharing the same subject, representing a chemical element with the chemical symbol *Fe*. Giving that element a distinct identity, it is referencing to the URI “http://www.example.org/Fe”. By this allocation of a URI to a resource, the resource achieves the status of an “individual”. In *RDF* every individual is made distinct by URIs, whether it is a material resource, e.g. a chemical element, a person, a book, or an immaterial resource, such as an idea or specific unit of knowledge.

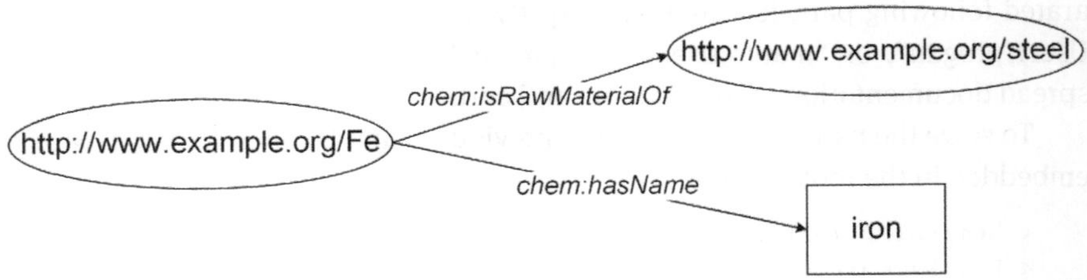

Fig. 3.2: *RDF* graph.

The edges between the nodes of the *RDF* graph correspond to the predicate statements connecting subject and object. Each of these relations is adding a particular property to the subject, hence, these relations are named “properties”. In Figure 3.2 the properties of both triples are allocated to the namespace, referenced by the prefix chem. The semantics of the properties are provided by the verbalized annotations *chem:isRawMaterialOf* and *chem:hasName*.

The object closes a triple statement and is also referencing to a URI, presupposed that it is an individual. This seems to apply to the upper triple of Figure 3.2, in which the object is referenced to the URI “http://www.example.org/steel”. Thus, the upper graph represents a predicate relationship between two individuals. Due to the property semantics, the triple can be verbalized as: “http://www.ex-ample.org/Fe” is a raw material of “http://www.example.org/steel”.

However, in the lower graph the object is not referencing to a URI, but to the character string “iron”. In this way, a simple data value named “literal” is allocated to the subject and can be interpreted as a specific subject attribute. Again, the property semantics allows us to verbalize as follows: “http://www.example.org/Fe” has the name “iron”. Such data values are no resources but simple string representations by which resources can be described. Consequently, literals in *RDF* triples can never appear as subjects or properties, but only as objects.

For enabling an effective, automatic processing of *RDF*, the graphic representation models shown in Figure 3.2 have to be translated (the technical term is "serialized") into linear syntax. Each triple of an *RDF* graph is listed according to specific syntactic requirements. Several triple syntaxes have been developed, e.g. Notation3 (Berners-Lee & Connolly 2011) or Turtle (Beckett & Berners-Lee 2011). Following the modularized skid of Figure 3.1 the only reasonable approach lies in the *RDF* serialization by *XML* syntax, since only the common *XML* standard provides adequate compatibility within the WWW. Hence, every *RDF/XML* encoded document is also a valid *XML* document. The *XML* outcome of the serialized two triple graph of Figure 3.2 is:

```
<?xml version="1.0" encoding="utf-8"?>
<rdf:RDF xmlns:rdf="http://www.w3.org/1999/02/22-rdf-syntax-ns#"
xmlns:chem="http://www.example.org">

<rdf:Description rdf:about="http://www.example.org/Fe">
<chem:isRawMaterialOf>
<rdf:Description rdf:about="http://www.example.org/steel"/>
</chem:isRawMaterialOf>
</rdf:Description>

<rdf:Description rdf:about="http://www.example.org/Fe">
<chem:hasName rdf:datatype="http://www.w3.org/2001/
XMLSchema#string">
iron
</chem:hasName>
</rdf:Description>

</rdf:RDF>
```

The used namespaces are declared in the start tag of the root element *rdf:RDF*. Besides our fictive example namespace that uses the prefix *chem*, an *RDF* namespace is declared, too. The *RDF* namespace uses the prefix *rdf*, so every tag initiated by that prefix will be validated against the *RDF* vocabulary, which is provided by the URI in the header of the above syntax example.

The *rdf:Description* tags are representing the individuals that appear as subjects and objects within the *RDF* triples of Figure 3.2. The properties, as can be easily seen, are represented by the tags *chem:isRawMaterialOf* and *chem:hasName*, in which the character string representation "iron" is modeled as an attribute *rdf:-datatype*. The attribute's value "iron" is specified by another URI that provides distinct information about the type of data, e.g., an integer or decimal number, some sort of calendar date or (being the case in the given example) a simple character string. Literals with such added information are named "typed", while literals without any information about their datatype are called "untyped". In contrast to untyped literals, the typed literals are distinctly interpretable and can be used for further automatic processing. Having regard to datatypes as properties of chemical elements, it could be useful to enable an automatic differentiation, e.g. between float or decimal numbers (for instance representing an atomic mass) and character string (for instance representing an element's verbalized appellation). A complete overview of valid datatypes in *XML* and *RDF* is delivered by Peterson et al. (2012).

While *RDF* is limited to the alignment of statements about resources, the *RDF* namespace *RDFS* goes beyond that and allows expressing semantic interdependencies between resources by providing a number of specific elements. In *RDFS* the modeling of classes and the assignment of individuals to those classes becomes possible. Taken as a whole, this paves the way for the construction of 'lightweight' ontologies (i.e. ontologies featuring poor or even no logical axioms and thus supporting only limited or even no automatic inferencing) (cf. de Bruijn 2003). The *RDFS* elements *rdfs:class* and *rdfs:subClassOf* are the essential instruments for constructing a hierarchical or polyhierarchical network of individuals.

```
<?xml version="1.0" encoding="utf-8"?>
<rdf:RDF xmlns:rdf="http://www.w3.org/1999/02/22-rdf-syntax-
ns#" xmlns:rdfs="http://www.w3.org/2000/01/rdf-schema#"
xml:base="http://www.example.org"/>

<rdfs:Class rdf:about="chemicalElement"/>
<rdfs:Class rdf:about="rawMaterial"/>

<rdfs:Class rdf:about="metallicElement">
<rdfs:subClassOf rdfs:resource="#chemicalElement"/>
</rdfs:Class>

<rdfs:Class rdf:about="Fe">
<rdfs:subClassOf rdfs:resource="#metallicElement"/>
<rdfs:subClassOf rdfs:resource="#rawMaterial"/>
</rdfs:Class>

</rdf:RDF>
```

First, please note the declaration of a "base" URI next to the URIs that are referencing to the *RDF* and *RDFS* namespaces. The base URI allows us to keep the attribute values of *rdf:about* and *rdfs:resource* short by referencing only to their relative parts, while the basic part "http://www.example.org/" is deposited in the header as a value of *xml:base*. For the sake of shortness, we will keep this practice in further examples, while the header will be omitted from now on. As a consequence of this procedure, single syntax examples could be incomplete and would not pass a syntactical validation check. However, if the following examples are read as fragments of larger *RDF/XML* files, they are wholly meaningful.

In the above example, the four *RDFS* classes *chemicalElement*, *rawMaterial*, *metallicElement*, and *Fe* (representing the element iron) are defined. The appearance of *rdfs:subClassOf* implicates a hierarchical structure, in which *chemicalElement* and *rawMaterial* are the two most general classes, while *metallicElement* is subordinate to *chemicalElement* and *Fe* is subordinate to *metallicElement* and *rawMaterial*. The derivable statements of this structure are:

- All metallic elements are chemical elements.
- The element *Fe* and all of its possible instances (which we don't know yet) are metallic elements and raw materials.

These statements are valid, since the property *rdfs:subClassOf* is transitive by definition. In the context of knowledge representation and in the artificial intelligence domain as well, the deriving of such statements in due consideration of the underlying logical axioms is referred to as 'inferencing'. However, not only classes, but also properties can be ordered hierarchically. Via *rdfs:subPropertyOf* a property can be subordinate to another.

```
<rdf:Property rdf:about="reactsWith"/>

<rdf:Property rdf:about="oxidatesWith">
<rdfs:subPropertyOf rdfs:resource="reactsWith"/>
</rdf:Property>
```

This can become of practical relevance when opening up a broader context of a given statement, e.g.:

```
<rdfs:Class about="Fe">
<chem:oxidatesWith>
<rdfs:Class rdf:about="O"/>
</chem:oxidatesWith>
</rdfs:Class>
```

If this statement, saying that iron (chemical symbol *Fe*) oxidates with oxygen (chemical symbol *O*) is available with the previous *subPropertyOf*-statement, it can be inferenced that the described relation between *Fe* and *O* is a special kind of chemical relation, as the property *oxidatesWith* is subordinate to the property *reactsWith*.

To ensure that only meaningful relations are built, the properties can be bounded to specified constraints about their domain of definition and range of values. By adding the attributes *rdfs:domain* and *rdfs:range* to a property, a variety of specifications can be defined, e.g. to which classes the individuals referring to the property shall be subordinated. Assuming that a collection of chemical elements is modeled as classes and a collection of chemical reactions is modeled as properties, it would then be useful to add via *rdfs:domain* the information to every property, between which elements a reaction can appear – e.g. an oxidation can only appear, when the element oxygen is involved. Consequently, only those elements could be related to each other that are matching the domain constraint of the property.

3.1.3 OWL

The ontology language *OWL* is based on predicate logic and provides a modeling power that is far more expressive than *RDF/RDFS* (cf. W3C OWL Working Group 2009). First, it can be differentiated between three sublanguages: *OWL Full*, *OWL DL* (i.e. OWL Description Logic) and *OWL Lite*.

As shown in Figure 3.3, *OWL Full* contains both *OWL DL* and *OWL Lite* and provides maximal expressiveness. *OWL DL* contains *OWL Lite* and provides medium expressiveness, whereas *OWL Lite* is the smallest *OWL* fragment and provides relatively poor expressiveness. The high expressiveness of *OWL Full* is attended by high complexity, which may lead to undecidable situations. In contrast, *OWL DL* and *OWL Lite* are of relatively poor complexity and based on decidable logic.

As described by the Semantic Web stack in Figure 3.1, *OWL* can be embedded into *RDF/XML* syntax for automatic processing in the *WWW*. Besides that, there are a number of alternative, less common syntaxes, e.g. the "functional syntax" (Motik, Patel-Schneider & Parsia 2012), or the "Manchester syntax" (Horridge & Patel-Schneider 2012).

An *OWL* ontology consists – like *RDF* – of individuals, modeled as instances, that are hierarchized via *rdfs:subClassOf* and between relations, modeled as *OWL* properties. But in contrast to *RDF/RDFS* the possible relations in an *OWL* ontology can reach a higher complexity. In the following, we give a brief overview of knowledge representation principles with *OWL*, without describing the full complexity of this powerful modeling language.

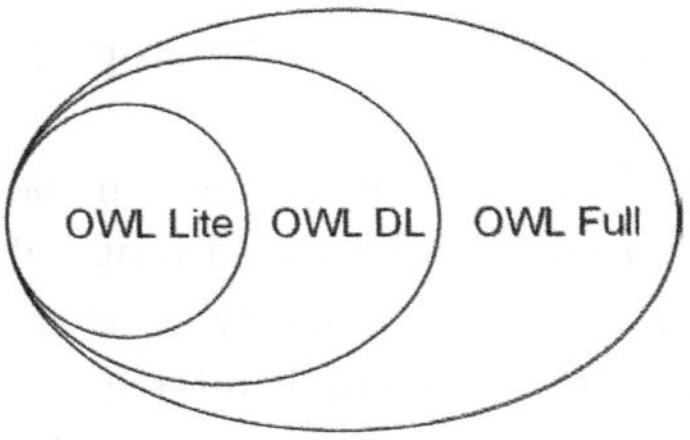

Fig. 3.3: *OWL* sublanguages.

An *OWL* class is defined by *owl:Class*, e.g. a particular group of the periodic table:

```
<owl:Class rdf:about="period8"/>
```

An instance is assigned to an OWL class according to *RDF/XML* syntax:

```
<group8 rdf:about="Fe"/>
```

Furthermore, abstract and concrete properties are differentiated. Abstract properties (*owl:ObjectProperty*) are connecting individuals with each other, while concrete properties (*owl:DatatypeProperty*) are connecting individuals with characteristic data values. For example, an abstract property may connect a chemical element with a certain aggregate state, while a concrete property may establish a relationship to the element's atomic weight, which is actually represented as a number. These pieces of knowledge modeled in *OWL* would lead to the following outcome:

```
<owl:ObjectProperty rdf:about="hasAggregateState"/>
<owl:DatatypeProperty rdf:about="hasAtomicWeight"/>

<owl:Class rdf:about="group8"/>

<group8 rdf:about="Fe"/>
<rdfs:label>iron</rdfs:label>
<hasAggregateState rdf:resource="#solid"/>
<hasAtomicWeight rdf:datatype="&xsd;float">55,845</
hasAtomicWeight>
</group8>
```

The above example shows the declaration of two properties, an abstract one (*hasAggregateState*) and a concrete one (*hasAtomicWeight*). An *OWL* class *group8* is defined and an instance, the individual *Fe*, is subordinate to that class. Subsequently, some additional information is given about the individual *Fe*. At first the verbalized appellation "iron" is assigned to *Fe* by using *rdfs:label* from the *RDFS* namespace. The aggregate state of *Fe* is provided via the property *hasAggregate State* that leads to the value "solid" as an *rdf:resource*. Finally, the atomic weight of *Fe* is provided via the property *hasAtomicWeight*. The value "55,845" is typed by *rdf:datatype* as a floating point number – note that the used prefix "xsd" in the example should reference the *XML Schema* namespace in the header, that differentiates between several number formats (Peterson et al. 2012).

In addition, an object property can also be complemented by its inverse object property via *owl:inverseOf*. Using the example of two properties *hasAggregateState* and *isAggregateStateOf*, their inversion can be defined as:

```
<owl:ObjectProperty rdf:about="hasAggregateState">
<owl:inverseOf rdf:resource="#isAggregateStateOf"/>
</owl:ObjectProperty>
```

While the above examples are syntactically correct, nevertheless the appearance of the *rdf:resource* value "solid" seems to be arbitrary. However, the number of meaningful values at this point is limited, since physical sciences differentiate only a few specific types of aggregate states.

To ensure that only meaningful values appear, the relevant knowledge about aggregate states needs to be added to the ontology. In the next step, this new piece of knowledge is being concatenated to the individual *Fe*. This leads to a more comprehensive example:

```
<owl:ObjectProperty rdf:about="hasAggregateState"/>
<owl:DatatypeProperty rdf:about="hasAtomicWeight"/>

<owl:Class rdf:about="AggregateState">
<owl:oneOf rdf:parseType="Collection">
<owl:Thing rdf:about="solid"/>
<owl:Thing rdf:about="liquid"/>
<owl:Thing rdf:about="gas"/>
</owl:oneOf>
</owl:Class>

<owl:Class rdf:about="group8">
<rdfs:subClassOf>
<owl:Restriction>
<owl:onProperty rdf:resource="#hasAggregateState"/>
<owl:allValuesFrom rdf:resource="#AggregateState"/>
</owl:Restriction>
</rdfs:subClassOf>
</owl:Class>

<group8 rdf:about="Fe">
<rdfs:label>iron</rdfs:label>
<hasAggregateState rdf:resource="#solid"/>
<hasAtomicWeight rdf:datatype="&xsd;float">55,845</
hasAtomicWeight>
</group8>
```

The newly established *OWL* class *AggregateState* contains the relevant knowledge about aggregate states. At this point the higher complexity of *OWL* becomes already apparent. The use of *owl:oneOf* allows to express that the class *AggregateState* can be related to three different individuals, namely *solid*, *liquid* and *gas*, that are modeled as instances of the predefined class *owl:Thing* (the most general *OWL* class under which every other *OWL* element is subordinated). The attribute *Collection* allows the modeling of this situation as an n-ary relation from the class *AggregateState* to the listed individuals. This means in consequence that no other individuals are allowed to occur in this particular context. One can say that the class *AggregateState* is built from the given list of individuals. Thus, *owl:oneOf* can be understood as a particular kind of a class constructor. More *OWL* specific class constructors will be introduced in the following. Note that the use of those class constructors is one of the core differences of *OWL* to the less expressive *RDFS*.

In the above example the concatenation of this new knowledge to the individual *Fe* is provided via the *OWL* class *group8*. This class is subordinated via *rdfs:subClassOf* to a more general class *owl:Restriction. owl:Restriction* is a predefined, anonymous class, in which a number of certain restrictions can be stated. Since *rdfs:subClassOf* provides a transitive hierarchy, the restrictions are not only valid in *owl:Restriction*, but also in all its instances, i.e. in the above example the class *group8*. The actual restriction and its range are defined by the two elements *owl:onProperty* and *owl:allValuesFrom*. While the first states the property to which the restriction shall be affected and references the previous defined property *hasAggregateState*, the latter states the kind of restriction and references the class *AggregateState*. Consequently, the appearance of the property *hasAggregateState* within the class *group8* must lead to the restricted range of valid values *solid, liquid* or *gas*, that are listed as individuals in the class *AggregateState*.

However, property restrictions in *OWL* are not limited to the range of expected values, but can also affect the cardinality of a property:

```
<owl:Class rdf:about="chemicalElement">
<rdfs:subClassOf>
<owl:Restriction>
<owl:onProperty rdf:resource="#hasAtomicNumber"/>
<owl:allValuesFrom rdf:resource="&xsd;integer"/>
</owl:Restriction>
</rdfs:subClassOf>
<rdfs:subClassOf>
<owl:Restriction>
<owl:onProperty rdf:resource="#hasAtomicNumber"/>
<owl:cardinality rdf:datatype="&xsd;nonNegativeInteger">
1
</owl:cardinality>
</owl:Restriction>
</rdfs:subClassOf>
</owl:Class>
```

The above example defines a class *chemicalElement*, which is subordinate to two restriction classes. The first restriction class focuses on the property, which leads to a chemical element's atomic number and prescribes the datatype "integer" for the expected values by referencing via the prefix "xsd" to the *XML Schema* namespace again. The second restriction class affects the cardinality of the same property. Here, the value "1" means that each individual of the class *chemicalElement* is allowed to have exactly one value of the property *hasAtomicNumber*. There is a sufficient reason to do so, since physical sciences have assigned exactly one atomic number to each chemical element.

Beyond that, some more general logical characteristics can be added to a property, depending on the particular ontology purposes. This comprises transitivity, symmetry and the global (i.e. class independent) cardinality restrictions of functionality and inverse functionality.

Transitivity was already mentioned in the context of the *rdfs:subClassOf* element. Building a transitive hierarchy in *OWL*, one is not limited to the *RDFS* vocabulary. *OWL* properties can also be modeled transitive by definition via *owl:TransitiveProperty*:

```
<owl:ObjectProperty rdf:about="isA">
<rdf:type rdf:resource="#owl:TransitiveProperty"/>
</owl:ObjectProperty>

<owl:Class rdf:about="chemicalElement"/>

<owl:Class rdf:about="metallicElement">
<isA rdf:resource="#chemicalElement"/>
</owl:Class>

<metallicElement rdf:about="Fe"/>
```

Symmetry is given when a property is bi-directional. This is the case, when both connected individuals have the same relationship each to the other. Thereby could be expressed that both iron (*Fe*) reacts with oxygen (*O*) and vice versa.

```
<owl:ObjectProperty rdf:about="reactsWith">
<rdf:type rdf:resource="owl:SymmetricProperty"/>
</owl:ObjectProperty>

<owl:Class rdf:about="metallicElement">
<owl:Class rdf:about="nonmetallicElement">

<nonmetallicElement rdf:about="O"/>

<metallicElement rdf:about="Fe">
<reactsWith rdf:about="#O"/>
</metallicElement>
```

Functionality allows the restriction of a property's cardinality to one single value. Hence, if a functional property is directed to multiple values, those values are stated as identical to each other.

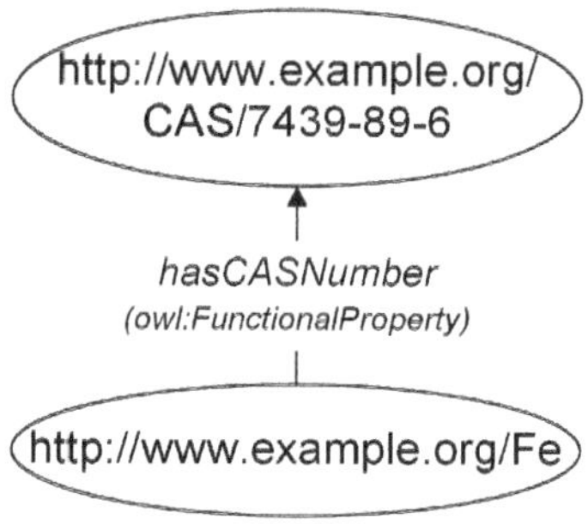

Fig. 3.4: *OWL* functional property.

This can be useful when establishing unique relationships between resources, e.g., the relation between the metallic element *Fe* and its *CAS* number as denoted in Figure 3.4 (note that both object and datatype properties can be declared as "functional", while the declaration of transitivity or symmetry is limited to object properties):

```
<owl:DatatypeProperty rdf:about="hasCASNumber">
<rdf:type rdf:resource="&owl;FunctionalProperty"/>
</owl:DatatypeProperty>

<owl:Class rdf:about="metallicElement"/>
<owl:Class rdf:about="CAS"/>

<CAS rdf:about="7439-89-6"/>

<metallicElement rdf:about="Fe">
<hasCASNumber rdf:about="#7439-89-6"/>
</metallicElement>
```

The relationship can be modeled vice versa using the inverse functional restriction:

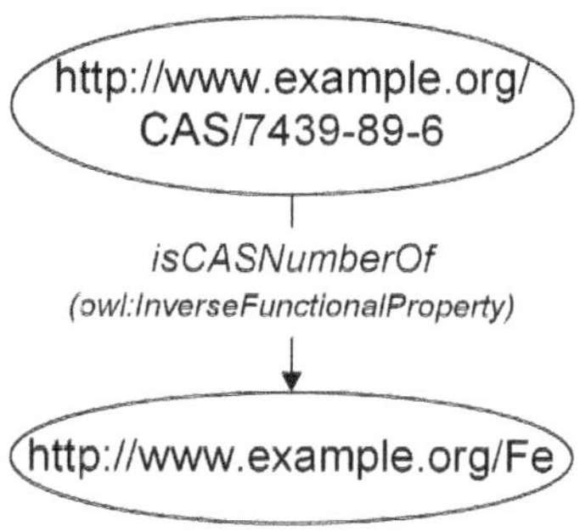

Fig. 3.5: *OWL* inverse functional property.

In an inverse functional property an individual can only be related to one particular other individual. The example in Figure 3.5 states that "7439-89-6" is the *CAS* number of the individual *Fe* and only of that individual.

```
<owl:ObjectProperty rdf:about="isCASNumberOf">
<rdf:type rdf:resource="&owl;InverseFunctionalProperty"/>
</owl:ObjectProperty>

<owl:Class rdf:about="metallicElement"/>
<owl:Class rdf:about="CAS"/>

<metallicElement rdf:about="Fe"/>

<CAS rdf:about="7439-89-6">
<isCASNumberOf rdf:about="#Fe"/>
</CAS>
```

Note also that in *OWL DL* only object properties can be declared as "inverse functional" – in contrast to the attribute "functional" that can be added to both object and datatype properties. The situation in *OWL Full* is even more confusing – here both object and datatype properties can be "inverse functional", since *OWL Full* datatype properties are modeled as instances of object properties.

Besides all that, *OWL* features a number of other class constructors, e.g. those which are enabling Boolean combinations of classes. Conjunctions (*owl:intersectionOf*), disjunctions (*owl:unionOf*), and negations (*owl:complementOf*) can be used for numerous differentiated statements:

```
<owl:Class rdf:about="transitionMetal">
<owl:intersectionOf rdf:parseType="Collection">
<owl:Class rdf:about="chemicalElement"/>
<owl:Class rdf:about="group8"/>
</owl:intersectionOf>
</owl:Class>
```

In this example a complex class *transitionMetal* was built as an intersection of the two elemental classes *chemicalElement* and *group8* (of the periodic table). By inferencing, it can thus be concluded that all chemical elements that belong to the group 8 of the periodic table are transition metals.

The design of *OWL* ontologies is essentially influenced by the paradigm of the *Open World Assumption (OWA)*. According to that, a particular fact or an actual situation is implicitly assumed as valid, as long as its invalidity has not been made explicit. Hence, the absence of an explicit statement about a particular fact or situation does not mean that it is not valid. The *OWA* paradigm follows a pragmatic approach of the WWW as an incomplete base of knowledge, which is continuously expanded by new knowledge. The impact of the *OWA* paradigm on the previous example of the complex class *transitionMetal* is that other chemical elements, which are not matched by the intersection, are not axiomatically suspended from that class. The relationship between those elements and the class *transitionMetal* is merely unknown. Only the explicit modeling of a disjunction between two classes via *owl:complementOf* allows to model the proscription of an individual's membership in both classes (note that the same effect could be reached by using *owl:disjointWith* instead of *owl:complementOf*):

```
<owl:Class rdf:about="alkalineEarthMetal">
<owl:complementOf rdf:about="transitionMetal"/>
</owl:Class>
```

The previous examples are only a small excerpt of possible approaches for knowledge representation with semantic technologies. Especially the rather complex languages *RDFS* and *OWL* cannot be discussed exhaustively without going too much into technical details.

3.2 Application-based Representation Languages

The web-based application languages we outlined in the previous section provide the fundament for a couple of application-based data models and encoding schemes. These offer additional (standardized) elements for representing existing KOSs adjusted to specific use scenarios. With Topic Maps and SKOS we introduce two of them in this section.

Topic Maps and the *XML*-based encoding scheme *XTM* (XML Topic Maps) have been constituted as a standard for knowledge representation by the seven part ISO/IEC 13250 (2006). Topic Maps emerged from a HyTime-application for the purpose of representing and merging digital back-of-book indexes and were continuously developed to a more general data model (Pepper 2010).

SKOS (Simple Knowledge Organization System) refers to a representation language that was developed for sharing and linking thesauri. Yet, it was extended in order to apply to other simple indexing languages as well. By now, the *SKOS* primer explicitly mentions "classification schemes, subject heading lists, taxonomies, folksonomies, and other similar types of controlled vocabulary" as additional application areas (Isaac & Summer 2009). Since its announcement as *W3C* recommendation in 2009, *SKOS* has become the de-facto standard for publishing indexing languages on the web. Many Linked Data applications revert to *SKOS*. Best practices for using *SKOS* to represent indexing languages viz. to convert existing indexing languages into *SKOS* are well documented (Leroi & Holland 2010), (Assem, Malaisé, Miles & Schreiber 2006), (Summers, Isaac, Redding & Krech 2008), (Zapilko & Sure 2009), (Zeng & Panzer 2009), (Putkey 2011).

Closely related to *SKOS* is the Metadata Description Schema in *RDF (MADS/RDF)*, a standard that is designed for authority and vocabulary data used within the library and information sciences community. It is maintained by the *MODS/MADS Editorial Committee* with the *Network Development and MARC Standards Office* of the *Library of Congress* and input from users. The data model is represented as an *OWL Full* ontology and has been fully mapped to *SKOS*. As it is more specific than *SKOS* and less applied, we will not discuss it in this book. Information about *MADS* can be found in the respective primer (MADS/RDF 2012) or on the corresponding official website.[9]

In the following, we will describe the range of possibilities *XTM* and *SKOS* offer for representing elements of knowledge and information resources. Yet these will be restricted to aspects we deem as being relevant for the discussion in Part C of this book.

3.2.1 XTM

The structure of *XML Topic Maps (XTM)* is determined by a subject-centric view and leads to a network of interconnected topics, which is serialized completely in *XML*. The TAO (topics, associations, occurrences)-model, announced by Pepper, illustrates the different core elements of Topic Maps (Pepper 2002). In the *TAO-model*, the topics are the nodes of the network, whereas associations and occurrences are two types of links. An association is linking two associated topics and can be seen as a network-internal link. Occurrences are linking topics with particular information resources, which are logically located outside the network. Figure 3.6 gives a visualization of that model.

The concept of a subject can be defined as anything whatsoever, regardless of whether it exists or has any other specific characteristics, about which anything whatsoever may be asserted by any means whatsoever (ISO/IEC 13250-2 2006). Thus, similar to an *RDF* individual, a Topic Map subject can be of material or immaterial kind, as well as fictive or non-fictive. Besides that, *RDF* data can also be integrated in Topic Maps (Pepper et al. 2006a), (Pepper et al. 2006b).

In the following, a brief overview is given on the construction of Topic Maps with the *XTM* specification.[10] Therefore the essential *XTM* elements are introduced using some minimal examples from the already known chemistry domain

---

9 http://www.loc.gov/standards/mads

10 The syntax examples are based on the *XTM 1.0* specification. Although *XTM 1.0* has long been revised by *XTM 2.0*, the *XTM 1.0* specification is still of practical relevance and well documented.

(cf. Hunting 2003 for a more instructive guidance and Pepper & Moore 2001 for a complete reference of XTM).

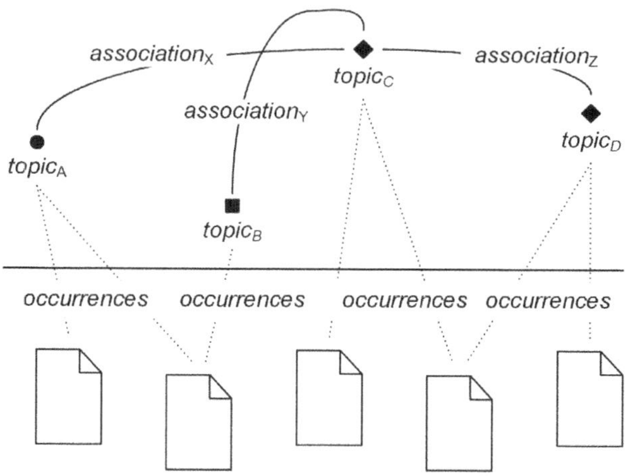

Fig. 3.6: The TAO-model (modified from Pepper 2010).

Topic in XTM

A topic can be interpreted as a subject representation in an information system. It is defined as a symbol, used within a Topic Map to represent one, and only one subject, in order to allow statements to be made about the subject (ISO/IEC 13250-2 2006). Thus, a Topic Map that covers a certain domain will include topics that represent the subjects of that certain domain. The *XTM* elements *topic*, *baseName* and *baseNameString* allow us to define topics and to give them verbal appellations:

```
<topic id="chemicalElement">
<baseName>
<baseNameString>chemical Element</baseNameString>
</baseName>
</topic>

<topic id="metallicElement">
<baseName>
<baseNameString>metallic Element</baseNameString>
</baseName>
</topic>

<topic id="iron">
<baseName>
```

```
<baseNameString>iron</baseNameString>
</baseName>
</topic>
```

The above example contains three topics. Each topic consists of an ID, which ensures the topic's uniqueness within the *XTM* file, and a base name, which is always a character string. Instead of the verbal IDs in the example, IDs can also be represented by alphanumeric strings, as long as the leading character isn't a digit. The base name of the topic, which is embedded in the elements ***baseName*** and ***baseNameString*** is a string character and will be used to label the topic, when running the *XTM* file in a Topic Map application.

Topics that represent narrower subjects can be typed by subordinating them to topics that represent broader subjects. Embedding the *instanceOf* element in a topic allows us referencing from that particular topic to another topic, which becomes the "topic type" of the referencing topic. By using *instanceOf* it can be declared that e.g. "chemical element" is the topic type of "metallic element", while "metallic element" is the topic type of "iron":

```
<topic id="chemicalElement">
<baseName>
<baseNameString>chemical Element</baseNameString>
</baseName>
</topic>

<topic id="metallicElement">
<instanceOf>
<topicRef xlink:href="#chemicalElement"/>
</instanceOf>
<baseName>
<baseNameString>metallic Element</baseNameString>
</baseName>
</topic>

<topic id="iron">
<instanceOf>
<topicRef xlink:href="#metallicElement"/>
</instanceOf>
<baseName>
<baseNameString>iron</baseNameString>
</baseName>
</topic>
```

Please note that from the above typification one cannot assert that "chemical element" is also the topic type of "iron", since the *instanceOf* element is not transitive by definition. However, efforts have been made for implementing description logics in Topic Maps environments, which enable machine-based reasoning (Rath 2003).

Every topic can be enhanced with machine-readable identities. The *subjectIdentity* element and its child element *subjectIndicatorRef* allows the embedment of URIs. In Topic Map context a URI functions as a "published subject indicator" (PSI), which can be defined as any resource that has been published in order to provide a positive, unambiguous indication of the identity of a subject for interchange and merging purposes (Vatant 2003, 73):

```
<topic id="iron">
<subjectIdentity>
<subjectIndicatorRef xlink:href="http://www.example.org/Fe"/>
</subjectIdentity>
<baseName>
<baseNameString>iron</baseNameString>
</baseName>
</topic>
```

Associations in XTM

An association is connecting two topics. Hence, it represents a relationship between the two subjects that are represented by the connected topics. As association members, these topics are referenced by the *member* element, which is a child element of *association*.

```
<topic id="iron">
<subjectIdentity>
<subjectIndicatorRef xlink:href="http://www.example.org/Fe"/>
<baseName>
<baseNameString>iron</baseNameString>
</baseName>
</topic>

<topic id="steel">
<subjectIdentity>
<subjectIndicatorRef xlink:href="http://www.example.org/steel"/>
</subjectIdentity>
<baseName>
<baseNameString>steel</baseNameString>
</baseName>
</topic>

<association id="steelProduction">
<member>
<topicRef xlink:href="#iron"/>
```

```
</member>
<member>
<topicRef xlink:href="#steel"/>
</member>
</association>
```

The above association *steelProduction* is connecting the two associated members *iron* and *steel*. However, this association doesn't hold much information about the relationship semantics. To make the association more meaningful, specific roles can be added to the association members. Consequently, these roles have to be modeled as topics, too:

```
<topic id="rawMaterial">
<subjectIdentity>
<subjectIndicatorRef xlink:href="http://www.example.org/
rawMaterial"/>
</subjectIdentity>
<baseName>
<baseNameString>raw material</baseNameString>
</baseName>
</topic>

<topic id="endProduct">
<subjectIdentity>
<subjectIndicatorRef xlink:href="http://www.example.org/
endProduct"/>
</subjectIdentity>
<baseName>
<baseNameString>end product</baseNameString>
</baseName>
</topic>

<association id="steelProduction">
<member>
<roleSpec>
<topicRef xlink:href="#rawMaterial"/>
</roleSpec>
<topicRef xlink:href="#iron"/>
</member>
<member>
<roleSpec>
<topicRef xlink:href="#endProduct"/>
</roleSpec>
<topicRef xlink:href="#steel"/>
</member>
</association>
```

The topics "rawMaterial" and "endProduct" are referenced within the roleSpec element for defining the particular role of the associated topics "iron" and "steel". Based on the above, the assertion can be made that in an association "steelProduction" the topic "iron" functions as a raw material, while "steel" functions as an end product.

Finally, associations can be modeled as instances, too. When building e.g. a Topic Map of the basic material industry domain, it could be useful to define a topic "production" and instantiate the association "steelProduction" to that topic:

```
<topic id="production">
<subjectIdentity>
<subjectIndicatorRef xlink:href="http://www.example.org/
production"/>
</subjectIdentity>
<baseName>
<baseNameString>production</baseNameString>
</baseName>
</topic>

<association id="steelProduction">
<instanceOf>
<topicRef xlink:href="#production"/>
</instanceOf>
<member>
<roleSpec>
<topicRef xlink:href="#rawMaterial"/>
</roleSpec>
<topicRef xlink:href="#iron"/>
</member>
<member>
<roleSpec>
<topicRef xlink:href="#endProduct"/>
</roleSpec>
<topicRef xlink:href="#steel"/>
</member>
</association>
```

Occurrences in XTM

Occurrences are references to resources that provide further information about a particular topic. These pieces of information are logically based outside the Topic Map, since they are not a not affecting the structure between associated topics. Physically an occurrence can be stored as a data string inside the Topic Map or point to a resource outside the Topic Map via a URI.

Initiated by the *occurrence* element, a resource, which is physically stored within the Topic Map can be referenced by using the child element *resourceData*:

```
<topic id="iron">
<subjectIdentity>
<subjectIndicatorRef xlink:href="http://www.example.org/Fe"/>
<baseName>
<baseNameString>iron</baseNameString>
</baseName>
<occurrences>
<resourceData>7439-89-6</resourceData>
</occurrences>
</topic>
```

For referencing an occurrence by pointing to an external URI, the element *resourceRef* is used:

```
<topic id="iron">
<subjectIdentity>
<subjectIndicatorRef xlink:href="http://www.example.org/Fe"/>
</subjectIdentity>
<baseName>
<baseNameString>iron</baseNameString>
</baseName>
<occurrence>
<resourceRef xlink:href="http://www.example.org/CAS/7439-89-6"/>
</topic>
```

By instantiating the occurrence to an appropriate topic, the semantics of the resource data becomes clear. In this example, the content that is embedded in the *resourceRef* element represents the iron-specific *CAS* number.

```
<topic id="CAS-Number">
<subjectIdentity>
<subjectIndicatorRef xlink:href="http://www.example.org/CAS"/>
</subjectIdentity>
<baseName>
<baseNameString>CAS-Number</baseNameString>
</baseName>
</topic>

<topic id="iron">
<subjectIdentity>
<subjectIndicatorRef xlink:href="http://www.example.org/Fe"/>
</subjectIdentity>
<baseName>
<baseNameString>iron</baseNameString>
</baseName>
```

```
<occurrence>
<instanceOf>
<topicRef xlink:href="#CAS-Number"/>
</instanceOf>
<resourceRef xlink:href="http://www.example.org/CAS/7439-89-6"/>
</occurrence>
</topic>
```

As Pepper concluded, the strength of Topic Maps lies in the ability of encoding arbitrary complex knowledge structures and linking them to information resources (Pepper 2002). By taking the generality and expressive power of the Topic Maps concept into account, Topic Maps are mainly discussed as a knowledge management tool for the constitution of corporate memory.

3.2.2 SKOS

Simple Knowledge Organization System (SKOS) builds on the *RDF* und *RDFS* standards and makes use of some *OWL* constructs to provide an additional set of elements for representing KOSs on the web. The main *SKOS* vocabulary supports modeling concepts and conceptual relations. An optional extension called *SKOS-XL* additionally allows describing relations between terms. In this section, we sketch central elements of the *SKOS* core vocabulary. For a more comprehensive insight into *SKOS*, see the respective *W3C* documents (Isaac & Summers 2009), (Miles & Bechhofer 2009a), (Miles & Bechhofer 2009b).

According to the *SKOS* core vocabulary, concepts are instances of the class *skos:Concept*. Via the relation *skos:inScheme*, they can be allocated to an individual knowledge organization system that has to be defined as instance of the class *skos:ConceptScheme* beforehand. *skos:Concept* and *skos:ConceptScheme* are declared as disjoint; no concept can be instance of both classes at the same time. Semantic relations between concepts – or more general: between instances – can be represented with recourse to a small set of pre-defined relation types. The example below gives a respective *SKOS* encoding for the concept "iron" modeled in the *Library of Congress Subject Headings.*[11]

```
<skos:Concept rdf:about="http://id.loc.gov/authorities/subjects/
sh85068131">
<skos:prefLabel xml:lang="en">iron</skos:prefLabel>
```

11 Please note that the encoding example does not fully comply with the *LCSH* encoding that is available within the frame of the *LCSH* Linked Data service. Thus not all semantic relations modeled in the *LCSH* are displayed here.

```
<skos:inScheme rdf:resource="http://id.loc.gov/authorities/
subjects"/>
<skos:broader rdf:about="http://id.loc.gov/authorities/subjects/
sh88003746"/>
<skos:narrower rdf:resource="http://id.loc.gov/authorities/
subjects/sh85050200"/>
<skos:related rdf:resource="http://id.loc.gov/authorities/
subjects/sh2003006396"/>
</skos:Concept>
```

As common within the frame of the Semantic Web, all concepts can be identified via URIs. The first URI in the above example ending with "sh85068131" represents a particular concept that is referenced in natural language for human understanding by the preferred label "iron". The label is connected with the concept by using *skos:prefLabel*, a subproperty of *rdfs:label*. The property *skos:inScheme* connects the concept "iron" to the concept scheme in which it is modeled, exposing it explicitly as an *LCSH* concept. The other *SKOS* elements refer to semantic relations.

Representation of semantic relations
The *LCSH* concept is linked via *skos:broader*, *skos:narrower* and *skos:related* to a number of other *LCSH* concepts, which are represented by URIs as well.

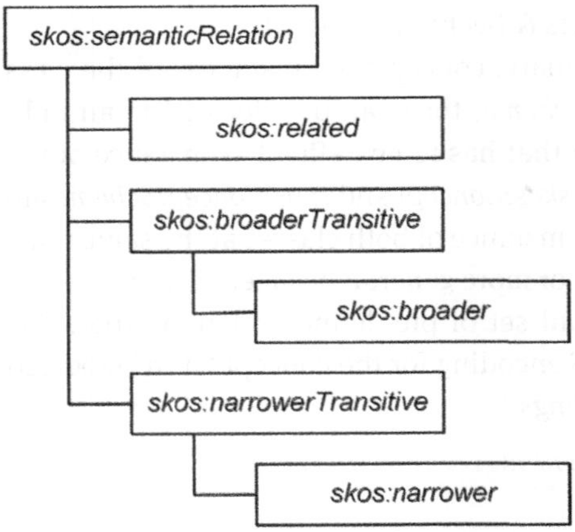

Fig. 3.7: Relationships between *SKOS* semantic relation properties (Miles & Bechhofer 2009a).

skos:broader and *skos:narrower* are connecting concepts having a broader scope of meaning with concepts having a narrower scope of meaning and vice versa, as these two *SKOS* elements are inverse to each other. Therefore, they represent hierarchical relationships.

skos:related denotes a symmetric associative relation. The semantic relations defined in *SKOS* are ordered in an *RDF* hierarchy, which allows drawing additional inferences. Figure 3.7 presents this hierarchy by sub- and superordination of *SKOS* properties, following application-oriented criteria.

skos:broader is modeled as a subproperty of *skos:broaderTransitive*, whereas *skos:narrower* is modeled as a subproperty of *skos:narrower:Transitive*. This makes all concepts being related via *skos:broader* also being related via *skos:broaderTransitive*, independently of whether or not this relation has been modeled explicitly. The same applies to *skos:narrower* and *skos:narrowerTransitive* respectively. Taking the aforementioned *LCSH* concept "iron" as an example, Figure 3.8 shows that the *skos:broader* property connects this concept with the *LCSH* concept "native element minerals", whereas the *skos:narrower* property connects it with the *LCSH* concept "Food--Iron content".

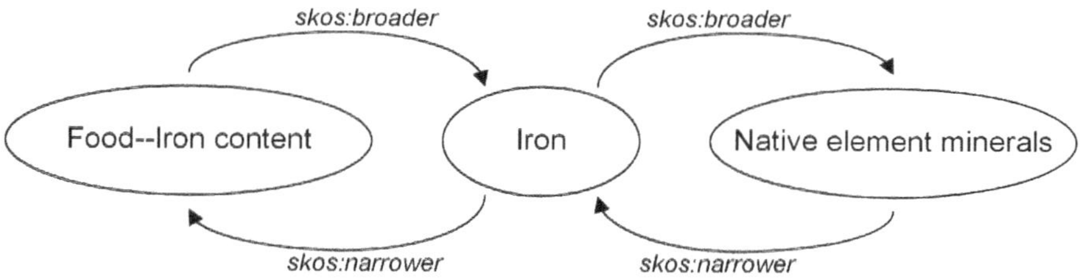

Fig. 3.8: Modeled *SKOS* properties between *LCSH* concepts.

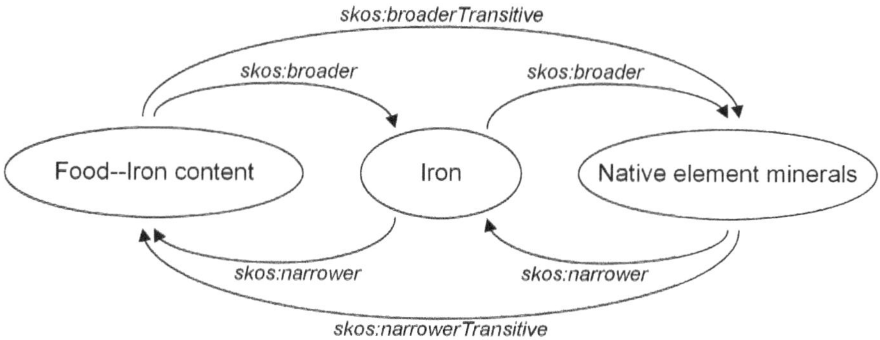

Fig. 3.9: Inferred transitive *SKOS* properties between *LCSH* concepts.

Due to the defined hierarchy, the respective transitive property can be inferred, allowing machines to automatically consider the indirect relation holding between the concept "Food--Iron content" and the concept "Native element minerals" as well and present respective associated information resources. From *skos:broader* the *SKOS* property *skos:broaderTransitive* can be inferred. This makes the concept "Food--Iron content" not only related to the concept "iron" via *skos:broader* but also via *skos:broaderTransitive*. Likewise the concept "iron" is related to the concept "Native element minerals". As *skos:broaderTransitive* is transitive, it can be deduced that the concept "Food--Iron content" is also related to the concept "Native element minerals" via *skos:broaderTransitive*. Equally, *skos:narrowerTransitive* can be inferred from *skos:narrower*. This means that "iron" is related to "Food--Iron content" and "Native element minerals" to "iron" not only via *skos:narrower* but also via *skos:narrowerTransitive*. As *skos:narrowerTransitive* is a transitive property, it can be concluded that the concept "Native element minerals" is related to the concept "Food--Iron content" via *skos:narrowerTransitive* as well (cf. Fig. 3.9).

4 Information Retrieval and Knowledge Exploration

In this chapter, we will give a brief introduction in information retrieval (IR) and some related aspects of knowledge exploration. Both of these processes constitute the major focus of this book and can therefore be seen as core activities. The enhancement of these processes by using models, procedures, and instruments of semantic knowledge representation will be discussed in Part C. Prior to this, the basic retrieval paradigms and scenarios are outlined in this preliminary chapter for providing a comprehensive understanding of these essential issues.

4.1 Information Retrieval Essentials

The term *information retrieval* was introduced by *Mooers* in the early 1950's, who stated it as "a finding or discovery process with respect to stored information", which "embraces the intellectual aspects of the description of information and its specification for search, and also whatever systems, techniques, or machines that are employed to carry out the operation" (Mooers, 1951). As a matter of course, the associated activities (i.e. the searching and finding of relevant information to a given information need) were also practiced before *Mooers* characterized them as "information retrieval". However, once this label was applied, it was used by the upcoming research in the late 1950's and 1960's, when for the first time computers were used for the automatic characterization of document contents and the "retrieving" of certain contents from document collections (Cool & Belkin 2011).

The idealized process of IR, as stated by van Rijsbergen (1979, 3) can simply be described as a stored collection of documents and a person (i.e. a user of the store), who formulates a question (i.e. a query) to which the answer is a result set of documents satisfying the information need expressed by the user's question. Therefore the retrieved documents have to be some kind of "relevant" to the information need. This notion of *relevance* is essential to every form of IR (ibid., 4) and it is determined by the extent of accordance between the formulated query, which represents the manifested information need and the content of each retrieved document. Hence, the degree of matching between query and document indicates the document's supposed relevance to the information need. Apart from that, every match in a retrieval process is providing an access point to some more or less relevant information. This conception of a retrieval process can also be characterized by a *lookup-based* retrieval model, which can be seen as a generic prototype for modeling specific IR systems over the last decades (Bates 1989, 408).

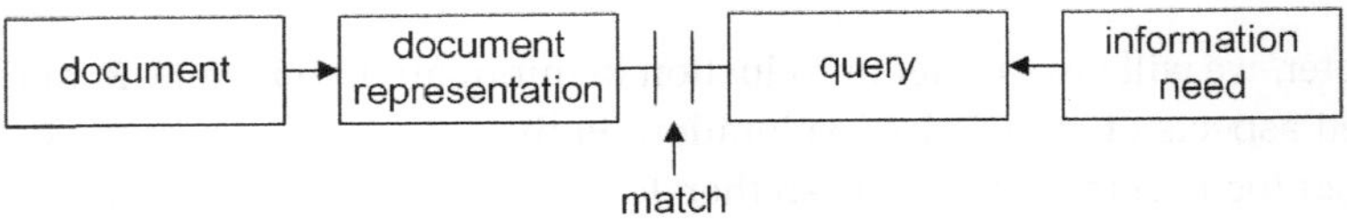

Fig. 4.1: Lookup-based retrieval model (Bates, 1989).

In the following, we will shortly describe how this lookup-based process of matching between the query and the document resp. the document representation was designed by developing various models of IR. Afterwards we will discuss the shortcomings of the lookup-based paradigm and introduce some alternative approaches in the context of knowledge exploration.

4.1.1 Exact Match Paradigm

Assuming that a document (whether full-text documents or merely their documentary representations) consists of terms, the relevance of a document can be stated if the terms contained in it are matching the query's terms. This imagination of a *string-based query* (Glossary B1) is based on the *exact match* paradigm which is based upon a dichotomic principle, as either relevance is given (in the case of matching), or it is not (in the case of mismatching). The functionality can be provided by the *Boolean model* of IR. A query is constructed as a restrictive search argument, using Boolean logic, and matched against the document collection, which is usually represented by an index-based access structure for providing a fast lookup processing. The Boolean operators *AND*, *OR*, and *NOT* are used for processing set intersection, set union, and set difference operations (Kowalski 2011, 16):

Tab. 4.1: Boolean search arguments.

Search arguments	Operation
Chemistry *AND* physics *NOT* mechanics	Select all documents containing "chemistry" and "physics" that do not contain "mechanics".
Chemistry *OR* physics *NOT* mechanics	Select all documents containing "chemistry" and/or documents that contain "physics" and do not contain "mechanics".
Chemistry *OR* chemical *OR* chemically	Select all documents containing "chemistry" and/or "chemical" and/or "chemically".

In Table 4.1 some typical Boolean search arguments are shown. Usually, a Boolean search argument is processed in the order of the operator's precedence, so that *AND* resp. *NOT* take precedence over *OR*. Please note that the Boolean *OR* is not to be confused with the colloquially used or, which means either/or. In contrast, the Boolean *OR* can be put on a level with the colloquial and/or, as it is used to build set union operations.

Hence, the search argument in the first row of Table 4.1 retrieves a set intersection of documents containing the terms "chemistry" and "physics", while all documents containing "mechanics" are excluded from that set intersection. The argument in the second row retrieves a set union of documents containing the term "chemistry" and/or documents containing the term "physics", but not "mechanics". Thus the set difference operation is effected only to the set of documents containing "physics", and not to the set union operation as a whole. The argument in the third row retrieves a set union of documents containing "chemistry" and/or "chemical" and/or "chemically" – three terms, which are semantically near to each other. Those search arguments can emerge from the assumption, that documents containing the terms "chemical" or "chemically" are relevant to the same information need, as documents containing "chemistry" are relevant to. Thus, the construction of large set union operations is one Boolean search technique for obtaining more access points to desired information. It should be mentioned that these set operations affect only a formal level, as e.g. the search argument "chemistry *AND* physics" retrieves documents containing both terms "chemistry" and "physics", but not necessarily documents about "chemical physics" or similar.

Many search environments also obtain the functionalities of truncation and proximity, which allow a less restrictive formulation of Boolean search arguments. While truncation allows the placement of a wildcard character at the left or right end of a search term (e.g. if "*" would be the wildcard character, the search argument "chem*" would match all search terms of the third row in Table 4.1), proximity search enables a pattern recognition for searching terms that occur near to each other. Nevertheless, the exact match paradigm hardly provides an adequate IR, as it comes down to finding simple matches to patterns, instead of finding relevant documents (Grossman & Frieder 2004, 1). Therefore, van Rijsbergen distinguishes between "data retrieval", based on exact matching, and genuine IR, based on partial matching (van Rijsbergen 1979, 1–2).

4.1.2 Partial Match Paradigm

With regards to the shortcomings of exact matching, IR research has developed a number of models that execute a *partial matching*. In doing so, the notion of relevance as a dichotomic factor is replaced by a more complex relevance perception, which is based on the assumption that a document isn't absolutely relevant or non-relevant, but only relatively relevant (resp. non-relevant) to a user's query. However, those more elaborated models are still based on terms and the common notion, that the more often terms are found in both the document and the query, the more relevant the document is to the query (Grossman & Frieder 2004, 9).

The *vector space model* and the *probabilistic model* are probably the most prominent examples of retrieval models, allowing a partial match search. The vector space model can be seen as a geometric approach. In a given collection, each document is represented by a vector, consisting of the document's terms. The query is also considered as a document and therefore the query terms are represented by a vector, too. Hence, documents and query are represented together in the vector space, so it becomes possible to compare the similarity between the query and each document by the extent that their vectors point into the same direction (Salton, Yang & Wong 1975). The closeness of a document vector to the query's vector indicates the assumed relevance of the represented document to the query. Obviously, this relevance judgment is influenced by the similarity coefficient that is being used to measure the closeness. Several measures have been developed, which partially consider automatically or manually assigned term weightings for document or query terms (Kowalski 2011, 144–147; Grossman & Frieder 2004, 18–21).

The probabilistic model determines the similarity between a query and a document as the probability of the document's relevance to the query. It should be mentioned that probabilistic relevance judgments don't refer to the degree of relevance of a document to a given query, but only to the degree of probability to which a document is relevant or not (Robertson 1997, 281). Therefore, a matching process between the query and the document collection is executed, following the simplifying assumption, that the distribution of terms over the collection is independent, so that there's no interrelation between two terms in the same document (Robertson & Sparck-Jones 1976, 132). Initially, all documents are assumed to be relevant or non-relevant by equal probability and a document is stated as non-relevant, if it doesn't at least partially match the query. Subsequently, the user can refine the obtained result set, giving some intellectual relevance judgments by selecting those documents that fit best the information need. The IR system will consider the selected documents as highly relevant and execute another matching process, based on the *relevance feedback* received from the user. To do so, a weighting function is used to set up the weights of the terms, contained in the relevant documents. A number of such weighting functions have been established and their effects on IR was discussed extensively (cf. e.g. Harman 1992). Eventually, the probability of appearance of terms in relevant documents is relativized to their probability of appearance in non-relevant documents and in the whole collection, which is expected to lead to increasingly precise probabilistic relevance judgments of the IR system.

Besides the vector space model and the probabilistic model, numerous alternative models were developed, e.g., the *Latent semantic indexing model* (cf. Deerwester et al. 1990) and the language model (as further developments of the vector space model resp. the probabilistic model), Boolean indexing and fuzzy set models (both further developments of the Boolean model, which transform Boolean search arguments by term weighting resp. by fuzzy logic), or several network-based models, using inference or neural networks. An overview, including these more sophisticated retrieval models is provided by Grossman and Frieder (2004, 9–92) or Rasmussen (2011, 95–111). With the upcoming of web search engines and particularly *Google*, the field of index-based retrieval environments was also notably developed by sophisticated ranking algorithms (cf. Grossman & Frieder 2004, 281–284 for a compact overview or Langville & Meyer 2006 for a vivid introduction to search engine rankings).

4.2 Measuring Effectiveness in Information Retrieval

Returning to van Rijsbergens idealized definition, the goal of IR lies in the answering of a users query by retrieving a result set of documents containing relevant information for satisfying the user's information need. Therefore the IR system must deliver all relevant documents and discard all non-relevant documents. As we have seen in the previous section, IR research made several attempts in developing various models to reach this goal. But contrasting the idealized view with practice, it becomes obvious that no retrieval model can raise this performance completely, so the formulated goal of IR is stated to be hypothetical. How retrieval models really outperform is continuously tested and evaluated against several test collections.

These test collection-based evaluations can be traced to the 1950's, when the first tests were conducted. The *Astia* test and the *Cranfield-Uniterm* test, carried out in the United States and Britain, tested the retrieval performance of several indexing approaches compared to the performance of a simple single term (uniterm) indexing in a given document test collection (Ellis 1996, 1–3). Later on, a larger scaled retrieval test, the *Cranfield I* test, was executed. Cranfield I focused on the comparative performance of four indexing approaches: the *Universal Decimal Classification (UDC)*, an alphabetical subject index, a faceted classification scheme, and, again, the *Uniterm* indexing approach. By searching a test collection of 18,000 documents with a set of 1,200 questions, the results showed only little differences between the tested approaches (ibid., 3–6). Eventually, a test series named *Cranfield II* was conducted to investigate the effect of varying index language features on the retrieval performance. For this purpose, 33 different types of indexing languages were built using manifold terminologies and structures. Beyond that, the measure of effectiveness in *Cranfield II* was an explicitly relevance-based measure (ibid., 6–7), represented by the two essential ratios precision and recall.

Precision represents the degree of soundness of a retrieval result. To obtain precision the number of relevant documents retrieved is related to the total number retrieved. Thus, a high precision indicates a high number of relevant documents in the result set. Yet, the total number of relevant documents in the collection must not be ignored, since one cannot infer from a high precision value to a high IR performance. A result set may obtain predominantly relevant documents, but the IR performance would be poor, if the bigger part of relevant documents remained untraceable in the document collection. *Recall* considers this factor, as it is the ratio of the number of relevant documents retrieved to the total number of relevant documents in the collection (Grossman & Frieder 2004, 2–5).

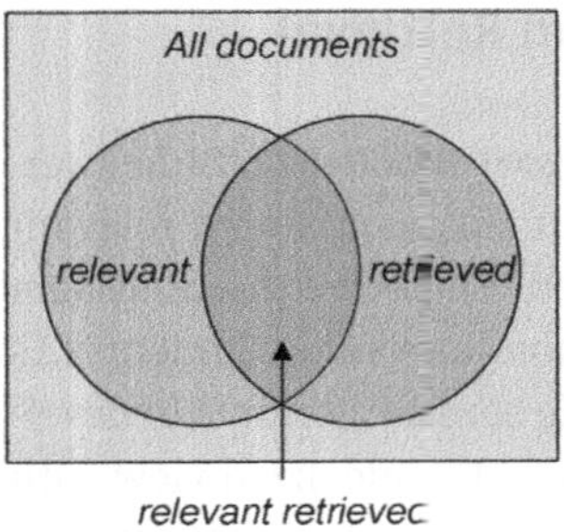

$$\text{precision} = \frac{\text{relevant retrieved}}{\text{retrieved}}$$

$$\text{recall} = \frac{\text{relevant retrieved}}{\text{relevant}}$$

Fig. 4.2: Precision and recall (Grossman & Frieder 2004).

As shown in Figure 4.2, precision and recall are determined by four elementary parameters: (1) the number of relevant documents, (2) the number of retrieved documents, (3) the number of relevant retrieved documents, (4) the number of not relevant, not retrieved documents. Parameter (1) (i.e. the number of relevant documents), which is needed to calculate the recall, is typically unknown and can only be approximated (cf. Fuhr & Nottelmann 2003 for a methodological overview on this task). Concerning the combined consideration of precision and recall, Grossman and Frieder (2004, 4) discuss a typical precision/recall graph, as shown in Figure 4.3, and point to the correlation between these two ratios, which can be described as inverse proportional. While an increasing recall can only be reached by retrieving more documents, this is accompanied by the increasing probability of retrieving more non-relevant documents. In turn, this must lead to a decreasing precision, since the quality of a retrieved result set decreases, the more non-relevant documents are obtained. The understanding of this inverse proportional relationship between precision and recall, which was also observed in the results of the *Cranfield II* test series (Ellis 1996, 7), is essential to every user of an IR system for formulating adequate queries and retrieving satisfying result sets. A comprehensive overview that outlines the numerous empirical studies on the relationship between precision and recall is provided by Buckland and Gey (1994).

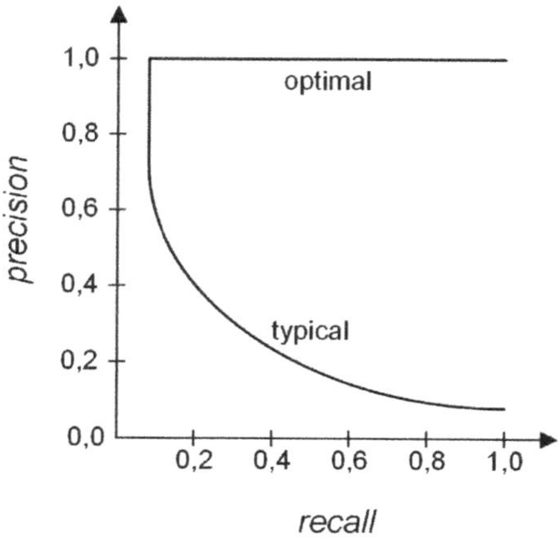

Fig. 4.3: Typical and optimal precision/recall graph (Grossman & Frieder 2004).

The difficulty of understanding this opposed effects can be seen as a fundmental motivation for questioning the traditional lookup-based model of IR and for acquiring a broader comprehension of how to satisfy information needs. Beyond analyzing the user's search behaviour, the improving of retrieval processes is crucial. The more successful matches between query and documents are obtained, the more access points to relevant information are provided, and the better recall will perform. Several attempts of improving retrieval processes have been made, mostly concerning the query processing in various ways by developing more effective retrieval models (cf. the examples in the previous section, e.g. models based on latent semantic indexing, fuzzy logic, etc.). Since the early 1990's, those approaches have been tested and evaluated against large test collections in the context of the annual *Text REtrieval Conference (TREC)* (cf. http://trec.nist.gov and for an introduction to the work of TREC cf. Grossman & Frieder 2004, 291–298).

In the next section we will point out strategies for improving IR and thereby multiplying access points to relevant information, not by focusing on the algorithmic side, but on conceptual aspects. We will introduce an enhanced understanding of terms and discuss the outcomes of word-based and conceptual retrieval processes, as well as of conceptual and topical exploration processes. With the notion of exploration a new retrieval paradigm is addressed, which no longer focuses on the retrieving of information, but on the exploring of knowledge.

4.3 From Retrieving to Exploring

To begin with, it seems useful to carve out the differences between conventional, lookup-based IR and the rather vague conception of "exploring" (Glossary B4) through information spaces. The well established works of Bates (1989) and Marchionini (2006) both stress these differences by describing "berrypicking" resp. exploratory-like searches and seem to provide adequate theoretical frameworks for embedding our further considerations.

As Bates (1989, 408) emphasizes, the lookup-based model promoted the understanding of IR in many ways. However, the reduction of the user's information need to the one-time conception of a query is contradictory to real-life searches, which contain typically multiple query iterations, postquery browsing, and detailed result examination, all of which, as White and Roth (2009, 4) determine, are not captured in the lookup-based model.

Based on this insight, it emerged the idea of a less restrictive model, which is not limited to a linear query-answer-process, but considers more exploratory searches. The conception of satisfying a rather precise or vague information need by "exploring" an information space resp. a document collection, is particularly addressed by the *berrypicking* model (Bates 1989). With the "berrypicking" model, *Bates* formulated an alternative draft to the lookup-based model of the traditional IR research. As Bates explains, real-life searches may begin with just one feature of a broader topic, or just one relevant reference, and move through a variety of sources, in which each encountered piece of information gives new ideas and directions to follow and, consequently, a new conception of the query (ibid., 409–410). Hence, the query will not prove satisfactory by a single result set, but by a series of selections of individual references and bits of information at each stage. Bates characterizes this search process as a "bit-at-a-time retrieval" and subsumes it under the label "berrypicking" (ibid.).

Closely related to the "berrypicking" model, Marchionini (2006) raises the conception of an *exploratory search*. Initially, he introduces a hierarchy of information needs, which ranges from basic facts for guiding short-term actions, to networks of related concepts for understanding and executing complex tasks, to complex networks of tacit and explicit knowledge for accreting a lifetime's expertise. Based on these different kinds of information needs, three kinds of search activities are identified: "lookup" (i.e. the established lookup model of IR), "learn" (i.e. developing new knowledge through cognitive processing and interpretation of the objects resp. documents contained in a retrieved result set), and "investigate" (i.e. analyzing, synthesizing and evaluating extended knowledge in the sense of a long-term task) (ibid., 42–43). Pointing to the differentiation between simple "lookup" activities and the more complex activities of learning and investigating, Marchionini characterizes the both latter activities as "exploratory" searches.

In Figure 4.4 we adopt Marchionini's classification of search activities. However, since the term "exploratory search" is rather common in describing a user's search behaviour, we prefer the term *knowledge exploration* (Glossary B4) as we are focusing not only on user-system interaction, but also on system support. For giving a more vivid impression, Marchionini characterized each search activity by a number of attributes (cf. Fig. 4.4). A "lookup" search covers known-item searches, which are executed by data or information retrieval (supported by some navigational features if applicable) for the purpose of verifying or answering a given information need. It becomes apparent, that "learn" and "investigate" search activities are affected by more abstract attributes, which can mostly be assigned to specific tasks, e.g., the acquisition or aggregation of knowledge. As White and Roth (2009, 13–14) point out, there is generally interplay between these activities, as for example "lookup" searches are embedded in learning or investigation, and again learning is an important part of investigation (the dotted arrows in Fig. 4.4 represent these interactions).

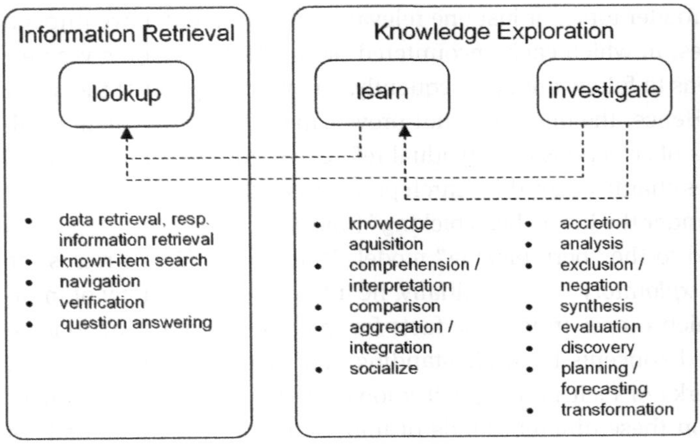

Fig. 4.4: Search activities in IR and knowledge exploration (modified from Marchionini 2006).

It is obvious that the more complex search activities are, the more support by adequate retrieval features is required. While "lookup" searches basically may be well executed by a common fulltext information retrieval, this probably won't suffice, when it comes to learning or investigating activities. Thus for providing an adequate support of these knowledge exploration tasks, more elaborated retrieval features seem to be required. In the following we will adopt a term-based perspective of retrieval processes and introduce a differentiation into four types of support:
- string-based retrieval processes
- conceptual retrieval processes
- conceptual exploration processes
- topical exploration processes

In Figure 4.5 the retrieval process types are represented in ascending order of their retrieval coverage. We speak of *retrieval coverage* for describing the degree of scope by which a retrieval or exploration process can be supported through an underlying conceptual knowledge structure. While string-based retrieval processes are simply matching query strings against the document collection, conceptual retrieval processes are recognizing the word and its underlying conceptual meaning. Processes of conceptual exploration are relating this meaning to its semantic environment, considering these relations for improving retrieval results. At the top of this hierarchy stands the notion of topical exploration processes. Compared to conceptual explorations, processes of topical exploration are not limited to the retrieval of single concepts and their a priori defined conceptual environments, as they are able to recognize document-specific topics via an a posteriori combination of one or more concepts. Subsequently, we will discuss these process types from minimal, string-based to maximal, topical coverage of retrieval in detail.

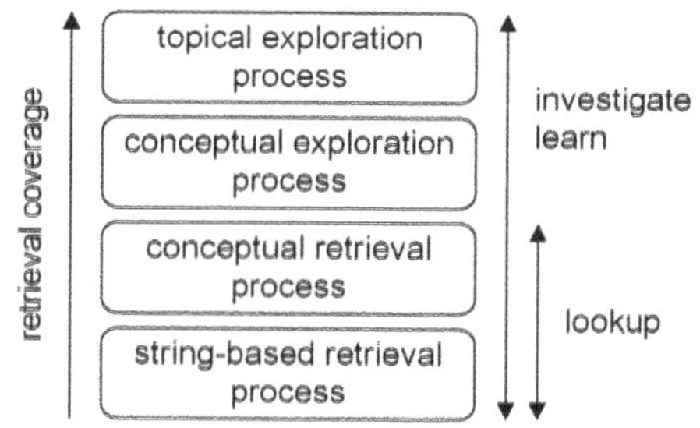

Fig. 4.5: Retrieval process types and search activities.

Beyond that, Figure 4.5 shows a proposed assignment of the retrieval process types to the three search activities of "lookup", "learn" and "investigate". Thus string-based and conceptual retrieval processes are limited to lookup search activities, due to the adequate support of known-item-searches and the navigation between a concept and its various expressions. In contrast, it can be assumed that conceptual and topical exploration processes provide support of both lookup searches and learning and investigation tasks. The navigation not only between concepts and their appropriate expressions, but also between several concepts by considering their semantic relatedness and the considering of even document-specific topics seem to be reasonable features for supporting knowledge acquisition, interpretation, analysis and evaluation tasks, etc. (cf. Fig. 4.4). When focusing on the introduced retrieval process types in the following, we will prove these statements by presenting some examples of use cases.

4.3.1 String-based Retrieval Processes

The *string-based retrieval process* is of the most simplest kind. The string sequences contained in the entered query are matched against the string sequences contained in each stored document resp. in each documentary unit. This can be processed by an exact or partial matching.

Figure 4.6 shows an example of an exact matching procedure. The query string "iron" retrieves a result set of documents, which are concerning "iron" as well as other topics that contain the searched string, too. It becomes obvious, that string-based searches often lack precision, if e.g. a search for the chemical element "iron" returns documents about "irony". On the other hand it is to fear that a number of relevant documents concerning the element "iron" are not found by the simple query string "iron".

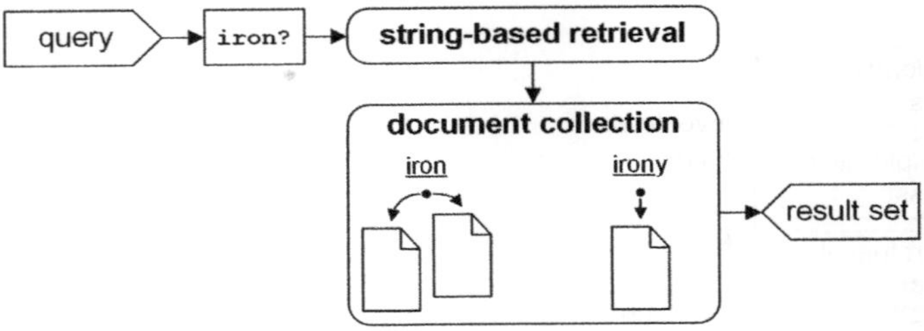

Fig. 4.6: String-based retrieval process.

For reducing this lack of recall in string-based retrieval, one can broaden the rather restrictive query by adding some alternative, but semantically identical query terms. Figure 4.7 shows a modified query that uses the Boolean *OR* operator for adding alternative appellations of the element "iron". In Boolean IR systems, this expanded query can be processed as a set union operation.

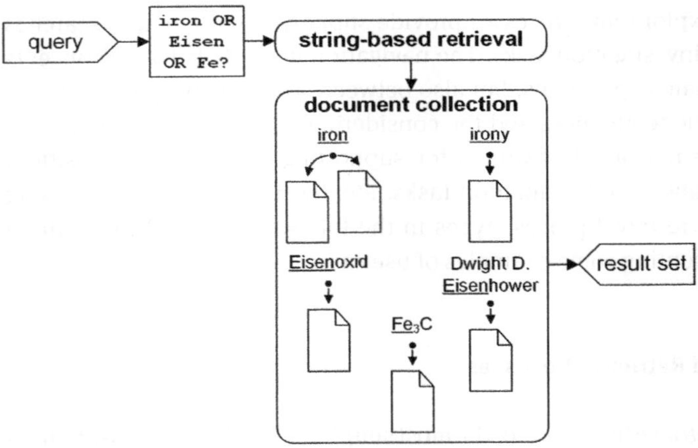

Fig. 4.7: Expanded string-based retrieval process.

The broader query formulation, which is now enhanced by the terms "Eisen" (the German translation of iron) and "Fe" (the standardized element symbol of iron in the periodic table of elements), may lead to an increasing recall, but likewise to a decreasing precision, as more documents are retrieved, but not all of them can be deemed relevant to the query. This effect was already pointed out in Section

4.2 as an inverse proportional correlation between precision and recall. Within the string-based approach, this situation cannot be reasonably improved. Therefore the simple matching of string sequences should be supported by appropriate knowledge about the term semantics. Initially, we will focus on "lexical" knowledge, i.e., the consolidation of various different terms that share the same conceptual meaning.

4.3.2 Conceptual Retrieval Process

As we have seen in the previous section, string-based retrieval processes may cause an extensive intellectual effort of query formulation for achieving a satisfying precision. To relieve the user from this time-consuming task, the appropriate query vocabulary can be structured proactively. We speak of *conceptual* retrieval, when the user-side efforts for collocating synonymous terms to broader search arguments are automatically adopted by the IR system. This can be achieved by modeling those strings that refer to the same concepts as classes of semantic equivalence. One can use these classes as *synsets* (sets of synonyms) for an adequate query formulation. In Figure 4.8, a Boolean search argument using the terms "Fe" and "C" leads to a result set of documents containing the term "iron" as well as the term "carbon". This becomes possible by recourse to the conceptual knowledge, which is provided by appropriate synsets.

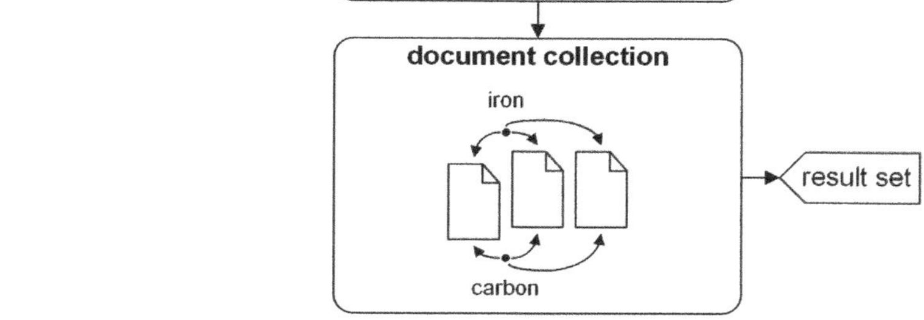

Fig. 4.8: Conceptual retrieval process.

In this example of modeling, the terms “carbon”, “silicon”, and “iron” are related each to a number of synonymous terms, representing the status of *semantic equivalency*. These semantic equivalences can be defined by annotating the in-between relations. However, the annotation “use synonym” in Figure 4.8 not only constitutes synonymy, but can also be recognized as a role statement. In an indexing process an indexer would learn from this synsets that e.g. “carbon” should be used as the preferred term for describing a document concerning the chemical element of carbon as a topic.

For providing an automatic conceptual retrieval, this conceptual knowledge must be considered somehow automatically in a retrieval process. Basically two approaches are conceivable for this purpose. One approach lies in an automatic *query expansion* in the sense of supplementing the initial query with additional terms (Efthimiadis 1996, 122). This can be done by using the synsets of terms as knowledge structures – when entering a query term, a check routine is initiated, proving if the entered term is related to any other semantically equivalent terms. If so, these related terms are added to the query.

The other approach can be characterized as a kind of *query modification* in the sense of adding terms to or removing terms from the initial query (ibid.), and it stands to reason, if the underlying document collection was indexed with controlled vocabulary. In this case, a replacing routine based upon the synset structure could be initiated for changing the entered query term with the particular synonym that was used as the preferred term in the indexing process.

4.3.3 Conceptual Exploration Processes

In the sense of *Marchionini's* framework of search activities (cf. Fig. 4.4), the increasing complexity of information needs and search activities becomes manifest in the shift from lookup-oriented retrieval processes to learn- or investigate-oriented explorative processes. This increasing complexity of information needs and search behavior is attended by increasing requirements on the applied IR systems. For providing an adequate support of this higher level of complexity, we perform a paradigm shift from the conception of a query-response retrieval process to the notion of a more openly designed process of knowledge exploration. Therefore it becomes of interest to focus not only on concepts and their synonymous expressions, but to their conceptual environment as a whole. In Figure 4.9, a knowledge structure is chosen as the starting point of this consideration. Three types of semantic relations commonly appear in those structures. Besides the *use synonym* relation between a preferred term and number of corresponding synonymous terms, a knowledge structure is constituted by hierarchical *broader term / narrower term* relations and *related term* relations, defining a rather vague kind of semantic association between a pair of terms (in Chapters 8 and 9 of this book we will provide a detailed discussion on these different types of relations in indexing languages).

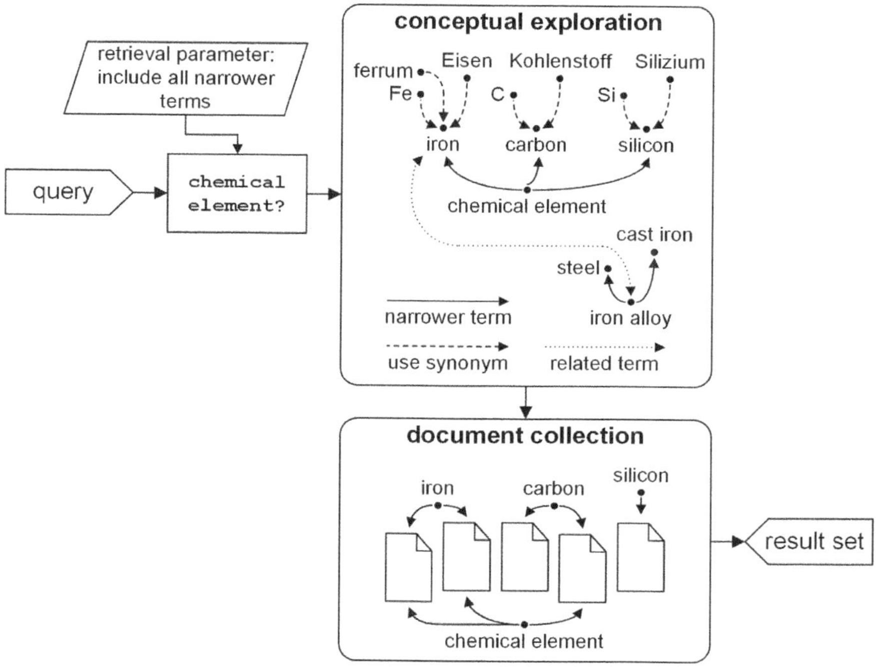

Fig. 4.9: Conceptual exploration process.

Figure 4.9 shows the well-known synsets of the chemical elements carbon, silicon, and iron as introduced in Figure 4.8, which are enriched by hierarchical and associative structures. Each element is now modeled as a narrower term of the broader term “chemical element”. Beyond that, the term “iron” is modeled as a related term to the term “iron alloy” and vice versa.

How this semantic network can be embedded in retrieval resp. exploration processes, is demonstrated by the entered query in Figure 4.9. Initially, this query is targeted on the term “chemical element”. As denoted, the result set of this quite restrictive query would contain three documents. None of these three documents is concerning chemical elements in general, but more specific topics, namely iron and carbon as concrete instances of chemical elements. Having asserted this fact, the user could wish to expand the query, so that documents concerning chemical elements as well as documents concerning only one or more instances of chemical elements are retrieved. This can easily be reached by recourse to the hierarchical *narrower term* relations.

For the consideration of the hierarchical relations, an appropriate parameter could be added to the query, which particularly defines the range of consideration. The example in Figure 4.9 is executed with a maximal range, as all narrower terms shall be included. However, this parameterization could be adjusted by hierarchical levels for including e.g. only the narrower terms of the next hierarchical level (i.e. the immediate narrower terms) or the narrower terms of the next two hierarchical levels etc.

Ideally, this conceptual exploration process would lead to an increasing recall, as denoted again in Figure 4.9, where the result set for the term "chemical element" including all narrower terms obtains more documents, than a search with "chemical elements" only would obtain. The underlying assumption is that most of these additionally obtained documents should be relevant to the query due to the semantic relatedness of the used query terms. Beyond that, the exploration could also be based upon associative relation types. However, one can argue that the rather vague semantic relatedness between associated terms leads to a decreasing precision of the retrieved result set. This becomes apparent in the example of the associative relation between the terms "iron" and "iron alloy" (cf. Fig. 4.9). Though it is basically possible to retrieve documents with these two terms that are relevant to the same information need, this is not very likely. In an IR system this phenomenon can be accommodated by the implementation of relation specific weighting factors, so that a stronger semantic relatedness, e.g. synonymous relations, will be weighted higher, and a lesser relatedness, e.g. hierarchical or associative relations, will be weighted lesser (Bayer et al. 2005).

The use of knowledge structures for supporting conceptual retrieval and exploration processes as described beforehand, were extensively examined by IR research and has been implemented in many retrieval environments as a feature, often referred to as *explosion, expansion, search down,* or similar. Early approaches can be traced back to the 1970s and 1980s and are reviewed by Efthimiadis (1996) or more recently with a focus on the search interface design by Shiri, Crawford and Chowdhury (2002). Performance measurements of these approaches are amongst others provided by Kekäläinen and Järvelin (1998). Some attention was also devoted to the fundamental question, if the knowledge structures, on which the retrieval resp. exploration processes are based upon, should be provided by collection-independent KOSs (i.e. classification systems, thesauri, ontologies), or if collection-dependent KOSs should be preferred, which would be statistically generated from the collection's vocabulary. Mandala, Tokunaga and Hozumi (1998) provide an overview with regard to the use of the natural language thesaurus *WordNet* (Fellbaum 1998) for supporting retrieval processes and state that the collection-independent structure of *WordNet* should at least be amended by a collection-dependent vocabulary.

Through the emerging vision of a *Semantic Web*, which becomes increasingly more concrete, thesauri and other semantic models have become of interest for supporting these visionary developments. While the Semantic Web and its underlying technology and standards were outlined in the previous chapter, we will now focus on the associated idea of augmenting semantic relationships for the purpose of obtaining new retrieval possibilities. Amongst others Tudhope, Alani and Jones (2001) gave an essential overview of these issues. This augmenting leads to a further development from rather thesaurus-like structures to more ontology-like structures and promotes the notion of conceptual exploration.

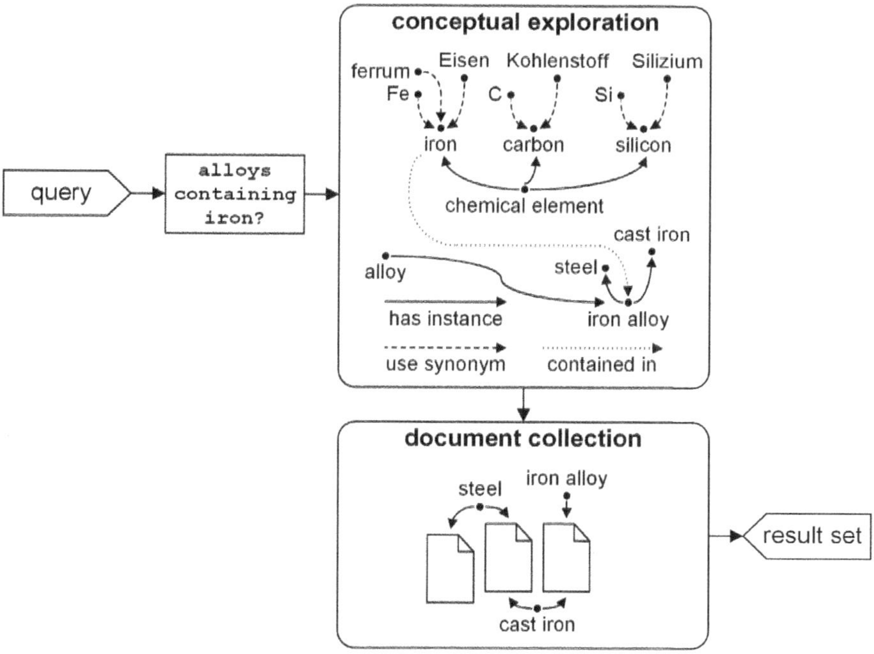

Fig. 4.10: Ontology-based conceptual exploration process.

First, the determination of semantic relationships (Glossary C3.1) allows a more differentiated query formulation and more selective exploration processes. Beyond that, the augmenting holds the potential of reasoning mechanisms that provide a completely new level of exploration. This is denoted in Figure 4.10, where the former unspecific, bi-directional, associative relationship between the terms “iron” and “iron alloy” was modified into a specific, uni-directional relationship, which is annotated with the statement “contained in”. The hierarchical *broader term / narrower term* relationships were modified into more specific *class / instance* relationships.

Assuming that the IR system is able to interpret the meaning of these relationships correctly, it becomes possible to formulate far more specific queries and to initiate more sophisticated exploration processes. So the query in Figure 4.10, which asks about alloys containing iron, can be processed due to the provided ontology-based knowledge structure and not only due to exact or partial matching. The query term “alloy” can be recognized as a class, comprising the instance “iron alloy” and it can be considered that the concept iron points to iron alloy via the “contained in” relation. Hence, “iron alloy” matches the query. But besides that, these properties of “iron alloy” are also valid to all its instances, such as “steel” or “cast iron”. So the result set may also obtain documents concerning one or more of these instances (cf. Fig. 4.10). In Chapter 3 we demonstrated how these reasoning features work on the basis of Semantic Web standards. Examinations of ontology-based retrieval approaches, including performance measurements are e.g. provided by Paralic and Kostial (2003), Stojanovic (2005) or Castells, Fernández and Vallet (2007).

4.3.4 Topical Exploration Processes

While the earlier described approaches of retrieval and exploration are representing the status of common practice or, regarding to the processes of conceptual exploration, at least the status of work under development, processes of *topical exploration* in the following sense must be understood as a desirable vision. We speak of topical exploration, when exploration processes are not only determined to a priori defined knowledge structures, but can also be expanded to those relations that were built a posteriori during the indexing process of the underlying information resources. Consequently, this means that the initial point of a topical exploration process doesn’t lie in a concept of a knowledge structure, but directly in a document topic. These document topics can be represented by concepts that are defined either a priori by given knowledge structures or a posteriori by combining multiple single concepts to a more specific conceptual expression. This means, strictly speaking, that we must distinguish between two approaches of allocating descriptors for the representation of document topics – either a descriptor is simply made up by using an appropriate a priori defined concept from a given knowledge structure or a descriptor is constructed by an a posteriori combination of concepts. Processes of topical exploration as we think of them support both of these approaches.

Figure 4.11 gives a demonstration of the latter approach. The document collection obtains three documents concerning the topic of "iron-carbon alloy". As previously described, conceptual retrieval and exploration processes can be supported by a given knowledge structure, however, the structure in Figure 4.11 provides no adequate concept for representing the topic of "iron-carbon alloy". Thus, a query formulation that is targeted on this particular topic cannot refer to an a priori defined concept and the information need has to be somehow circumscribed.

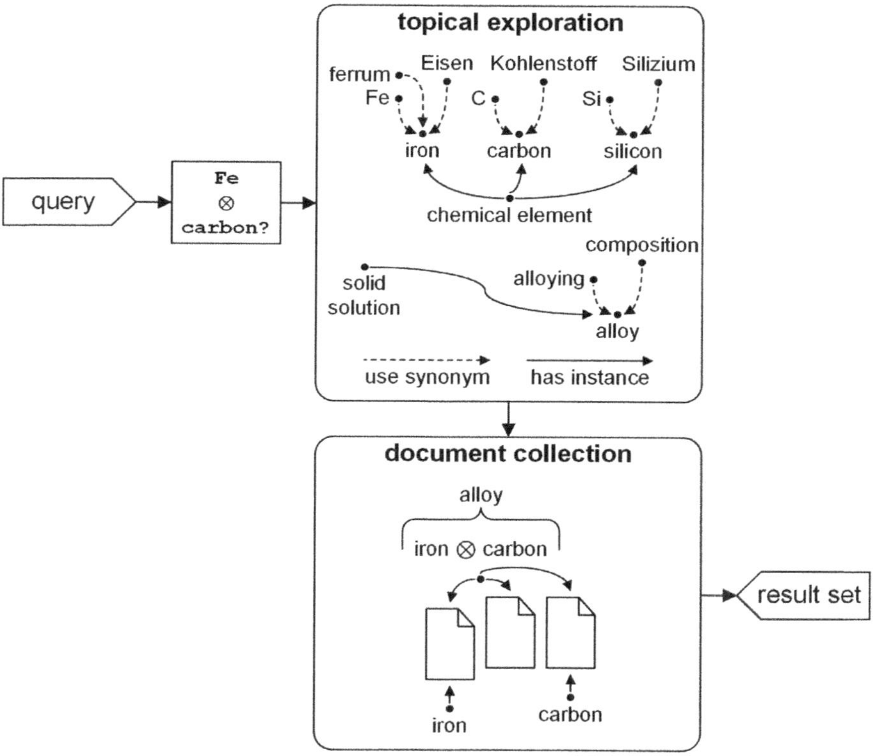

Fig. 4.11: Topical exploration process.

Therefore, the underlying document collection has been indexed by descriptors, which were built a posteriori as conceptual combinations. These conceptual combinations, which are constituting the descriptor of a document topic, follow specific syntactical rules. This is denoted in the example of Figure 4.11 by the operator symbol that is connecting the concepts iron and carbon. These two concepts and the in-between operator must be read as one syntactic expression: "iron X carbon".

The operator establishes a specific syntactical relationship between the two concepts, which is not provided by their particular conceptual contexts within the given knowledge structure. In our example let the meaning of this relationship be that of a product in the sense of an alloy. The two single concepts iron and carbon become constitutive components of this alloy, so the syntactic expression as a whole can be interpreted as the representation of the document topic of "iron-carbon alloy". An introduction into the theoretical background and some general thoughts about the establishing of those syntactical relationships is provided by Buchanan (1979, 18–21).

Ideally, this syntactic expression should be cognitively interpretable by the information seeker, as well as machine-interpretable by the IR system, and thus would close a gap between elaborated indexing methods and state-of-the-art semantic technologies. Assuming this, the expression could also be used in the query formulation (cf. Fig. 4.11). Hence, not only the indexer can interpret and use those syntactic elements for representing document topics, but also the information seeker who uses the same elements for transferring his information need into a valid query and the IR system that processes the entered query under the consideration of syntactic requirements. We will return to this notion of formalizing indexing languages for knowledge representation in Part C of this book.

It should be mentioned that this syntactical combination between single concepts is not to be confused with a Boolean combination. While the Boolean operators as introduced in Section 4.1 address a formal level, e.g. the common appearance of two terms in a set intersection, the here introduced operator refers to a level of content, as it can be read and understood as a statement about a specific semantic context between the connected concepts. In contrast, a Boolean search argument like "iron AND carbon" is targeted on documents concerning the topics of iron and carbon, but not on the specific topic of "iron-carbon alloy". This circumstance is also denoted in Figure 4.11, where the occurrences of single document topics as "iron" or "carbon" appear independently from the occurrence of the specific topic of "iron-carbon alloy".

4.4 From Homogeneous to Heterogeneous Information Spaces

Finally, we will shift our view from search activities and retrieval processes to the environment in which these processes appear. So far, we assumed that retrieval effectiveness depends especially on how successful an information need can be transformed into an adequate query and how this query can be processed by the IR system for retrieving an optimal result set. Of course, this perception isn't wrong, but with shifting the focus from rather laboratory search environments to more real situations, other influences have to be taken into account.

As described beforehand, retrieval processes are based on a matching process between the entered query and the document collection. We already outlined, how these matching processes can be executed on a string-based, a conceptual or even a topical level. Nevertheless, we assumed an underlying document collection that provides a consistent representation for each stored document. Yet, this assumption of a homogeneous information space may fit to a laboratory environment but not to reality, where most collections must be stated as heterogeneous.

Heterogeneity can be the result of inconsistent indexing decisions, when for instance, several indexing languages or indexing methods are used within one or between several document collections. Beyond that, heterogeneity can also be the result of multilingualism, i.e., the appearance of documents in two or more languages. All of these aspects must be taken into account for the understanding and interpreting the generation of a result set to a given query and for avoiding it to retrieve merely subsets of relevant documents within a heterogeneous collection.

A first simple impression of heterogeneity has already been given by Figure 4.7, which shows a string-based retrieval process. This process is initiated by a query that is formulated as the Boolean set union operation "iron OR Eisen OR Fe". A user would formulate this query in anticipation of a heterogeneous document collection, and therefore tries to give a broader description of his information need. The user assumes that the stored documents concerning the topic of iron or at least their documentary representations could contain the English term "iron", the German term "Eisen", or the element symbol "Fe". All of these three terms are referring to the same concept, yet using only one of these terms in a query would lead only to a subset of all relevant documents (cf. Fig. 4.7). As we have described in the previous section, this lexical heterogeneity can be handled by modeling synsets for each concept for facilitating conceptual retrieval processes.

However, in practice it often comes to distributed retrieval processes, where a query is run against more than just one collection. Imagine an IR system, which allows the querying of various document collections – some of them may be consistently, some of them inconsistently indexed with controlled vocabulary, some others may only provide uncontrolled keywords and some merely full text representations, some collections may be monolingual, other may contain documents resp. document representations in two or more languages.

Using one single concept for the query formulation in this situation, would not only – on the string-based level of retrieval – restrict the result set, but could lead to an even more complex effect on the conceptual level. In a knowledge structure that is developed and used as an indexing language for describing document topics, each descriptor term refers unambiguously to one concept and, in turn, the concepts and their in-between relations can be understood as surrogates for real world things. The information seeker, who uses the provided descriptor terms for his query formulation, relies on the unambiguousness of the thereby represented concepts. Yet this unambiguousness gets lost to a certain degree, when it comes to retrieval processes in a heterogeneous environment, as a descriptor term may now refer to several concepts, which are embedded in several knowledge structures.

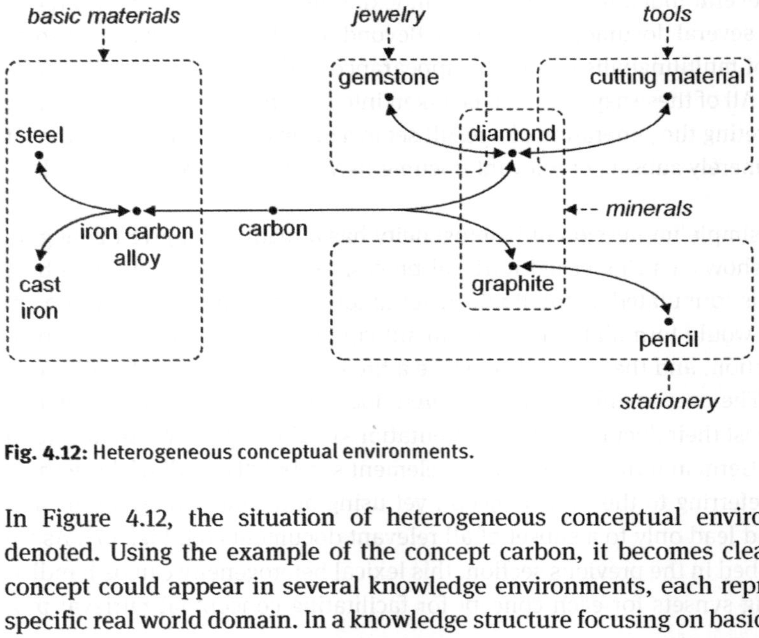

Fig. 4.12: Heterogeneous conceptual environments.

In Figure 4.12, the situation of heterogeneous conceptual environments is denoted. Using the example of the concept carbon, it becomes clear that this concept could appear in several knowledge environments, each representing a specific real world domain. In a knowledge structure focusing on basic materials, carbon could be modeled as a specific component, which allows the creation of various materials, like iron-carbon alloys for industrial purposes.

In contrast, in another knowledge structure, carbon could refer to its natural forms of appearance and therefore being modeled near to graphite or diamond. With regard to the possible usages of these minerals, the concept of carbon could be embedded in such different conceptual environments like stationery (as graphite is an important component of pencils), jewelry, or tools (as gemstones, as well as cutting materials can be made of diamonds).

If we now imagine an IR system, providing distributed retrieval processes over several document collections and therefore offering support via different knowledge structures, the expectable retrieval effects in such heterogeneous information spaces become apparent. Let the information seeker enter “carbon” as a query term and this term being matched against all available underlying knowledge structures. The term could be identified in several conceptual contexts about basic materials, stationery, jewelry, and tools and the result set could obtain documents concerning the carbon percentage in various steels, the hardness degree of pencils, the gemstone manufacturing or the risks of using diamond-based cutting tools.

As we have seen, homogeneous information spaces can affect retrieval processes in different ways. On a string-based level it can restrict the result set, as the query terms are matched against a collection of documents wherein the same topic is represented by various, homogeneous descriptors or keywords. On a conceptual level it can cause an unambiguousness of the concepts, to which the descriptor vocabulary is referred to and therefore lead to a lack of precision in the retrieved result set.

For characterizing possible conceptual differences in a heterogeneous environment, we can abstract from the previous example the more general statement that these conceptual differences often reflect specific viewpoints, which are influencing the conceptual meaning and may be grounded in a specific discipline (e.g. material science, where carbon is meant as a component or mineralogy, where carbon is meant as an element that appears in form of graphite or diamond), a specific culture, or religion.

Thus, the fundamental challenge of executing retrieval processes in heterogeneous information spaces lies not so much in lexical or lingual differences, but in the confrontation of different models of reality. For ensuring a comprehensive support of retrieval processes by using the various, heterogeneous indexing data and knowledge structures, it has to be somehow mediated between those models. For that purpose, we will introduce a number of approaches in the following part of this book that can be seen as possible attempts for handling heterogeneity in information retrieval environments. However, it should be mentioned that an optimal solution has not been found yet.

Part B
Status quo – Handling Heterogeneity in Indexing and Retrieval

5 Approaches to Handle Heterogeneity

In Part A of this book, we introduced the principles of indexing and knowledge organization, semantic technologies for knowledge representation and, finally, information retrieval and knowledge exploration. We concluded our considerations by exposing how exploring and retrieving information can be hindered by heterogeneity and multilingualism. Part B takes on these problems and presents an overview of the status quo in solving them. Therefore, this chapter will present three practical approaches that cope with heterogeneity and multilingualism with recourse to indexing languages and indexing data.

In the following, we will briefly sketch the so-called "citation pearl growing" approach and strategies of modeling multilingual indexing languages. Subsequently, we will introduce how semantic interoperability between indexing languages can be established, as this issue plays an important role when it comes to developing and enhancing indexing languages based on semantic technologies.

5.1 Citation Pearl Growing

The so-called *Citation pearl growing* is a method for dealing with the heterogeneity of indexing data in information retrieval (Riesthuis 2008, 258). It offers possibilities for expanding initial queries based on hyperlinks and existing indexing data from different indexing languages assigned to information resources. These possibilities are based on the principle that "documents, which have subject assignments in common, are logically relevant for the same question" as "if two documents have the same classification code or the same subject heading then they deal with the same subject" (ibid.).

A subject indicator of an information resource, relevant to a given information need, is used as an initial point for a query. If subsequently relevant information resources with different subject indicators are retrieved, these subject indicators are likewise used for query expansion and modification. Let us for example assume that the following information resource with its assigned indexing data is deemed to be relevant for the information need at hand:

Staab, S., & Studer, R. (2004). Handbook on ontologies. Berlin: Springer.
LCSH [Library of Congress Subject Headings]:
Knowledge representation (Information theory)
Conceptual structures (Information theory)
Ontology
Database design
Expert systems (Computer science)

SWD [Headings from the German subject headings authority file, Schlagwortnormdatei]:
Informationssystem
Wissenstechnik
Ontologie <Wissensverarbeitung>
Semantic Web
Wissensbasierte Systeme
Konzeptionelle Modellierung
Aufsatzsammlung

DDC [Classification number from the Dewey Decimal Classification]:
003.54 – ddc22 [Information theory]

Citation pearl growing encourages information seekers to use the provided hyperlinks in the subject indexing data for initiating additional queries and expanding the result set. As not all information resources are indexed with recourse to the same indexing language, a search with similar concepts from different indexing languages may yield different results that may likewise be relevant for the given information need. Taking the *LCSH* term *Ontology* and the *SWD* heading *Ontologie <Wissensverarbeitung>* as examples, we can assert that both terms represent the concept "ontology", which is the central topic of the mentioned information resource. Let a conceptual query using the *SWD* heading *Ontologie <Wissensverarbeitung>* in a database focusing on library and information science lead to the following result set:

1. Stuckenschmidt, H. (2009). Ontologien: Konzepte, Technologien und Anwendungen [Ontologies: concepts, technologies, applications]. Berlin: Springer.
2. Staab, S., & Studer, R. (2004). Handbook on ontologies. Berlin: Springer.
3. Aberer, K. (2007). Semantic Web: 6th international Semantic Web conference. 2nd Asian Semantic Web conference, ISWC 2007 + ASWC 2007, Busan, Korea, November 11–15, 2007: Proceedings. Berlin: Springer.
4. Harmelen, F. v. (2005). Information sharing on the Semantic Web. Berlin: Springer.

Let a conceptual query with the *LCSH* heading *Ontology* on the other hand lead to the following result set:

1. Davies, J. (2003). Towards the Semantic Web: ontology-driven knowledge management. Chichester, Wiley.
2. Raskin, V., & Nirenburg, S. (2004). Ontological semantics. Cambridge, Mass.: MIT Press.
3. Staab, S., & Studer, R. (2004). Handbook on ontologies. Berlin: Springer.

The result set of both conceptual queries slightly differ from each other. Some resources are found with the query term *Ontologie <Wissensverarbeitung>* that are not found with the term *Ontology*. Nevertheless, these could be likewise relevant to satisfy the underlying information need about ontologies. We can assume that the two result sets complement each other in satisfying the information need and this is exactly what citation pearl growing builds upon.

Commonly, information seekers conduct citation pearl growing intellectually by following presented hyperlinks in the indexing data of retrieved information resources. Yet, it is imaginable that automatic mechanisms can be developed, providing a more efficient support in applying this strategy. The effectiveness of citation pearl growing depends on the character of the applied indexing languages. It can be assumed that the method is most effective if the respective indexing languages exhibit similar characteristics and if the produced indexing data constitute coextensive representations of the content of an information resource.

Citation pearl growing relies on the application level of indexing languages and therefore neither supports the initial query formulation nor the process of knowledge exploration, as the support of exploration processes requires relational structures, which are modeled within the process of indexing languages design and are not reflected in the indexing data.

5.2 Modeling Multilingual Indexing Languages

On the level of individual indexing languages, the problem of *multilingualism* can be coped with integrating additional linguistic representations of existing concepts in an indexing language. In a retrieval process, these can be used as additional terminological access points to information resources. This may also be adequate when it comes to query formulation in heterogeneous information spaces. However, this approach is based on the assumption that all considered indexing languages have a common structure. This gets the more questionable the more language terms from different cultures are added that may be associated with concepts whose connotation scope may differ slightly.

If a classification exhibits an index, multilingualism can be achieved by expanding the vocabulary of the index. The *Dewey Decimal Classification (DDC)* and the *Universal Decimal Classification (UDC)* represent two impressive examples for multilingual classification schemes. The *DDC* has been translated into more than 30 languages. Its top three levels are online available and reusable in eleven languages.[12] The *UDC* has been published in 40 languages, a summary can be viewed online in 27 languages.[13]

12 http://dewey.info
13 http://www.udcc.org/udcsummary/php/index.php

Similar approaches are suggested for multilingual thesauri – one language may be defined as the main language that also crucially contributes to the modeling of the relational structure. Expressions of other languages are added as synonyms resp. near synonyms. Alternatively, all languages may be equally treated for the modeling of the relational structure, which requires structural similarity between these languages. In symmetric thesauri an equivalent (or near equivalent) expression in every considered language is set for every concept. In asymmetric thesauri neither the whole number of preferred terms have necessarily to be the same in each language nor the way they are related (Riesthuis et al. 2009).

In the course of the creation of a German *DDC* edition, a proposal was made to combine multilingualism and localization in different *DDC* translations and their corresponding indexes (cf. Gödert 2007, 2008), characterized as follows (Gödert 2008, 234) :

> The local perspectives are uncoupled from the key system and added back to the localized systems, both in the form of pre-combined built numbers but also in the form of document specific synthesized notations to support document retrieval for localized subject matters. Therefore on has to isolate facts and concepts into linkable elements and the process of localization should be supported continuously by systematic actualization of instructions for notational synthesis. For instrumental clarity of the procedure, instructions for synthesis as model examples of the localization should be developed.

However, a complete integration of all requirements of localization for subject query and knowledge exploration cannot be achieved in this way, since many local viewpoints require alternative, local-specific structures[14].

5.3 Establishing Semantic Interoperability between Indexing Languages

Pushed by the vision of a Semantic Web and the Linked Data Movement that promise new forms of information and knowledge exchange, establishing semantic interoperability between common traditional KOSs has become the most popular method to deal with heterogeneity in recent years. In order to enhance access to heterogeneously indexed information resources resp. to improve the recall of topical queries, concepts of different indexing languages are connected, whereas the local structures of the individual systems remain untouched and thus may still be utilized for local query and exploration processes. The term *semantic interoperability* is often associated with two types of interoperability,

14 Cf. also our discussion in Section 10.2.1.

which are tightly interwoven but nevertheless have to be kept apart for developing a consistent model of semantic interoperability. On the one hand, semantic interoperability refers to the error-free connection of data resp. the encodings that facilitate adequate automatic processing and interchanging of concepts. On the other hand, it refers to the semantic equivalency or at least to a high degree of semantic similarity in respect to the meaning of concepts modeled in KOSs, which can only be properly perceived and created intellectually. Conceptual relations, as the results of localized aspects, cannot be represented in a one-to-one correspondence by mappings between subject headings of authority files or mappings between subject headings and classes of a classification to that we are accustomed, as a sufficient semantic correspondence between the individual semantic containers does not exist, and, even more important, as the respective conceptual structure cannot be represented within a mapping process.

5.3.1 Structural Models

According to part 2 of the ISO 25964 standard (ISO 25964-2 2013) for thesauri and interoperability with other vocabularies, two structural models can be distinguished that may be adopted for establishing semantic interoperability between indexing languages: the non-equivalent pairs model and the backbone model.

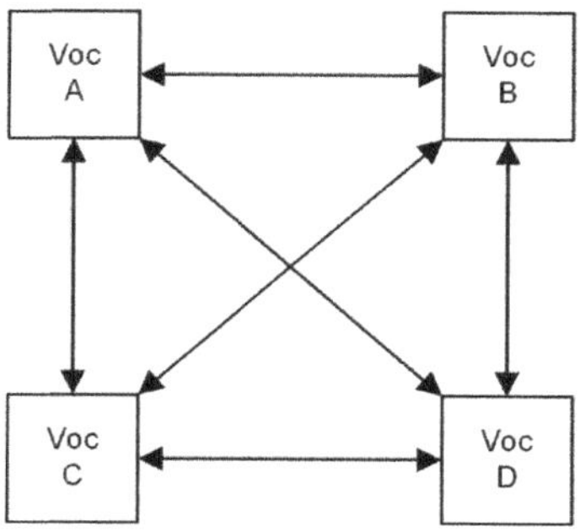

Fig. 5.1: Non-equivalent pairs model.

Many cross-concordances follow either strictly or at least as far as possible the non-equivalent pairs model that aims at establishing direct linkages between concepts of all indexing languages (Fig. 5.1). This is very useful for processes of query expansion, because irrespective which language is used for the initial query formulation, precise enhanced access points can be provided. However, it does not solve the problem of structural differences and distinct viewpoints. The more structural dissimilar concept schemes from different countries are involved in cross-explorative processes, the more difficult it is for information seekers to get familiar with the cultural viewpoints that are reflected in the schemes, especially if concept schemes due to their historic development lack a gapless and consistent relational structure.

The backbone, spine or switching model aims at keeping the efforts coming along with establishing and maintaining intersystem relations to a minimum. One indexing language is designated as the backbone to which all other vocabularies are linked. This is advantageous, as the number of links to be established can be kept to a minimum. In retrieval processes, the core vocabulary functions as a switching language. As a result, precise enhanced access points, which may also be used for automatic processes of query expansion, are primarily provided in respect to those concepts that are directly linked to the core language. Indirect linkages from one knowledge system through the core system to another knowledge system might cause a loss of precision (Probets, O'Brien & Si 2010). Nevertheless, such indirect linkages may be utilized to support cognitive query expansion. With the definition of a core system, a basic orientation resp. reference point for exploratory processes is given.

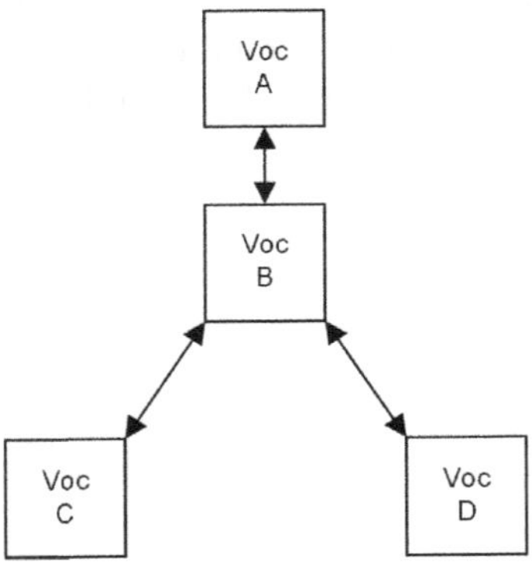

Fig. 5.2: Backbone model.

It should already be noted that we will broaden this two-model spectrum in Part C of this book by introducing a third, more sophisticated structural modeling approach. This approach intends to make use of a de-localized KOS, most preferably a classification, as a backbone, which mediates between several local indexing languages and therefore provides a gapless and consistent relational structure with logical valid relations, reflecting the diverse local needs and viewpoints. In this context, we will speak of a spine and its surrounding "satellites". However, the following discussion of mapping levels will be based on the two established approaches, as illustrated in Figures 5.1 and 5.2.

5.3.2 Mapping Levels

Against the background which linking strategies are applied to and which implications these have for supporting specific information retrieval features, three levels of semantic interoperability between concepts of KOSs can be distinguished[15]:

- string-based interoperability
- conceptual interoperability
- differentiated interoperability

All levels have in common that their data can be utilized for automatic or cognitive expansion of initial conceptual queries (or string-based queries whose initial search term complies with the representation of a linked concept) and hence for improving recall. The precision of automatically expanded queries, however, in principle differs with respect to the specific interoperability level and may be additionally influenced by an assigned directionality of linkages. Thus, uni-directional linkages established between a source and a target language may result in a significant loss of precision and functionality when used opposite. Within the frame of Semantic Web and Linked Data activities, linkages are commonly created reciprocal and bi-directional to enable a wider range of possible usage, sometimes even a certain exchangeability of data. To which extend intersystem relations also contribute to processes of knowledge exploration, depends on the description of their expressivity and additionally on the characteristics of the individual KOS. The association of a particular retrieval paradigm with a respective model of semantic interoperability is not to be understood as a rigid one-to-one attribution, but rather as a loose allocation.

Sometimes, economic or legal issues force linking activities to be restricted, which may lead to a so-called "high-level mapping" approach, as the counterpart of "deep-level mapping". Both strategies are commonly used in connection with a mapping to a classification that is characterized by a strong hierarchical structure. Whereas deep-level mapping considers all concepts represented in the corresponding classification scheme, high-level mapping constricts the number of entities looked at by taking only those entities into account that are located at higher hierarchical levels.

15 These concepts will here only be introduced, a more detailed discussion is given in Chapter 6.

String-based Interoperability

The most basic method for establishing semantic interoperability uses techniques of automatic pattern matching, which are rather easy to implement and cost-effective. Main reference objects for declaring similarity between concepts of different indexing languages are the strings of the main representations of concepts (i.e. preferred labels, notations or class headings). Synonyms or near synonyms are often not at all or at least not equally taken into account, particularly as they are sometimes deemed to be less reliable although they are likewise expressions of the same concept. Parameters of similarity either rely on the information inherent in the individual indexing language (scheme level) or on further data associated with the subject indexing data (application level).

Automatic linking techniques lead to a string-based interoperability that is characterized by rather unspecified and usually undirected one-to-one linkages, connecting concepts that do not have the same or even a similar meaning. As a result, conceptual queries remain confined to singular indexing languages in the first instance. Nevertheless the intersystem relations provide useful additional access points and may especially assist information seekers in processes of cognitive query expansion. If they are applied for automatic query expansion to improve recall, initial conceptual queries are in principle expanded by string-based queries with controlled terms (or notations) that do not necessarily reflect what was originally meant, leading perhaps to an unsatisfying precision in respect of the additionally obtained result set. Due to their semantic inaccuracy, intersystem relations that are created mainly on the basis of the comparison of strings cannot be utilized to adequately assist information seekers in processes of knowledge exploration.

Conceptual Interoperability

Conceptual or concept-based interoperability not only allows to improve the recall of initial conceptual queries in heterogeneous information spaces but also enables information seekers to obtain a quite satisfying degree of precision, when the query is automatically expanded with recourse to the established intersystem relations. Fairly precise enhanced access points are provided, making conceptual queries no longer limited to a single indexing language. This is achieved by adopting a cognitive linking approach in which the best-possible connection between concepts is established. On the basis of all relevant information that is stored within the corresponding concept schemes, the document-independent, system-specific meaning of the concepts is elicited and compared. Semantic interoperability is defined as identity of or at least as significant similarity or congruence in the meaning of concepts. Missing definitions and lack of modeled semantic relations often place high demands on the expertise of the person(s) who create the linkages. Intersystem relations may be modeled uni- or bi-directionally, depending on the characteristics of the indexing languages and the envisioned application of the data.

If bi-directional linkages are established, concept schemes are used as a source as well as a target language. As a result, precise enhanced access points in both directions are provided. Uni-directional linkages are established exclusively from one source vocabulary to one target vocabulary. In information retrieval, their functionalities can only be exploited to the full if a query is expanded in respect to the concepts of the target language. One concept of one scheme can be connected with one or more concepts in another scheme. Simple one-to-one mappings can be used for automatic query expansion; they may support interchangeability of concepts in processes of information retrieval. Yet, significant structural, typological and linguistic differences as well as differences in scope and depth of concept schemes often require a one-to-many mapping. The more concepts in a target language are connected with one particular concept in the source language, the less suitable created intersystem relations are for automatic query expansion. Still, one-to-many linkages enhance access to schemes and information resources considerably; they should be in any case presented to information seekers for processes of cognitive query expansion.

Differentiated Interoperability

Differentiated interoperability is a special type of conceptual interoperability and as such does not only share the same understanding of semantic interoperability as the basic type of conceptual interoperability outlined beforehand, but also the fundamental functionalities that are associated with it[16]. It goes beyond the basic type by exposing characteristics of the established linkages and representing them in a way that they are cognitively and/or machine-interpretable, thus enabling refined or even additional application and usage. Depending on the kind and on the degree of expressivity of the assigned properties, differentiated intersystem relations may allow additional regulation of the recall of enhanced conceptual queries. They may also foster ranking mechanisms in respect of information resources that are retrieved subsequent to an automatically expanded query. If their semantic content is reflected appropriately and human understandable in their description, differences in the meaning of concepts and in the viewpoint of the different knowledge systems may be quicker to recognize, facilitating a more efficient use of the connected concepts in assisted strategies of cognitive knowledge exploration and in query expansion. If on top of that

16 We will give a more detailed discussion of this concept in Section 6.2.2.

valid logical attributes are provided, inferences can be drawn on behalf of the machine, preparing the ground for more sophisticated processes of information retrieval in heterogeneous information spaces. Whether intersystem relations can ever be standardized, is an open question (Dextre-Clarke 2011).

5.3.3 Vocabulary Linking Projects

In this section, we sketch some respective vocabulary mapping projects that expose significant characteristics being representative for many others. Further linking projects are described in Vizine-Goetz et al. (2004), Chang and Zeng (2004) and Clavel-Merrin, Žumer and Landry (2006). Macgregor and McCulloch (2008) outline linking projects with focus on specific intersystem relations, the *W3C* provides a list of mapping projects that adopt Semantic Web techniques to support interoperability.[17]

Multilingual Access to Subjects (MACS)

The *MACS project* was one of the earliest projects in librarianship that aimed at overcoming linguistic barriers in information retrieval. It was initiated by the *Conference of European National Libraries (CENL)* in 1997/1998 and has been conducted by the *Swiss National Library (SNL)* in cooperation with the *French National Library (BNF)*, the *British Library (BL)* and the *German National Library (DNB)* ever since. Topical headings of the German subject headings authority file, *Schlagwortnormdatei (SWD)* – since 2012 integral part of the German *Integrated Authority File, Gemeinsame Normdatei (GND)* – are intellectually linked to the headings of the French *Répertoire d'autorité-matière encyclopédique et alphabétique unifié (Rameau)* and the English language *Library of Congress Subject Headings (LCSH)*. The linking process as well as the maintenance of the established linkages take place in the Link Management Interface (LMI), a web-based software application that has been developed especially for this purpose (Hoppenbrouwers 2001). The LMI is synchronized with the master authority files weekly or monthly (Jahns & Karg 2011, 55).

In the *MACS* project, all subject headings are treated equally. Whether an indexing language constitutes the source or the target language depends on the person who conducts the mapping. The direction of the conducted mapping is not reflected in the stored mapping data. In information retrieval, connected concepts are conceived as clusters. According to Landry (2009, 35), linkages may be established:

17 http://www.w3.org/2005/Incubator/lld/wiki

> [...] based on an analysis at the terminology level (subject heading), at the semantic level (authority record), and at the syntactic level (indexing). A match or link is considered successful when a concept represented by similar headings in the different SHLs [subject headings lists] [...] returns the most closely relevant result (titles) through subject retrieval.

The different reference points of the mappings are not made explicit with the result that it is not clear which mapping refers to which level. Likewise, different degrees of equivalence are distinguished in theory (Jahns & Karg 2011, 60) but in practice the same relation type, an unspecified intersystem relation, represents all established linkages. Linked concepts are stored in tabular form. Incomparable characteristics of indexing languages are compensated by auxiliary constructions. Thus, *MACS* allows the creation of one-to-many mappings where one subject heading of a source language is connected to a compound concept of a target language that is created within the frame of the mapping process. The compound concept consists of two or even more subject headings that are combined via Boolean operators, whereby the Boolean operator AND is most frequently used. The compound concepts are stored in the LMI. Table 5.1 gives respective examples for *MACS* linkages.

Tab. 5.1: *Rameau-LCSH-SWD* linkages from the *MACS* project.

Rameau	LCSH	SWD	Domains	MACS Links
Théâtre	Theater	Theater	790	MACS0000455
Rôle – [Nom du rôle]	--	Rolle AND Theater	790	MACS0000318
Théâtres – Effets sonores	Theaters – Sound effects	Geräuschkulisse AND Theater	790	MACS0000254
Théâtre – Censure	Theater – Censorship	Theater AND Zensur	--	MACS0000198
Droit d'autheur – Droits de representation	Copyright – Performing rights	Aufführungsrecht AND Theater	340 700 801	MACS0000047
Théâtre AND Bibliographie	Theater – Bibliography	Theater AND Bibliographie	790	MACS0000194
Théâtre – Objets de collection	Theatrical paraphemalia	Theater AND Sammlung	790	MACS0000265
Théâtre AND Prix et récempenses	Theater -- Awards	Theater AND Kulturpreis	790	MACS0000193
Théâtre AND Aspect moral	Theater – Moral and ethical aspects	Theater AND Moral	--	MACS0000209
Théâtre AND Espositions	Theater -- Exhibitions	Theater AND Ausstellung	790	MACS0000199

According to Jahns and Karg, the *MACS* data "is freely accessible via LMI to interested parties. Links can be downloaded from the LMI-database as *XML*-file and converted to other formats. DNB [The German National Library] has published the mappings as Linked Data [...] and has planned to integrate them in its own portal to offer its users a multilingual search over the collections" (ibid., 61).

KoMoHe project

The *KoMoHe project*, whose abbreviation stands for *Competence Center Modeling and Treatment of Semantic Heterogeneity*, ran from 2004 to 2007. It was funded by the *German Federal Ministry of Education and Research (BMBF)* and conducted at the *GESIS Social Centre* in Bonn. *Cross-concordances* between 25 controlled vocabularies were built manually. 13 German vocabularies, 8 English, 1 Russian and 3 multilingual concept schemes were taken into account. In the end, 64 cross-concordances were established. Yet, not all concepts of the involved vocabularies were linked but only those that were deemed to be relevant for the domain of Social Sciences. In the established net of mappings the *Thesaurus for Social Sciences (ThesSoz)* takes over a central role.

Most mappings are modeled bilateral and bi-directional, some exclusively uni-directional. Differences in the indexing languages are compensated in the form of one-to-many mappings connecting one concept of the initial language to a compound concept of the target language. The compound concept was created within the frame of the mapping process and consists of two or more concepts of the target language that are combined with encodings similar to Boolean operators. It is stored with the mapping data.

Established intersystem relations are differentiated in form of encodings that refer to semantic relation types common in thesauri. The sign "=" stands for an understanding of an equivalent relation that links identical, synonymous or quasi-synonymous concepts, the signs "<" and ">" describe hierarchical relations that hold between concepts being broader or narrower in scope, whereas the sign "^" denotes an association relation connecting concepts that are in one way or another similar. Besides, a Null (0) relation exposes that one term could not be mapped to another (cf. Tab. 5.2). A relevance ranking was added to every intersystem relation as a kind of secondary and relatively weak expression of its quality (Petras & Mayr 2009).

Tab. 5.2: Linkages from the *KoMoHe* project (Petras & Mayr 2009).

Start term TheSoz	Relation	End term	End vocabulary
Weiterbildung [further education]	=	Weiterbildung	Psyndex, STW, Infodata, SWD, BISp, DZI
	^	Berufsforbildung	FES
		Further education	CSA-ASSIA
		Continuing education	CSA-PEI
		Adult education	CSA-SA
		Education	CSA-WPSA
		Erwachsenenbildung	IBLK

The concordances are implemented in the *German Science Information Portal Sowiport.*[18] In the real-life application of *Sowiport*, however, the equivalence relations are exclusively used for the enhancement of queries. Yet, all semantic relations apart from the relevance parameters can be viewed in the thesaurus and the concordances module of the portal.[19]

CrissCross project

The *CrissCross* project was funded by the German research foundation *Deutsche Forschungsgemeinschaft (DFG)* and ran from 2006 to 2010. It was conducted by the *German National Library (DNB)* in cooperation with the *Cologne University of Applied Sciences*. To our knowledge, it is the only project that faced the challenge of establishing semantical interoperability between typologically distinct indexing languages on a large scale. 150.000 subject headings of the German *Schlagwortnormdatei (SWD)* – that have by now been integrated in the German *Integrated Authority File, Gemeinsame Normdatei (GND)* – were intellectually linked to classes of the *Dewey Decimal Classification (DDC)*. Additionally – as contribution to the *MACS* project – 70.000 German subject headings were linked to their equivalences in the French indexing language *Rameau* and the English language indexing language *LCSH*. In this chapter, we focus on the *SWD-DDC* linking approach being specific for the *CrissCross* project.

In view of the peculiarities of *SWD* and *DDC*, a uni-directional, differentiated mapping approach was adopted in which the *SWD* served as initial and the *DDC* as target system. The linkages were established based on the document-indepen-

18 http://www.gesis.org/sowiport
19 http://www.gesis.org/sowiport/nc/de/suche/thesaurus.html

dent a priori meanings of the represented concepts. The mapping process followed three principles:

1. *One-to-many mapping*: In order to support comprehensive access to *DDC* and *DDC*-indexed information resources, one *SWD* heading could be mapped to several *DDC* numbers. In information retrieval, linked notations can be combined with the Boolean OR. Those additional *DDC* numbers could serve the information seeker as alternative suggestions which may also or even better match the seekers's information need.
2. *Deep level mapping*: Within the frame of the mapping process, built numbers were created – always by following the *DDC* number building instructions – in order to establish the best possible connection between *SWD* heading and *DDC* number. *DDC* built numbers that were created in the course of the *CrissCross* project were stored in the German classification tool *MelvilClass*[20] together with their component parts, adequate class headings and index terms. In the long turn, they will be integrated into the knowledge base of the German *DDC* edition.
3. *Mapping with degrees of determinacy*. Due to structural and typological differences of *SWD* and *DDC*, modeled concepts are never fully equivalent. In the *CrissCross* project, different types of equivalency were distinguished in the form of four numbers that express so-called "degrees of determinacy" (D)[21]. D4 applies if the *SWD* heading fully corresponds to the topic that is emphasized in the *DDC* class heading. D3 applies if the *SWD* heading refers to a topic that – in terms of the *DDC* – approximates the whole of the respective *DDC* class. D2 applies if the *SWD* heading refers to a topic that is logically part of the *DDC* class but less extensive in scope than the concept represented by the class number. D1 applies if the topic the *SWD* heading describes is only to a small part included in the *DDC* class. The degrees of determinacy are intended to be used for structuring and ranking *DDC*-indexed information resources (Jacobs, Mengel & Müller 2010, 2011).

```
Eingabe: 1250:18-05-98 Änderung: 1150:14-02-14 09:18:58 Status:
9999:17-01-09
005 Ts1
006 http://d-nb.info/gnd/4502849-7
008 saz
```

20 *MelvilClass* was replaced by *WebDewey Deutsch* in the end of 2012, cf. Fig. 5.3. Detailed information on *WebDewey Deutsch* is given on the *DDC Deutsch* website by the *German National Library*: http://www.ddc-deutsch.de/Subsites/ddcdeutsch/DE/DDCprodukte/WebDeweyDeutsch/webdeweydeutsch_node.html

21 Cf. also the discussion in Section 8.3.3 and – in a more generalized fashion – in section 10.2.2.

```
011 s
012 w;z
035 gnd/4502849-7
039 swd/4502849-7$vzg
065 30;31.9b
083 006.246$d2$t2014-02-14
083 621.384192$d2$t2014-02-14
089 621.38419$d1$t2009-10-28$g2014-02-14
150 Kontaktlose Chipkarte
450 RFID$xChipkarte
450 Radio frequency identification$xChipkarte
550 !041477235!Chipkarte$4obal
550 !997599162!Nahfeldkommunikation$4vbal
670 Vorlage, Def. B 1996 unter Chipkarte
750 Radio frequency identification systems$uhttp://lccn.loc.gov/
sh93005118$SDLC$0sh 93005118$2lcsh$vMACS-Mapping. Bitte keine
Änderungen vornehmen.
750 Systèmes d'identification par radiofréquence$uhttp://data.
bnf.fr/13749199$SFrPBN$0FRBNF13749199X$2ram$vMACS-Mapping. Bitte
keine Änderungen vornehmen.
903 $eDE-101
903 $rDE-101
913 $Sswd$is$aKontaktlose Chipkarte$04502849-7
```

The linked *DDC* numbers and the corresponding degrees of determinacy are stored with the respective *SWD* headings in the *SWD/GND* data record together with a time stamp that guarantees the precise transition from *SWD/GND* data record to *DDC* over time; mappings are intended to be adjusted to *DDC* updates. The above example gives an impression of a subject heading data record that has already gone through an updating process due to changes in the *DDC*. Field 083 contains the present valid linked *DDC* numbers with the respective degrees of determinacy (contained in subfield $d) and the date when the mapping has been

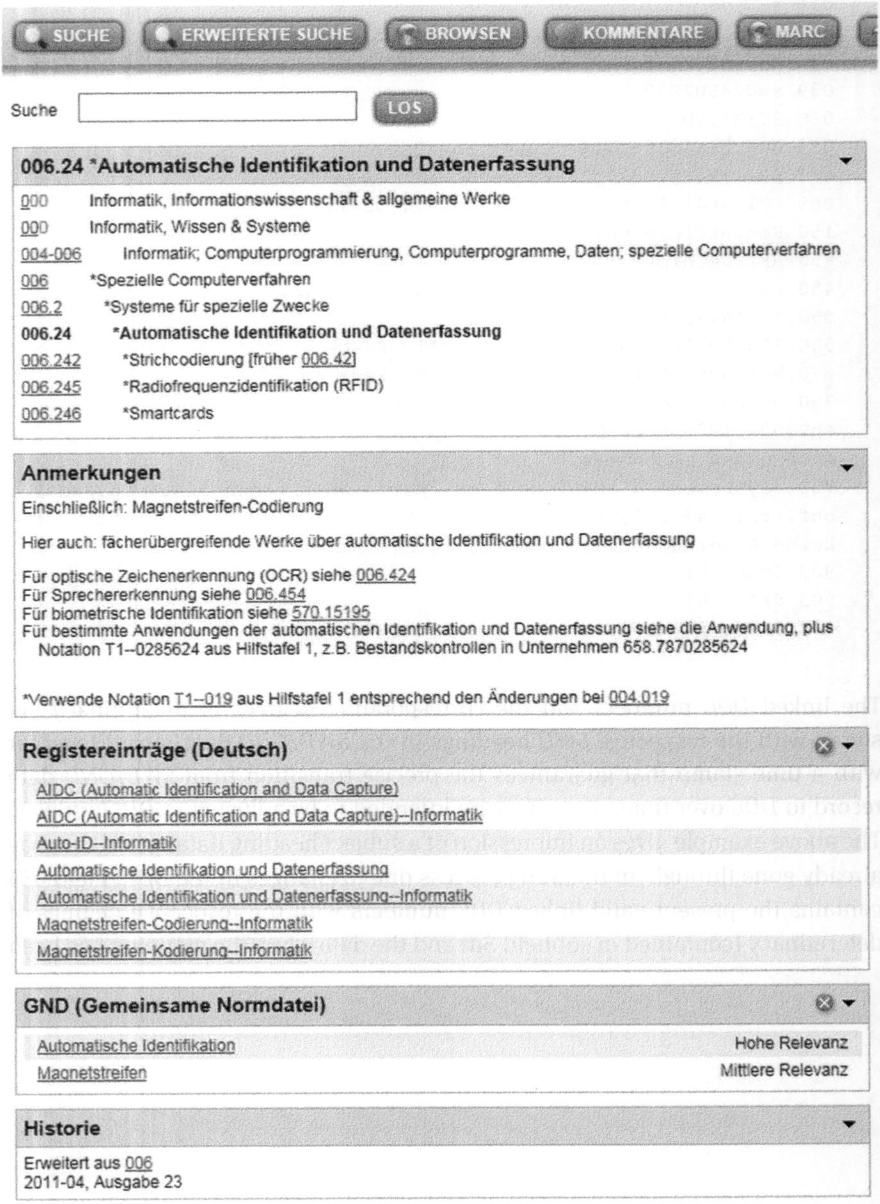

Fig. 5.3: Linked *SWD* headings in *WebDewey Deutsch*.

proved valid (contained in subfield $t). Field 089 contains the former *DDC* number and the respective degree of determinacy that have been valid before the updating process. Subfields $t and $g give information on the period in which the linkage has been valid.

Figure 5.3 shows how *SWD/GND* headings that are linked to *DDC* classes are visually integrated in *WebDewey Deutsch*, a German *DDC* classification tool.

High-Level Thesaurus (HILT)

The *HILT* project, which ran from 2000 to 2009, was funded by the *Joint Information Systems Committee (JISC)* and partly involved collaboration with *EDINA*, a UK national academic center situated at the University of Edinburgh. It consisted of a series of research projects that were conducted at the *Center for Digital Library Research (CDLR)* at the University of Strathclyde with the aim to develop solutions for cross-searching and browsing in a heterogeneous information space. This included building a web-based pilot terminology server and developing an adequate retrieval model to access concepts of different subject schemes. The *DDC* was taken as spine whose hierarchical structure can be used for browsing. For the research, existing indexing data by *OCLC* between *DDC* and *LCSH* was taken into account as well as linkages between several terminologies and the high-level *DDC* captions that have been newly created manually, following primarily a high-level-mapping approach (Nicholson, Dawson & Shiri 2006; Nicholson 2003; Nicholson & Wake 2001).

Tests were conducted with intersystem relations that were specified according to the – at that time developing – *Simple Knowledge Organization System (SKOS)* Core Mapping Vocabulary Specification (MVS). This provided the following matching types: *exactMatch* to describe concepts that may be used interchangeably, *broadMatch* and *narrowMatch* to describe hierarchical relations between concepts, *majorMatch* and *minorMatch* to describe concepts whose meaning is overlapping (Miles & Brickley 2004). Within the context of the *HILT* project, however, these relation were deemed to be "probably inadequate to express equivalence relationships between mapped terms from different terminologies since the five types of relationship within the *SKOS Core MVS* are conceptually based and broad, and so do not account for more subtle variations relating to lexical differences such as spelling variations or singular/plural matches." (Nicholson, McCulloch & Macgregor 2007, 9; Macgregor & McCulloch 2008, 89). As a reaction to this conclusion, an additional set of match types, originally been developed by Chaplan (1995) and mainly focused on expressing linguistic differences of the main representation form of the concepts, was tested. From the given set of 19 match types a total of nine could be verified.

6 Problems with Establishing Semantic Interoperability

After the presentation of some examples and concrete projects for handling conceptual interoperability in the previous chapter, we will now describe these approaches on a more abstract level and thereby identify problems that will be the starting points for a modeling approach given in Chapter 10.

Interoperability of data, in the broadest sense understood as their processing in other environments than their development environments, is an important subject for the study of semantic issues (Harken et al. 2006). One encounters a wide spectrum of the understanding of interoperability. The following quotations give impressions from the spectrum of typical interpretations.

> Semantic interoperability refers to the ability of computer systems to transmit data with unambiguous, shared meaning. Semantic interoperability is a requirement to enable machine computable logic, inferencing, knowledge discovery, and data federation between information systems.[22]

Particular attention is given to issues of interoperability regarding the creation of a *Semantic Web*. Here, the technical interchangeability of data is often transferred to the level of content and so an expectation of a kind of conceptual interoperability arises:

> Beyond the ability of two or more computer systems to exchange information, semantic interoperability is the ability to automatically interpret the information exchanged meaningfully and accurately in order to produce useful results as defined by the end users of both systems. To achieve semantic interoperability, both sides must refer to a common information exchange reference model.[23]

This kind of understanding then extends to any information system that serves content-oriented search purposes:

> Search interoperability refers to the ability of two or more information collections to be searched by a single query.[24]

A similar interpretation can be found in an actual and important standard for questions of interoperability, the *ISO 25964-2* (2013, 6):

22 Cf. http://en.wikipedia.org/wiki/Semantic_interoperability
23 Cf. http://en.wikipedia.org/wiki/Interoperability
24 Cf. http://en.wikipedia.org/wiki/Interoperability

> The aim of interoperability between vocabularies is to enable an expression formulated using one vocabulary to be converted to (or supplemented by) a corresponding expression in one or more other vocabularies, typically during the exercise of an application such as information retrieval.

In summary, two prototypical interpretations can be indicated for an understanding of (semantic) interoperability:

- Conditions for sharing or reuse of data that can be interpreted semantically. *Semantically* not necessarily implies that a conceptual meaning in terms of a cognitive interpretation exists. It may be sufficient that the data are interpretable for a defined process. This interpretation needs to be known or to be mutually agreed upon.
- Entities as content-based metadata are considered semantically interoperable if their joint use within search operations results in meaningful extensions of the search results.

We will set the focus of our considerations to the second interpretation and understand the first interpretation as a necessary technical framework condition but not as a guide for conceptual design considerations.

Beyond the closed representation space of an indexing language, modeled terms lose their uniqueness and are no reliable indicators for identity or differentness of entities. This becomes most apparent when comparing indexing languages that are based on different natural languages, but it is also true for linguistically similar schemes. Due to missing definitions and insufficiently designed semantic relations, making precise statements about the degree of semantic similarity of entities remains a complex cognitive task that requires much expertise and familiarity with the indexing languages at hand. Yet, significant semantic congruence of entities is the decisive factor for any kind of conceptual interoperability, especially if regarded as basis for semantic interoperability (Glossary E1).

Sometimes the understanding of semantic interoperability is based on the linguistic representation of the entities, the terms or character strings. One could then speak of *Term-based interoperability* or of *String-based interoperability* (Glossary E1.1). This understanding will not be object of our discussion. We will focus on an understanding of semantic interoperability that is based on the conceptual content of the entities and that will be called *Entity-based interoperability* or *Conceptual interoperability* (Glossary E1.2).[25]

---

25 Cf. also the introduction of this concepts in Section 5.3.2.

6.1 Conceptual Interoperability between Entities of Indexing Languages

To begin with, we will consider problems of identifying conceptual interoperability between single entities of different indexing languages. We will introduce the discussion of criteria for such an identification in the context of search interests. Some examples will be given to illustrate this approach. Section 6.2 will enhance this discussion to interoperability problems for indexing results and in Section 10.1 this discussion will be taken up again by more formal considerations.

Let us first consider an example that should illustrate the basic problems of identifying conceptual interoperability. Let us take as an example three concepts that have been modeled as entities in two different thesauri. The concepts are:
- *Library*
- *Public library*
- *Documentation center*

At the moment the reader will have its own imagination about the content of the three concepts and their relationships to any other. In Table 6.1 different representations in two fictional thesaurus structures are given:

Tab. 6.1: The problem of interoperability for near synonyms: an example (1).

Thesaurus 1		**Thesaurus 2**	
Library		**Library**	
BF	Public library	UB	**Public library**
	Documentation center	VB	**Documentation center**

In each of the structures, different decisions on the contextual relationships of the involved concepts and their respective semantic content were made. The importance of these modeling decisions is perhaps better visible in the graphical presentation of Figure 6.1.

Without being bound to a particular purpose, the results of each of the two decisions could be part of a valid thesaurus structure. What are the consequences for interoperability issues? If only descriptors are permitted for establishing interoperability connections, all descriptors of *thesaurus 2* must be mapped to the one descriptor of *thesaurus 1*. Such an approach will be accompanied by a great loss of expression and differentiation ability. Generally speaking, this effect causes the least semantically differentiated structure to become the structural basis of all related knowledge representations. *Thesaurus 2* permits to express more conceptual diversity by connections to any of the three descriptors. This diversity cannot be prevented by considering the descriptors of both thesauri as interoperable.

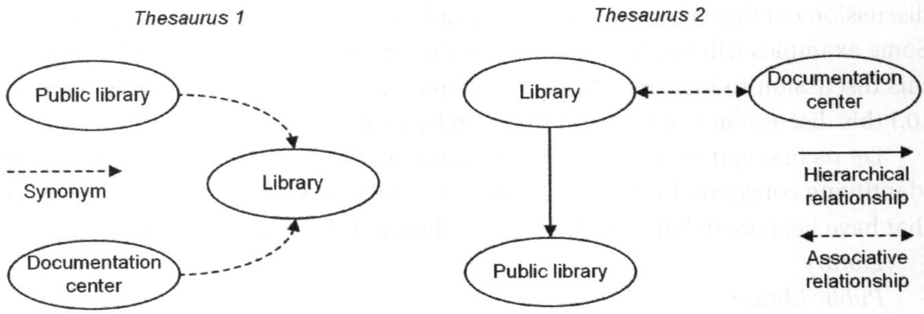

Fig. 6.1: The problem of interoperability for near synonyms: an example (2).

At least we can conclude from this example that for any decision of conceptual exchangeability it is not sufficient to regard the entities as context-independent. The relationships within the structure of each knowledge representation must also be considered, since these relationships provide a major contribution to the meaning of the entities.

6.1.1 Focused and Comprehensive Mapping

Basic parameters for regarding entities as conceptually interoperable are the scopes of their meaning being independent from any information resource to which their terms are assigned. It seems appropriate that a connection between mapping approaches and understanding of conceptual meaning is established. Therefore, we will distinguish between *core meaning* (Glossary C1.3) and *contextual meaning* (Glossary C1.4) of entities. In their core meaning, entities refer to concrete or abstract, real-life or fictive things in the world. Their core meaning is independent of the information resources to which the entities are assigned. In their contextual meaning, entities refer to aspects of concrete or abstract, real-life or fictive things in the world, putting things in relation to other. Their contextual meaning can be dependent of the information resources to which the entities terms are assigned. Both forms may be relevant for supporting conceptual queries. Based on this, we will now differentiate between two mutually exclusive cognitive linking approaches that we call *entity-based mapping approaches* (Glossary E2). The two types to be differentiated refer to the attributes *focused* and *comprehensive*.

Focused mapping (Glossary E2.1) focuses on the core meaning of entities, keeping the number of intersystem relations to be created to a minimum. Aspects of represented things are neglected as long as the core meaning of the entity in the initial language corresponds to the core meaning of an entity in the target language. Only if this does not apply, the contextual meaning of the entity is considered – if at all. For creating equivalent linkages between entities, the contextual meaning of one entity has to comply at least with the core meaning of the other entity. *Comprehensive mapping* (Glossary E2.2) on the other hand takes into account the core as well as the contextual meaning of the concepts represented in the initial language in any case, provided that both turn out to be important for the envisioned retrieval scenario.

An example taken from the *CrissCross*[26] project will illustrate the problems more clearly. One of the project's tasks was the enrichment of the *Relative Index* of the German edition of the *Dewey Decimal Classification (DDC Deutsch)* by entries from the German subject headings authority file *Schlagwortnormdatei (SWD)*[27]. The example refers to the subject field of zoology. Although the example may seem very challenging, it is neither artificial nor untypical for the problems that are considered in our context.

In the German subject headings authority file *Schlagwortnormdatei (SWD)*, the heading *Papageien* reflects the concept *parrots*, referring to the corresponding animals in general. The *Dewey Decimal Classification (DDC)* includes *parrots* in this object-based meaning in class *598.71 Psittaciformes*. This class also includes *parrots living in the wild*. Yet, *domestic parrots*, viz. *parrots raised by humans or living with humans as pets* are part of class *636.6865 Parrots*, a subordinate class of *636 Animal husbandry* that includes *pets* in its object-based meaning. The *SWD* represents the concept *pets* with the descriptor *Haustiere*.

Let us first consider a focused mapping approach. This approach takes the *SWD* as initial and the *DDC* as target language and links the *SWD* heading *Papageien* exclusively to *DDC* class *598.71*.

Based on such a mapping, information seekers conducting a conceptual query with *Papageien* retrieve respective *SWD*-indexed information resources and additionally *DDC*-indexed information resources dealing with *parrots* in general

---

26 Cf. http://ixtrieve.fh-koeln.de/crisscross/index_en.html. A description of the project, its aim and methods has already been given in Section 5.3.3.

27 Cf. Ref.: http://melvil.dnb.de/gnd. We will not continuously repeat that the headings of the *SWD* have by now been integrated in the German *Integrated Authority File GND*, cf. the remarks given in Section 5.3.3 when introducing the *CrissCross* project.

or with *wild-living parrots* in particular. They miss *DDC*-indexed information resources that deal with domestic parrots like parrots as pets – a fact of which they may even not be aware. Yet, if they intend to find all information resources that deal with *parrots* regardless where they live as the *SWD* heading implies, they have to conduct additional queries to find the excluded set of *DDC*-indexed information resources. If they are just familiar with the *SWD*, this can turn out as quite complicated, particularly as in this case neither the relational structure of the *SWD* nor the relational structure of the connected *DDC* class provide any support. The *SWD* only displays narrower terms of *Papageien* referring to types of parrots, whereas the connected *DDC* class provides access to subordinate or superordinate classes of *598.71*. Yet, the *SWD* heading *Papageien* has a scope note that contains, inter alia, a reference to the *SWD* heading *Papageienhaltung* (*keeping of parrots*) which may be helpful in this case. Unfortunately, scope notes are primarily written for indexers, so that information seekers seldom encounter them. Besides, only humans can interpret and utilize the information contained in such notes, as they are insufficiently machine-accessible and machine-interpretable.

If information seekers use *Haustiere* (the German term for *pets*), as additional query term besides *Papageien* to find information resources dealing with *parrots as pets*, they get no hits on behalf of *SWD*-indexed information resources, since *Papageien* and *Haustiere* are rarely used together in subject indexing. On the part of the *DDC*, they retrieve two distinct sets of *DDC*-indexed information resources, one indexed with the aforementioned *DDC* number *598.71*, the other indexed with *DDC* number *636* to which the *SWD* heading *Haustiere* is linked in a focused mapping. The *DDC* class that includes *parrots as pets*, however, is *636.6865*. Information seekers not knowing the *DDC* might stop searching before finding the adequate DDC class and the information resources associated with it, unless they have access to a *DDC* edition in a familiar language and the *DDC's* relational structure. Automatic truncation of the *DDC* numbers does not provide a satisfying solution to the problem, as it leads to a set of information resources that includes those indexed with the respective *DDC* number among many others. Extracting these can be exhausting, particularly as information seekers are not assisted in this process and neither know nor expect that relevant information resources might also be listed after or between a potentially great number of irrelevant ones. It is likely they will stop scanning the list of bibliographic data before encountering them.

Secondly, we will consider the comprehensive mapping approach that takes the *SWD* as initial and the *DDC* as target language. It connects the *SWD* heading *Papageien* not only to the *DDC* number *598.71*, but also to the *DDC* number *636.6865*.

Based on this, information seekers searching with the *SWD* heading *Papageien* can retrieve *SWD*-indexed information as well as *DDC*-indexed information resources that in one way or another deal with *parrots*, be it *parrots* in general or *wild-living* or *domestic parrots* in particular. Problems like those described above do not occur. It is imaginable that linked notations and corresponding headings, that help understanding the meaning of the classes, are displayed to information seekers in order to enable them to omit information resources indexed with one or the other *DDC* number if necessary.

The definition of entities can be based on a set of properties. These properties may provide adequate parameters for determining different degrees of conceptual identity to another concept. Unfortunately, neither thesauri nor classification systems make explicit all characteristics and components underlying the definition of their entities. In indexing languages, near synonyms or index terms even have influence of the definitional scope. By lack of formal parameters, it remains to justify conceptual similarity by cognitive interpretation of the entities. This way bears some problems that will be tackled in the following discussion.

By a deeper and more abstract discussion of the given example, requirements can be identified that may cause foundations of a modeling of indexing languages. Complemented by formal attributes these foundations will be the basis to develop a concept of an ontology-based indexing and retrieval including an understanding of semantic interoperability in the sense of conceptual similarity, as will be shown in detail in Part C of this book. Before doing so, we will present these requirements in more detail.

The different semantic reference points that focused and comprehensive mapping take as a basis for linkages to be established reflect their different understanding of *semantic or conceptual identity*. This different understanding will have an effect on all degrees of conceptual congruence that may be derived. In focused mapping, entities are regarded as semantically identical if they have the same core meaning. Comprehensive mapping, however, requires relevant aspects to be included in the meaning of the corresponding entities as well for regarding them as semantically identical. Consequently, some entities deemed as semantically identical in the view of focused mapping are just strongly similar from the perspective of comprehensive mapping. By the progress made so far, we can summarize the understanding of *conceptual identity* in tabular form:

Tab. 6.2: Conceptual identity in focused and comprehensive mapping.

	Focused mapping	**Comprehensive mapping**
Semantic identity	Identical core meaning	Identical core meaning + Identical contextual meaning

Consideration of further examples give rise to differentiate this understanding by evolving the concept of *semantic* or *conceptual congruence of entities*.

6.1.2 Conceptual Identity and Semantic Congruence

As indexing languages usually describe extracts of reality from a (culture-) specific point of view, adjusted to local needs and originally envisioned applications, entities of different indexing languages seldom represent exactly the same concept. In order to promote conceptual queries in heterogeneous information spaces, they can nevertheless be regarded as conceptually interoperable if they have strongly similar meaning, viz. if the things to which they refer have major characteristics in common.

It is a priori not possible to address the issues of interoperability or mapping approaches between entities under the same point of view as the question of identity or similarity of concepts themselves. Interoperability decisions regarding entities have to consider benefits for retrieval tasks and can be lead back to our discussion on focused and comprehensive mapping in the previous section.

Entities can only be seen as *conceptually identical* if they are of the same type and share the same context. Entities of different types like a) instances on the one hand and classes on the other hand, or b) entities of different complexity exhibit different characteristics, just allowing statements about degrees of semantic congruence at the most. Conceptual identity of entities is based on the core meaning of different entities and leads to a focused mapping.

For example, an exact one-to-one correspondence is to negate for entities embedded in different relational structures that reflect incomparable localized aspects, particularly as it is impossible to represent conceptual structures in a mapping[28]. The term *Legislation* in the *Library of Congress Subject Headings (LCSH)*, for instance, appears at first sight to describe a concept that also the term

28 The aspect of *Localization* for establishing conceptual structures will be discussed in more detail in Section 10.2.1. This discussion will also come back to the example.

Gesetzgebung in the German subject headings authority file *Schlagwortnormdatei (SWD)* represents. The linguistic level alone – a mere translation – cannot be sufficient for an answer. Otherwise, the entire approach of terminological control would be excluded. A closer look at the semantic environment, however, reveals significant differences. An example is shown in Figure 6.2.

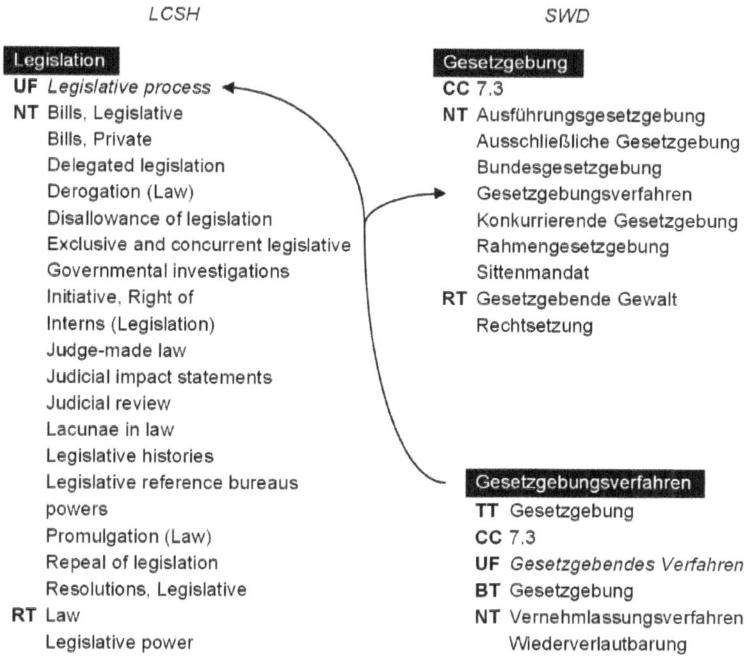

Fig. 6.2: Comparison of localized entities: *SWD* heading *Gesetzgebung* and *LCSH* term *Legislation.*

We can observe the following conceptual differences:

- The *LCSH* heading *Legislation* has a narrower *LCSH* heading *Judge-made law* representing an entity that does not exist in the context of German *legislation* and has no counterpart on behalf of the *SWD.*
- The *LCSH* views the concepts to which the terms *legislative process* and *legislation* refer as conceptually identical, they are seen as synonyms and represented by the entity *legislation.* In the *SWD,* the terms *Gesetzgebung* (legislation) and *Gesetzgebungsverfahren* (legislative process) refer to hierarchically related concepts that represent different *SWD* entities.

If the semantic environment of entities is regarded as being constitutive for their meaning, such differences cannot be neglected. When comparing entities, however, it must be kept in mind that indexing languages do not necessarily model all essential a priori relations of the represented concepts. From a strict semantic point of view, entities that do not share all characteristics are not identical. Yet, they may still be similar enough to regard them as equally useful for purposes of information retrieval.

Another case of semantically non-identical entities is described by the next example, we will call it *semantic* or *conceptual congruence*. Conceptual congruence is based on the contextual meaning of different entities and leads to comprehensive mapping approaches.

The example is taken from the *Dewey Decimal Classification (DDC)*. The *DDC* lists a number of index terms connected with the *DDC* class *598.97 Strigiformes (Owls)*, giving examples of concepts included in the class. Two of these, *tydonidae* and *barn owls*, correspond to the heading *Schleiereulen <Familie>* and its synonymous term *Tydonidae* in the German subject headings authority file *Schlagwortnormdatei (SWD)*, cf. Table 6.3. Yet, some *SWD* entities also refer to concepts that are not reflected in any *DDC* index term but are nevertheless conceptual part of the *DDC* class. For example, the *SWD*-heading *Schnee-Eule* describes the concept *snowy owls* which is also included in *DDC* class *598.97*, though the *DDC* does not address it explicitly.

Tab. 6.3: *DDC* class *598.97* and corresponding *SWD* headings.

DDC classes		SWD headings
598	*Aves (Vögel)	|s| Eulen
598.5-598.9	Landvögel	|s| Eulenvögel
598.9	*Falconiformes (Greifvögel), Strigiformes (Eulen), Caprimulgiformes (Nachtschwalben)	|s| Amerikanischer Uhu |s| Bartkauz
598.97	Strigiformes (Eulen)	|s| Fleckenkauz
598.97097	Eulen--Nordamerika	|s| Habichtskauz
		|s| Kuckuckskauz
		|s| Mandschurischer Fischuhu
		|s| Ohreulen
		|s| Otus flammeolus
		|s| Raufußkauz
		|s| Schleiereule
		|s| Schleiereulen <Familie>

In general, we mean by *semantic congruence* (Glossary E1.3) that entities can be regarded as conceptually interoperable to a comparatively high degree for search interests. Semantic congruence is given if the meaning of one entity is fully included in that of the other. When comparing entities modeled in indexing languages, near synonyms or index terms refer at least to some concepts that are included in the corresponding entities that can provide valuable reference points.

In the example of Table 6.3, the *SWD* descriptor *Schleiereulen <Familie>* represents a concept whose meaning is fully included in the *DDC* class *598.97*. When linking the *SWD* to the *DDC*, the *SWD* heading is exclusively connected to the *DDC* number *598.97*. This one-to-one mapping in principle allows for an automatic query expansion that adds the *DDC* number *598.97* to the initial query term *Schleiereulen <Familie>* to retrieve *DDC*-indexed information resources besides *SWD*-indexed. The *DDC*-indexed information resources, however, do not all deal with topics that refer to the thing described by the *SWD* entity. Some of them deal with *owls* in general, others with some owl types like *snowy owls*. Some may be relevant or interesting for the information need at hand, others may not.

Yet, a better precision in respect to the *DDC*-indexed information resources is not possible due to the semantic differences of the *SWD* and the *DDC* entity. When treating the *DDC* as initial and the *SWD* as target language, a one-to-many mapping provides the basis for enhanced retrieval processes in heterogeneous information spaces. The *DDC* class *598.97* is connected to several *SWD* entities, of which only one is represented by the aforementioned *SWD* heading *Schleiereulen <Familie>* (cf. Tab. 6.3). To find *SWD*-indexed information resources dealing with topics that are in some way related to the concept expressed by the initial *DDC* number *598.97*, all connected *SWD* entities have to be considered. In this specific example, all connected *SWD* entities represent concepts that are included in the *DDC* class.

If information seekers get the possibility to select those *SWD* entities being relevant for them, they can positively influence the precision of the set of *SWD*-indexed information resources retrieved. If information seekers are exclusively interested in documents associated with *ural owls*, they can initiate an additional conceptual query with the corresponding *SWD* entity *Habichtskauz*, excluding all other *SWD* entities.

Especially when linking indexing languages that exhibit different relational structures and contain entities of different types and with different degrees of precombination, an entity of the initial language is often neither equivalent to nor fully included in an entity of the target language. For retrieval purposes, however, entities can also be regarded as conceptual interoperable if they have strong overlapping meaning viz. if they share major significant characteristics. In this case, an entity of one indexing language is partially included in an entity of the other indexing language and differs from the latter in at least two ways. For instance, this applies to the aforementioned heading *Papageien* in the *Schlagwortnormdatei (SWD)* that is connected to the class *636.6865 Parrots* in the *Dewey Decimal Classification (DDC)* in a comprehensive mapping approach.

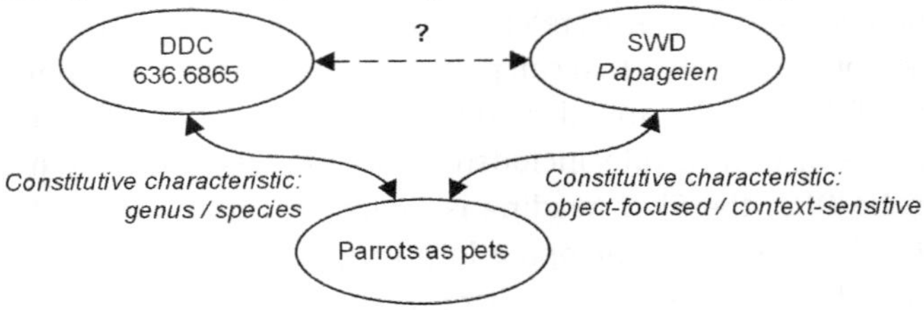

Fig. 6.3: The concept *parrots as pets* as conceptual connection between *SWD* and *DDC* entities.

The two entities can be best compared with reference to their mapping concept *parrots as pets* that is included in both entities but is related to the *SWD* heading in another way than to the *DDC* class when looked at in detail (cf. Fig. 6.3). A perspective hierarchy that indicates a shift in the point of view (Svenonius 2000) characterizes the relation between the concept *parrots as pets* and the *SWD* heading. First, *parrots* are seen from an object-focused point of view, whereas the second view focuses on a context-sensitive perspective. The connection between the concept *parrots as pets* and the *DDC* class in turn essentially constitutes a generic genus-species relation. A third distinguishing feature between *SWD* and *DDC* entity being independent from the linking concept is the number of concepts these include. Whereas the *SWD* heading just includes one animal type, *parrots*, the *DDC* class in addition includes an indefinable number of animal types belonging to the class *psittaciformes* that in itself constitutes one concept among many others like *lories, lovebirds, macaws or parakeets*, to mention only a few. All this makes the concept the *SWD* heading *Papageien* represents, in some way broader and at the same time narrower than the connected *DDC* class. That it nevertheless makes sense to regard it as conceptually interoperable to the *DDC* class has already been outlined in detail in Section 6.1.

We can summarize the formal content of the discussed examples using a set-theoretic nomenclature for representing the conceptual connection.

An entity E_A modeled in or with means of an indexing language *A* fully includes an entity E_B (modeled in or with means of an indexing language *B*) if it includes a concept C_A that is semantically identical to E_B.

$$E_A \supseteq C_A,$$
$$E_B \supseteq C_B$$

and

$$C_A = C_B$$

then

$$E_A \supseteq E_B$$

We can say that the conceptual content of E_B is fully represented by E_A.

The situation becomes more complex if there are more than one conceptual component defining the scope of the entities, as it is normally the case. We will consider a typical case as a pattern for the general case.

Let E_A and E_B once more be entities of indexing languages A and B and C_{Ai} their conceptual components. Additionally, the conditions should hold that

$$E_A \supseteq C_{A1}, E_A \supseteq C_{A2}, E_A \supseteq C_{A3}.$$
$$E_B \supseteq C_{A1}, E_B \supseteq C_{A2}$$

Then one can conclude

$$E_A \supseteq E_B$$

With respect to real indexing languages the given conditions are hard to verify, especially the condition $C_A = C_B$. Indexing languages make seldom explicit statements about the defining conceptual components of their entities. Normally, it remains a cognitive effort to get an impression about the conceptual scope of an entity.

Generally speaking, a term modeled in an indexing language A may represent a concept or several terms taken together that may represent it. It may also happen that it is not modeled at all, being just implicitly a semantic part of the respective entity. The semantic congruence that occurs commonly expresses itself in a one-to-one mapping in one direction and a one-to-many mapping in the other direction. The entity E_B from indexing language B is exclusively linked to the entity E_A from indexing language A, whereas the entity E_A is commonly linked to several entities from indexing language B. Only if those concepts that are included in entity E_A besides entity E_B are not sufficiently similar to any entity modeled in or with means of the indexing language B, a one-to-one mapping in both directions is imaginable. In all cases, the result set of information resources additionally accessed in an enhanced conceptual query exhibits a different precision than that retrieved with the initial query. Automatic query expansion achieves fairly satisfying results primarily in the case of one-to-one mapping.

Let us assume the following search situation. Entity E_A is utilized for enhancing an initial conceptual query based on entity E_B. The result set of information resources additionally accessed is likely to have a lower precision than that of the initial query, since entity E_A has a broader scope of meaning than entity E_B. Yet, it is impossible to achieve a better precision based on the respective subject indexing data. An interactive query expansion yields the same results as an automatic query expansion. If a conceptual query using entity E_A should be expanded to also retrieve information resources indexed with terms of indexing language B, all connected entities of indexing language B have to be taken into account. The connected entities from indexing language B not necessarily represent concepts that are fully included in entity E_A. Some may be just partially included, having overlapping meaning, a case we will describe later on. Moreover, not all may be relevant for the specific information need at hand.

Further types of intersystem relations used to establish interoperability links between different indexing languages are expressed as hierarchical or associative connections. By this method, the understanding of equivalence between entities of two indexing languages is transferred to an understanding of an equivalence of terms seen from the perspective of a special type of relationship without establishing a precise formal meaning. We refrain from further considerations and attempts to give any formalized descriptions. Such attempts cannot support solving the basic underlying problems.

Summarizing our discussion of examples, we can state that many cases are imaginable to regard entities as conceptually interoperable due to their strong overlapping meaning. We suspect that these cases differ when regarding the types of hierarchical relationships indirectly involved and that perspective hierarchies may play an essential role. Yet, all are likely to be associated with a one-to-many mapping in both directions. When used in information retrieval for conceptual query expansion, a loss of precision is unavoidable in any case.

6.2 Equivalent Intersystem Relationships

Practical interoperability decisions between different indexing languages show features that must be seen as unusual comparing them with intrasystem relations. We will call this form of relationship *equivalent intersystem relation*.

In this section, we will describe characteristics of these relations and their understanding, outlining main differences to common intrasystem relations. They are seldom established on the basis of precise formal considerations comparing the conceptual identity of the entities. Instead, entities of different indexing languages are regarded as semantically equivalent by cognitive interpretation and they are connected by links to indicate their interchangeability. With respect to information retrieval purposes, equivalence in this context is often interpreted as conceptual identity between the entities or at least it can be deemed as semantically identical for search purposes. We will show how intra- and intersystem relations complement each other for information retrieval purposes and distinguish between different types of equivalent intersystem relations.

6.2.1 Intersystem Relations Compared to Intrasystem Relations

Equivalent intersystem relations constitute a priori relations between entities of different indexing languages that are either truly semantically equivalent or at least deemed as semantically equivalent for retrieval purposes (Glossary E3). They share main characteristics with common intrasystem relations but also exhibit significant differences. Like equivalent intrasystem relations, they provide additional terminological access points to promote *entity-based queries* (Glossary C4.1). By entity-based queries we understand entity-based searches (Glossary C4) that are performed by direct search formulations using entities of an indexing language or knowledge representation. We will differentiate entity-based queries from *entity-based exploration* (Glossary C4.2), a type of entity-based searches that supports query enhancement by user-machine feedback on the basis of the conceptual structure underlying the indexing language or knowledge representation.

Equivalent intersystem relations facilitate and also enhance queries, leading not only to one but to two types of terminological entries. The terms they connect represent the same concept or at least strongly similar concepts. They do not necessarily have different character strings and they never represent the same entity, since entities are specific for each indexing language.

Like hierarchical or associative intrasystem relations, equivalent intersystem relations are deemed to hold between entities, though they are commonly designed as linkages between preferred terms. They are seldom modeled uni-directional (Glossary E3.3, E3.4). Even though they establish connections that should represent conceptual equivalence, they link preferred terms of different indexing languages. The equivalence relationship as intrasystem relation establishes links between non-preferred and preferred terms of the same indexing language and has always to be interpreted as uni-directional with respect to the conceptual meaning. From the perspective of one indexing language, however, linked preferred terms of a different indexing language are comparable to alternative terms that are not allowed to be used when indexing with the respective indexing language. An initial language can never accept back-linked terms of a target language as conceptual equivalent.

The two sets of information resources to which they lead as result sets via bi-directional linking are distinct in respect to their subject indexing data but may be overlapping in respect to the topics with which the contained information resources deal. Some information resources may be included in both sets. To which extent equivalent intersystem relations support query expansion, query modification or knowledge exploration depends heavily on the conceptional characteristics of the connected indexing languages. At the worst, they do not facilitate such search processes at all. From the perspective of one indexing language, however, the entities of a different indexing language may be not entities. All entities of a target language are in a way alien to the representational space of an initial language, since they are not an integral part of it. The represented concepts, however, may be familiar but represented by other terms.

If the linked entities are regarded as semantically identical, the entities of the target language refer to concepts that are modeled as entities and represented by respective terms in the initial language as well. Entities of the target language that represent concepts that are (fully) included in the concepts the respective entities of the initial language reflect are not modeled as entities but can nevertheless be modeled as terms in the initial language. If the linked entities have (strongly) overlapping meaning, the entities of the target language represent concepts that are not modeled as entities or terms in the initial language. They are neither explicitly nor implicitly part of the representational space of the initial language and do not smoothly fit into its relational structure. They remain foreign particles for the initial language that are difficult or even impossible to integrate, unless the initial language is significantly modified. The same naturally also applies vice versa.

The given arguments disclose some essential difficulties for pursuing a vice versa connection between entities of different indexing languages. We will come back to this question when considering uni- or bi-directional interoperability connections in Section 10.2.

Table 6.4 summarizes the outlined characteristics of intrasystem relations in condensed form and compares them with equivalent intersystem relations.

Tab. 6.4: Characteristics of intrasystem and equivalent intersystem relations.

Intrasystem relations		**Equivalent intersystem relations**
Hierarchical or associative intrasystem relations	Equivalent intrasystem relations	
Link preferred terms of the same indexing language.	Link non-preferred to preferred terms of the same indexing language.	Link preferred terms of different indexing languages.
Hold between entities of the same indexing language that represent different concepts. Fit into the relational structure of the indexing language.	Hold between terms of the same indexing language that represent the same entity but possibly different concepts in the real world (near synonyms). Fit into the relational structure of the indexing language.	Hold between entities of different indexing languages that can represent the same concept as well as different concepts. Do not inevitably fit into the relational structure of the respective indexing language.
Are bi-directional with respect to conceptual meaning	Are commonly uni-directional with respect to conceptual meaning	Can be used as uni- or bi-directional
Facilitate query expansion, query modification and knowledge exploration.	Promote conceptual queries.	Enhance conceptual queries by promoting cross-lingual conceptual queries.
Lead to two distinct result sets of information resources depending on the relational direction.	Lead to one result set of information resources.	Lead to two result sets of information resources that may be overlapping.

6.2.2 Interoperability and Search Tactics

We build on the presentation of types of search processes given in Section 4.3 and connect them with interoperability issues to get impressions of possible benefits for search outcomes by combining the use of retrieval tools and interoperability consideration for the design of search processes. The aim of this section is to derive propositions whether an expectation of conceptual interoperability for search results using different indexing languages can be made compatible with formal characteristics of entities and derived indexates representing the topics of information resources. In doing so, we are especially interested in deriving statements to what extent conceptual interoperability decisions could be based on formal and not only on cognitive criteria.

The information and the functionality equivalent intersystem relations offer are in a way complementing that of intrasystem relations. This makes it worth while

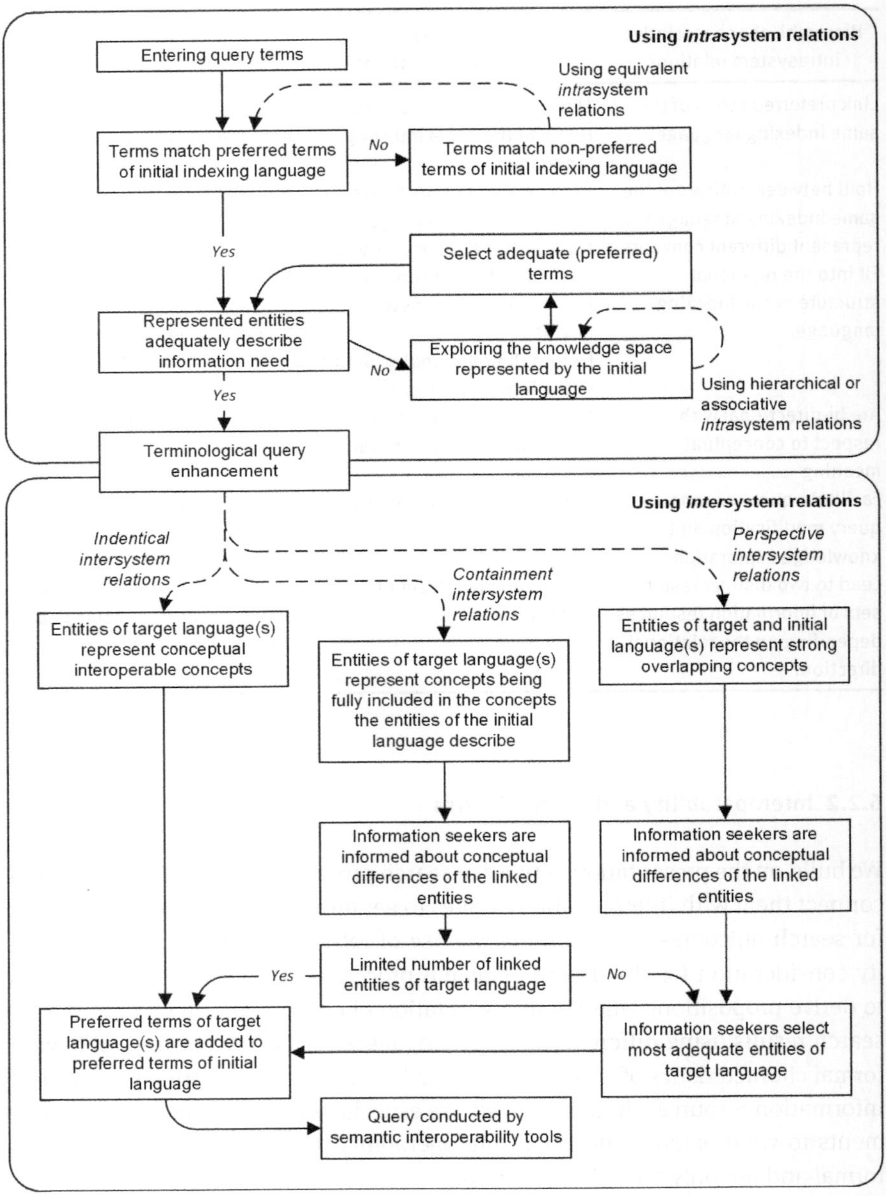

Fig. 6.4: Information retrieval model combining intra- and intersystem relations.

using both in conjunction for supporting retrieval processes in heterogeneous information spaces as has been shown by presenting the various vocabulary linking projects in Section 5.3.3. Afterwards we combine our findings with questions of conceptual interoperability. Figure 6.4 shows an abstract flow chart for illustrating design options for a search process with user-system-feedback. It is shown how terminological enhancement, search expansion and interoperability links between indexing languages can be thought as combined tools conducting a search. This chart can be taken as background for subsequent discussions. We think that it is not necessary to explain all details for the familiar reader. The three types of relationships, *Identical intersystem relations, Containment intersystem relations, Perspective intersystem relations* shown in the lower half of Figure 6.4 are introduced and explained in Section 6.2.3 as *Specified intersystem relations.*

Conceptual Queries

We start considering *conceptual queries* (Glossary B2). By this we mean queries that are explicitly directed towards concepts and that are possibly represented by more than one term in everyday language. For such cases terminological control within the indexing language is unavoidable but should be complemented by terminological hints for performing the search. At first, we will restrict our setting to searches for only one concept that can be thought to correspond to *elementary indexates* (Glossary D1.1).

Equivalence relations in general are deemed to promote conceptual queries in first place. Equivalent intrasystem relations lead information seekers from non-preferred terms of an initial language to corresponding preferred terms of the same indexing language, as shown in the first step in Figure 6.4. By this, they counteract to "zero hit" results. The information resources found, however, remain restricted to those indexed with terms of the initial language. Equivalent intersystem relations provide bridges from entities and terms of the initial language to entities and terms of target languages, as shown in the second step in Figure 6.4. This enables information seekers to retrieve information resources indexed with linked target terms as well.

The result set of a conceptual query that uses an entity of an initial language in query formulation is not necessarily directly comparable to that of a conceptual query that uses a conceptually interoperable entity of a target language even if the entities are cognitively interpreted as semantically identical. The reason for this lies in different characteristics of the subject indexing data. These characteristics influence the result of a conceptual query that is based on two or even more indexing languages and combines the respective conceptually interoperable elementary entities in a Boolean *OR* search. The results of such a conceptual query may not comply with the expectation of information seekers who are familiar with one indexing language. This is especially precarious if they are missing something without knowing about it.

Topical queries

We will now enhance our setting for search interests to *topical queries* (Glossary B3) combining more than one concept to complex thematic statements. For our interoperability considerations, we must then take into concern that the indexing results may be formulated as built indexates (Glossary D1.2) with a more complex structure combining the entities of an indexing language.

Regarding topical queries in general it is necessary to distinguish the following aspects:

- the conceptual complexity of the search topic
- the complexity of indexates representing such a topic by using elements, principles and rules of a certain indexing language
- the complexity of a formulated search question by using elements and tools of a certain retrieval system

Complexity should always mean that a whole can be thought as constructed by parts without requiring explicit use of syntactical devices. It remains open to the specific situation whether the conceptual components are represented by separate terms and whether they can be combined in a combinatorial fashion to represent the complex topic by its parts. As already mentioned, it must be permitted to compare pre-combined entities with built indexates for conceptual interoperability.

Any abstract discussion must refrain from giving details of a specific indexing language or retrieval system. We can only illustrate the situation by some examples. The indexates of the following example have been assigned to the same book so that they can be regarded as interoperable by a finding interest for the respective book[29].

Example 1
320.60973 – Policy making. United States (*DDC*)
JK468.P64 – Political planning. Public policy (*LCC*)
Policy networks--United States (*LCSH*)
Information networks--United States (*LCSH*)
Policy sciences (*LCSH*)

---

29 Cf. also the discussion about the method of *Citation pearl growing* in Section 5.1.

Example 2
004.6/2 – Interfacing and communication protocols (standards)(*DDC*)
TK5105.55 – Computer network protocols. Standards. General works (*LCC*)
Computer networks--Standards--Government policy (*LCSH*)
Computer networks--Standards--Political aspects (*LCSH*)
Computer networks--Standards--Economic aspects (*LCSH*)
Internetworking (Telecommunication)--Technological innovations (*LCSH*)

Example 3
025.0643 – Information storage and retrieval systems devoted to specific disciplines and subjects. Germanic (Teutonic) languages (*DDC*)
PD73.G36 – Languages. Treatises (General) (*LCC*)
Germanic languages--Electronic information resources (*LCSH*)
Electronic information resources (*LCSH*)
German language--Electronic information resources (*LCSH*)

As conclusion obviously emerges that a decision for conceptual interoperability based on built indexates requires a deeper analysis of the formal structure of the indexates.

Take as first case an indexing language A that allows indexers to create *composed indexates* (Glossary D 1.2.2) to represent topics of information resources. These composed indexates are built indexates constructed by terms each representing an entity for the conceptual components they contain. Let I_A be such a composed indexate with three terms t_{A1}, t_{A2} and t_{A3}, each representing one of the entities E_{A1}, E_{A2} and E_{A3}. The situation can then formally presented as follows, the equal sign should indicate identity on the respective terminological or conceptual level

$$I_A = t_{A1}\, t_{A2}\, t_{A3} \text{ with conceptual entities } E_{A1}, E_{A2}, E_{A3},$$

where

$$E_{A1} = t_{A1}, E_{A2} = t_{A2}, E_{A3} = t_{A3}.$$

The symbols t_{A1}, t_{A2} and t_{A3} can be interpreted as individual terminological and simultaneously conceptual components of I_A that can be chosen separately by using or omitting respective terms.

If the entity E_{A1} is used in conceptual query formulation, it is commonly associated with one elementary and at the same time with several composed indexates. Current information retrieval systems mostly do not distinguish between information resources indexed with elementary indexates and those indexed with composed indexates having the elementary one as a part. In any case, they are unable to identify the different kinds of composed indexates. Assuming the indistinguishability of both cases, on the one hand, the entity E_{A1} leads to information resources indexed with the elementary indexate represented by the term t_{A1}. The information resources deal with a topic that corresponds to the thing the entity E_{A1} describes. On the other hand, it leads to information resources indexed with possibly different composed indexates. The information resources possibly deal with a variety of topics. All these topics have in common that they are more specific than the topic the elementary indexate represents. Some can be regarded as being in some way subordinate to the topic the elementary indexate reflects. Others, most likely even most, represent completely different topics whose relation to the topic the elementary indexate describes is difficult to determine, since the role the respective entity plays in the whole construct is concealed.

A different retrieval situation occurs in case of an indexing language *B* that allows indexers to create *compound indexates* (Glossary D 1.2.1) to represent topics of information resources. Compound indexates are characterized by simple terms that formally do not reveal all their conceptual components. Formally this can be represented as follows. I_B is represented by the fictive term $t_{B1}\{x\ y\}$. Whereas the first part of the string, t_{B1}, exactly matches the term of the entity E_{B1}, the following parts, *x* and *y*, cannot easily be attributed to any entities E_{B2} or E_{B3} that would represent the other conceptual components of the compound indexate I_B.

$$I_B = t_{B1}\,\{x\ y\} \text{ with conceptual entities } E_{B1}, C_{B2}, C_{B3},$$

where

$$E_{B1} = t_{B1}, C_{B2} = x, C_{B3} = y$$

The symbols *x* and *y* can be interpreted as terminological components of I_B that cannot be chosen separately by using or omitting respective terms. The conceptual components they represent are encapsulated and cannot be separately chosen by any retrieval feature. Typical examples for such constructs are adjectives or noun parts of compounds representing concepts by different aspects. In indexing languages they can be found primarily as pre-combined elements.

If the entity E_{B1} is used for formulating a conceptual query, it functions in the first place as access point to one elementary indexate. It leads to information resources indexed with the elementary indexate represented by the term t_{B1}. The information resources deal with a topic that corresponds to the thing described by entity E_{B1}. The conceptual query resembles a topical query with the indexate I_B used in query formulation.

If truncation from the right side is used for compound terminological strings, it provides the possibility also to address compound indexates. This can be seen as access to subordinate topics that correspond to:
- a thing that is described by the entity E_{B1}
- a thing that is subordinate to the thing that is described by the entity E_{B1}

It depends on the specific conceptual conditions whether this subordination can be seen as a form of hierarchical connections and whether the enhanced search outcomes are useful for the initial search interest.

We can even go a step further. The string t_{B1} may represent a subordinate entity to E_{B1}. Let us call it $E_{B11} < E_{B1}$. The entity E_{B1} now gives access to elementary and compound indexates associated with E_{B1} and E_{B11} that start t_{B1}. The list of retrieved items can now be even enhanced to topics that correspond to:
- a thing that is described by the entity
- a thing that is subordinate to the thing that is described by the entity
- a thing that is described by a subordinate entity
- a thing that is subordinate to the thing that is described by a subordinate entity

The next step will combine the findings so far with questions of conceptual interoperability in a more explicit way. Initial situation should be a setting typical for interoperability decisions between entities of indexing languages with different properties concerning the existence of pre-combined entities.

Let be given the two indexing languages *A* and *B*. The entity E_A of *A* may have no direct conceptual counterpart in *B* but may be seen as conceptual interoperable to a combination of E_{B1} and E_{B2} in *B*. The entity E_A is therefore a pre-combined entity and must be seen as composed of two conceptual parts. Formulated as above, this looks like:

$$E_A = t_A, E_A = C_{A1}\,C_{A2}$$
$$E_{B1} = t_{B1}, E_{B1} = C_{B1}, E_{B2} = t_{B2}, E_{B2} = C_{B2}$$
$$E_A \sim E_{B1}\,E_{B2}$$

The sign ~ should indicate conceptual interoperability.

Each of the conceptual parts may be organized in a separate hierarchical structure, representing subfields or aspects. A topical search should use the interoperable entities of both indexing languages, the entities E_A, E_{B1} and E_{B2}, combined in a Boolean OR search.

Evaluating the search outcomes for their conceptual attributes we may get items with topics that correspond to:
- a thing that is described by the entity E_A of indexing language *A*
- a thing that is described by a combination of the entities E_{B1} and E_{B2}
- a thing that is described by an entity E_{B1} or E_{B2} that represents an aspect of the topic

From the scenarios given a lot of further cases can be derived. We refrain from giving additional examples. They all would support that it is hard to imagine how to take this description as an initial situation for interoperability decisions on a formal basis. For being conceptually exchangeable, interoperable entities do not only have to be semantically identical but the respective indexing languages also have to be associated with identical indexing methods. Reliable decisions for two composed indexates require identity in number and conceptual content of their components. This setting does not fit to all practical situations. There are a lot of situations where the semantic content of the topics and their relations can only be recognized cognitively at most.

Entity-based conceptual exploration

A further use case for applying conceptual interoperability decisions is given by *entity-based exploration* (Glossary C4.2). By this we mean a form of query enhancement by user-machine feedback on the basis of the conceptual structure underlying the indexing language.

Besides the equivalence relationship this structure is mainly characterized by hierarchical and associative intrasystem relations. They facilitate (automatic) conceptual query expansion or (cognitive) processes of knowledge exploration. In particular, they offer information seekers paths they can follow when looking for additional entities being possibly relevant for their information need. This becomes especially useful if the relational structures of two indexing languages considered for interoperability statements differ to some extent.

We will discuss this option by presenting an example first. The example is taken from the outcomings of the the *CrissCross*[30] project for enrichment of the Relative Index of the German edition of the *Dewey Decimal Classification (DDC)* by entries from the German subject headings authority file *Schlagwortnormdatei (SWD)*[31].

The entities modeled in the initial language, the *SWD*[32], represent more specific concepts than the entities modeled in the target language, the *DDC*. Yet, they mostly refer to concepts that are not subordinate or somehow related to the concepts the *DDC* classes describe but that are – either fully or at least mostly – conceptually included in these. Established equivalent intersystem relations often connect many *SWD* entities to one single *DDC* class. This connection can be utilized for query expansion or knowledge exploration especially in those cases

30 Cf. http://ixtrieve.fh-koeln.de/crisscross/index_en.html. A description of the project, its aim and methods has already been given in Section 5.3.3.

31 Cf. Ref.: http://melvil.dnb.de/gnd

32 Cf. http://www.dnb.de/DE/Standardisierung/GND/gnd_node.html

where the *SWD* modeling of the semantic environment of entities is lacunary and incomplete.

Figure 6.5 shows an extract from the *SWD* with a poorly designed relational structure. It is not really necessary to understand the content-meaning of the German headings, since merely the numbers of edges between the headings are of relevance for our considerations[33]. Information seekers using one of the displayed *SWD* entities in initial query formulation do not find enough paths to follow. They are thrown back to their own knowledge of a subject field and its respective terminology if they want to enhance their search for additional entities. Processes of automatic conceptual query expansion are likewise restricted.

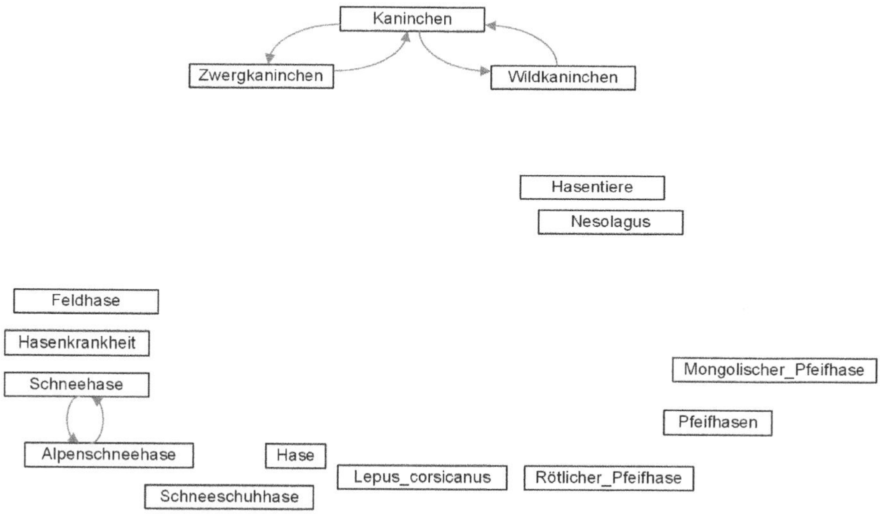

Fig. 6.5: Example for the sparse relational structure of the *Schlagwortnormdatei (SWD).*

If one looks for classes in the *DDC* that correspond to the *SWD* subject headings[34], a more elaborated relational structure will be found as shown in Figure 6.6. With the established *SWD-DDC* linkages, *SWD* entities being connected to the same *DDC* class can be subsumed and accessed as a cluster. Thereby missing relational structures are bridged. The clusters of *SWD* entities that emerge from the connec-

---

33 We provide a list with translations of the German headings: Kaninchen – rabbit, Zwergkaninchen – dwarf rabbit, Wildkaninchen – wild rabbits, Hase – hare, Hasentiere – hares (lagomorphs), Feldhase – European hare, Hasenkrankheit – rabbit disease, Schneehase – arctic hare, Alpenschneehase – mountain hare / Alps mountain hare, Schneeschuhhase – Snowshoe hare, Pfeifhasen – pikas, Rötlicher Pfeifhase – reddish pika, Mongolischer Pfeifhase – Mongolian pika.
34 Cf. Ref.: http://melvil.dnb.de/gnd

tion of several *SWD* entities to the same *DDC* class(es) may also be used for query expansion to improve *recall*. New connections valuable for knowledge exploration arise that could aid information seekers in cognitive conceptual search and orientation processes.

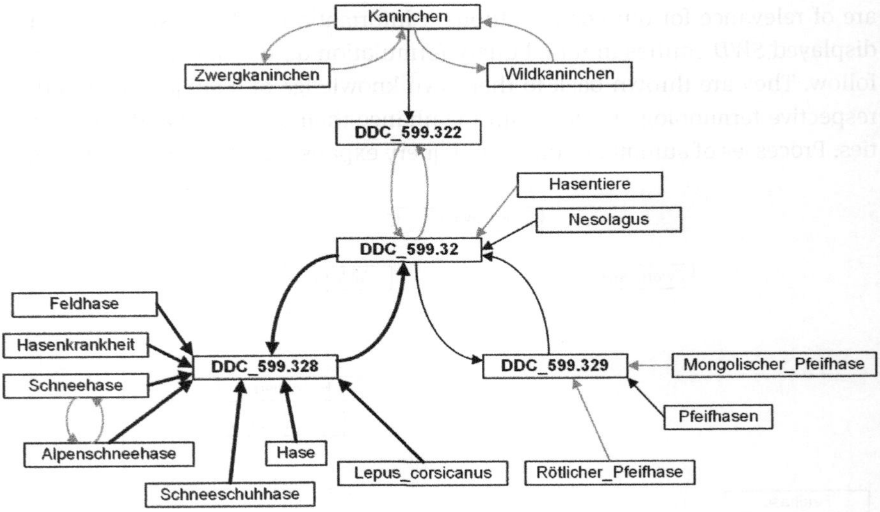

Fig. 6.6: More dense relational structure of the entities from Fig. 6.5 in the *DDC*.

Different shapes of the edges in Figure 6.6 indicate different types of relationship between *SWD* headings and *DDC* numbers. In Chapter 8, we will come back to this question and precise the understanding of a correspondence between classes of the *DDC* and headings of the *SWD*. At the moment, it is sufficient to recognize that an alternation between the knowledge structures can enhance one structure to further conceptual relationships by the other one.

Take as a further example the *SWD* entity represented by the heading *Schmetterlinge* (*butterflies*). This heading reflects an object-focused view on *butterflies* in general. It has eight headings as narrower terms and one heading as related term. It is connected to one *DDC* number, *595.78*. To the corresponding *DDC* class, 248 *SWD* headings are linked.

In a database that contains approximately 330.000 heterogeneously indexed information resources (a database that was created within the frame of the *CrissCross* project for test purposes), a conceptual query with *Schmetterlinge* yields 16 hits if the subject heading field is addressed and 17 hits if the title field is addressed. Query expansion with recourse to the paradigmatic intrasystem relations modeled in the *SWD* yields 23 hits if the subject heading field is addressed and 18 hits if the title field is addressed. The recall of the retrieval results can be improved further based on equivalent intersystem relations. If all *SWD* headings that are connected to the *DDC* number *595.78* are used as query terms, a query in the subject heading field yields 27 hits, in the title field even 39 hits (cf. Tab. 6.5).

Tab. 6.5: Hits of a conceptual query taking the *SWD* heading *Schmetterlinge* (*butterflies*) as initial query term.

Search term	***SWD* heading**	**Title**
Schmetterlinge	16	17
Hierarchical or associated *SWD* terms to *Schmetterlinge*	23	18
Backward cluster of (preferred) *SWD* headings for *DDC* number *595.78*	27	39

In the given example, the number of information resources associated with the cluster of *SWD* headings remains manageable. Yet, a larger number can be overwhelming for information seekers. In those cases, it would be advantageous to present a list of entities contained in the respective cluster from which information seekers may intellectually select to refine and extend the retrieval results.[35]

Processes of conceptual exploration, query modification or query expansion benefit most from established equivalent intersystem relations if these connect indexing languages with complementary relational structures whose entities are equally relevant or at least equally valuable for information retrieval in heterogeneous information spaces. Differentiated intersystem relations that adequately reflect the types of conceptual interoperability can indirectly reveal whether the direct semantic environment of linked entities is semantically compatible. If different types of semantic interoperability between entities are made explicit, we will call this feature *differentiated interoperability* (Glossary E3.2)[36]. As indicated by the above mentioned example, they may provide the basis for the development of more sophisticated information retrieval systems that utilize relational structures of linked indexing languages. Subtypes will be discussed subsequently. All other forms of interoperability with unclear semantic characteristic will be called *undifferentiated interoperability* (Glossary E3.1).

35 This method has been discussed in more detail in Boteram et al. (2009).

36 Cf. also the introduction of this concept in Section 5.3.2.

6.2.3 Specified Intersystem Relationships

We will summarize the discussion so far by introducing three basic types of specified intersystem relations:

- *Identical intersystem relations*
- *Containment intersystem relations*
- *Perspective intersystem relations*

We use the term *specified* for *inter*system relation in order to distinguish them from *typed* relations, a term that will be used in Chapter 8 for characterizing mainly *intra*system relations. There is no need to regard these types as disjoint, but it seems appropriate to make a terminological dictinction for their main application area.

These types take into consideration the semantic content of linked entities on the one hand and certain logical characteristics of the respective linkages on the other hand. They should describe the common types of expectations when linking indexing languages for bi-directional exchangeability of their entities regardless a deeper analysis of a conceptual exchangeability at first hand. Therefore, they should not be interpreted in a normative sense. They may serve as a set of types to describe the ways that are taken in order to plan or carry out practical projects implementing interoperability ideas. We refer to Figure 6.4 for a visualization. The set of types should be suitable to get insight into main characteristics of conceptual interoperability links or intersystem relations and must be complemented by means of a true conceptual modeling.

The first type of specified intersystem relations, the *identical intersystem relations* (Glossary E3.2.2), connect entities of different indexing languages that refer to exactly the same concept. This form of relationships does not only imply a certain degree of exchangeability in conceptual retrieval scenarios across more than one indexing language. It implies also a structural compatibility of the modeled conceptual environment of the respective entities. This type of intersystem relation resembles the equivalent intrasystem relation. It can be seen as the ideal form of conceptual interoperability with an imagination of conceptual identity and exchangeability. We can summarize as attributes: Identical intersystem relations are equivalent intersystem relations holding between semantically identical entities. If they are modeled according all formal requirements of equivalence relations they are reflexive, symmetric, and transitive. With these properties they are best suited for establishing inference processes that will be studied in more detail in Chapters 8 and 9.

Special benefit can be expected if the respective intrasystem relations for entities of an initial indexing language linked by identical intersystem relations to the entities of a target language may provide additional context for the entities of the initial language. New paths for explorative search processes occur from which processes of query modification or query expansion may profit as well. The logical property of transitivity becomes important if three or more indexing languages are connected, especially if the underlying framework does not follow a direct-linkages approach but a backbone- or switching model or even no structural model at all, since it allows drawing inferences across the entities of several indexing languages that need not to be structurally compatible.

The next type of specified intersystem relations is called *containment intersystem relations* (Glossary E3.2.3). Such relations connect entities of different indexing languages that refer to concepts that are fully included in one another. In other words, the concept one entity represents is contained in the concept the other entity represents.

Formally speaking, containment intersystem relations are asymmetric and consist of two inverse uni-directional intersystem relations that we call *is-contained-in-* and *contains-* relation. Both exhibit the property of transitivity with respect to their respective direction.

As the represented concepts differ in scope of their meaning, the respective entities are not exchangeable in retrieval situations across indexing languages but their direct semantic environment nevertheless is valid for both indexing languages. Modeled intrasystem relations and entities (and terms) directly connected with the linked entities of a target language may provide additional context for the corresponding entities of the initial language if they differ in number or specificity. This may be utilized for the support of explorative processes, query modification or query expansion.

If indexing languages differ in structure and typology, the more it is likely that entities regarded as being conceptually interoperable refer to concepts with strongly overlapping meaning that share major significant characteristics but that may differ in respect to their perspective. The underlying phenomenon was introduced in Section 6.1.2 as *semantic congruence*. We will now call the respective intersystem relation *perspective intersystem relations* (Glossary E3.2.4). Usually they involve a shift in the point of view.

The linked entities represent concepts as integral parts of the representational space of just one indexing language, the indexing language in which they were originally modeled. Consequently, the entities are not conceptually exchangeable in retrieval scenarios. Their direct semantic environments are not semantically compatible. Conceptual queries across the indexing languages require human interaction. Knowledge exploration, conceptual query modification or query expansion are not supported.

It is likely that perspective intersystem relations can be subdivided further by aspects that will be discussed in Section 8.1 after having introduced the concept of typed relationships for intrasystem relations. To explore the formal characteristics of this relation type and the possible benefit for retrieval processes across indexing languages connected by this type of relation is an outstanding issue for future research.

6.2.4 Conceptual Interoperability between Indexing Results

So far, we have considered the problems of conceptual interoperability of entities on an elementary conceptual level, we will now consider problems of identifying conceptual interoperability between entities of a more complex conceptual level. Entities of indexing languages may have a pre-combined conceptual structure although represented by a single descriptor or notation for example *American literature, German literature*. The question for conceptual interoperability between such pre-combined entities has strong resemblance to the question of conceptual interoperability between synthesized indexing results, composed explicitly from conceptual components, as for example *Literature – America, Literature – Germany.* An illustration of this feature is given in Figure 7.4 in Section 7.3. The similarity will justify to treat both cases within the context of this section. Once more, we have to discuss criteria for an identification of conceptual interoperability.

For ease of use, we call the results of an indexing process *Indexates*, regardless whether they can be seen as conceptually simple, pre-combined or synthesized.[37]

Indexates describing the content of information resources, however, often reveal all the entities of which they are composed. The relation between them as whole and their conceptual parts is not fixed in all cases. It depends on the *syntagmatic* or *a posteriori* relations that implicitly or explicitly connect the elements.

Indexates (*SE*) as synthesized products of entities, we call them *built indexates*, are conceptually identical if all their conceptual components (*C*) as well as all relations between these (⊗) are identical. Otherwise, they are semantically similar at the most in the sense that was introduced by the two types of relations in Section 6.2.3 called containment or perspective intersystem relations. Considering entities of two indexing languages *A* and *B*, in a formal manner this can be expressed as:

37 A more detailed presentation of this understanding is given in (Gödert 2010a, Gödert 2010b).

$$SE_A = C_{A1} \otimes_1 C_{A2} \otimes_2 C_{A3}$$
$$SE_B = C_{B1} \otimes_1 C_{B2} \otimes_2 C_{B3}$$

The symbol ⊗ should be likewise interpreted as implicit connection in a pre-combined entity (*German literature*) or as explicit syntactical connector between the components of a synthesized indexate (*Literature – Germany*). Then, one can say that SE_A and SE_B can be seen as conceptually identical, if the following two conditions are satisfied:

- The conceptual components are identical: $C_{A1} = C_{B1}$; $C_{A2} = C_{B2}$; $C_{A3} = C_{B3}$
- The syntax connectors $\otimes_2$, $\otimes_2$ have an identical meaning in each of their occurrences

Any decision for conceptual identity or interchangeability, at least its simplicity, depends on the transparency of the syntactic structure of the indexates. If there are no explicit syntactical connectors but only sequences of terms or helpful sequences or even pre-combined structures, the decision remains a task for cognitive analysis. It is much easier to come to an interoperability statement for built indexates with explicit syntactical devices – in Section 6.2.2 we have called such indexates as *composed indexates*. For such composed indexates the decision can be based on comparing the conceptual components and the meaning of the syntax connectors. For mere term sequences or pre-combined structures the situation remains more complex with a risk for uncertainty. Any idea for machine support requires at least sufficient transparency about the conceptual components and meaning of the connectors that need to be made explicit in a formal way.

The situation is different, if all interoperable entities show a kind of inclusion or overlapping meaning. Then the same may apply to the respective built indexates but generally it requires additional cognitive interpretation to determine the degree of semantic similarity being constitutive for the respective built indexates. This argument also sheds light on limits for any attempt of a computer based determination of the conceptual interoperability of built indexates from established equivalent intersystem relations between entities. Immediate necessary requirements are appropriate formal representations of the conceptual content of the entities and the built indexates and the syntax connectors.

The second form of built indexates we introduced in Section 6.2.2, the *compound indexates* present even more difficulties. They express conceptual complexity by single terms that do not clearly reveal their components. Decisions on conceptual similarity to other entities or indexates must be based on an intellectual analysis. Best expectation can be a resemblance in correspondence to containment or perspective intersystem relations. It cannot be automated with satisfactory results as long as the application rules are not available machine-accessible and machine-interpretable.

Some special cases remain even in the case of composed indexates. For composed indexates that are likely to have a similar meaning, it seems very plausible that interoperability may only be determined cognitively. For some indexing languages a close examination of their application rules will be recommendable to ensure that the corresponding composed indexates exhibit a similar syntax to avoid false statements about their conceptual interoperability.

Determining the conceptual interoperability between built indexates of different types like the conceptual interoperability between composed and compound indexates will remain a difficult cognitive task in any case. It presupposes well-founded knowledge of the respective (language-specific) application rules for building the composed indexates as well as knowledge about the conceptual compounds. Any support by machines seems fictitious as long as there is no transparency about the conceptual components. No statements can be made about ways pursuing this goal.

Concluding this section, we will give some typical abstract examples of indexates being *not* semantically identical.

Example 1

$$SE_A = C_{A1} \otimes C_{A2} \otimes C_{A3}$$
$$SE_B = C_{B1} \otimes C_{B2}$$

This example needs no further explanation: $SE_A \neq SE_B$

Example 2

$$SE_A = C_{A1} \otimes C_{A2}$$
$$SE_B = C_{B1} \otimes C_{B2}$$

with

$$C_{A1} < C_{B1} \text{ and } C_{A2} > C_{B2}$$

The symbols < and > should indicate the result of comparing the conceptual intension or scope of the entities regarded: $SE_A \neq SE_B$.

Example 3

$$SE_A = C_{A1} \otimes_1 C_{A2} \otimes_2 C_{A3}$$
$$SE_B = C_{B1} \otimes_3 C_{B2} \otimes_4 C_{B3}$$

with

$$C_{A1} = C_{B1};\ C_{A2} = C_{B2};\ C_{A3} = C_{B3}$$
$$\otimes_1 \neq \otimes_3 \text{ and } \otimes_2 \neq \otimes_4.$$

We refrain from giving further combinations of conceptual components that indicate semantic differences of syntactically built indexates.

6.2.5 Directedness of Intersystem Relationships

Analyzing entities of indexing languages for conceptual exchangeability, simple examples indicate that it may be wishful thinking assuming always a bi-directional exchangeability. The inspection even must not be restricted to a comparison between pre-combined and conceptually more elementary entities.

For estimating the potential quality of an interoperability design it is important to know whether equivalent intersystem relations or interoperability links can really be interpreted as truly *bi-directionally* interoperable or whether they should be seen as *uni-directional* in the sense of links between an access and a target vocabulary.

For the design of practical interoperability situations bi-directionality is often the guiding principle even for combinations of more than two indexing languages when planning practical search systems. As result one gets search results with conceptual fuzzyness and less precision. With respect to our three types of intersystem relations it must be said that identical intersystem relations with their strong requirement of conceptual identity too seldom are valid between the entities of different indexing languages. The two other types – containment and perspective intersystem relations are much more common but they do not guarantee the true conceptual exchangeability of the entities involved. The deeper reason is that it is not sufficient to base a decision for conceptual interoperability – even it is done cognitively – only on a context-free interpretation. Instead it is necessary to regard the relational structure for any of the two entities.

This aspect has already been mentioned when discussing the example at the beginning of this chapter, cf. Table 6.1 and Figure 6.1. The concept *library* was modeled as descriptor in two fictitious thesauri and by establishing different relations to other terms. We got two different contextual structures that had influence on the conceptual interpretation of the descriptor *library*. No criteria could be given that the descriptor *library* in Thesaurus 1 would be exchangeable with descriptor *library* in Thesaurus 2.

What would be the conclusive arguments? Does it make a difference to regard the links as *uni*- or *bi*-directional? Is it beneficial to make a switch from one structure to the other? What kind of search process would be supported by such a switch? If only descriptors are permitted for establishing interoperability, all descriptors of *Thesaurus 2* must be mapped to the one descriptor of *Thesaurus 1*. An approach like this must be accompanied by a great loss of expression and differentiation ability. Generally speaking, this effect causes the least semantically differentiated structure to become the structural basis of all related knowledge representations.

Assessing the example it seems obvious that *uni-directional* links provide better degrees of freedom for establishing search scenarios with transparent conceptual circumstances by switching from the entities of an initial indexing language to a target language. An understanding of conceptual interoperability in the sense of *bi-directional* connections requires a deeper analysis of the indexing languages involved including their relational characteristics.

Vocabulary linking projects do not always clearly specify the directionality of the links, bi-directionality is often assumed implicitly[38]. Such projects miss clear-cut semantic characteristics and do not allow for any formal representation. It must be regarded as questionable whether an interoperability link from an entity E_A to an entity E_B justifies the conclusion that the entity E_B may be connected in the same sense to entity E_A without analyzing the respective conceptual content. They only state that entities of different indexing languages are somehow related. They neither allow machines nor humans to immediately recognize semantic differences that may be valuable in view of retrieval processes that are based on two or even more indexing languages.

Uni-directional intersystem relations that are not specified in a certain sense contain first the information that an entity E_A of an indexing language *A* is in some way semantically interoperable to an entity E_B of indexing language *B* without making any statement about the kind of conceptual interoperability present. This means at first only, continuing a search that was started with E_A by using E_B may lead to useful results.

Intersystem relations can be seen as *specified* (Glossary E3.2.1) in more than one sense if the strong condition of conceptual equivalence must no longer be respected. We have discussed this in Section 6.2.3. For uni-directional relations the type of specification may refer either to the conceptual or to the application level of entities. It is also imaginable that they address both in the form of corresponding attributes. A further differentiation is possible for uni-directional intersystem relations on the application level. Such relations can be regarded between entities or between indexates or between entities and indexates.

An example of uni-directional intersystem relations that refer to application level of entities is given by the so-called *degrees of determinacy* (Glossary E3.2.5).

---

38 Cf. the presentations given in Section 5.3.3.

This methodological approach has been developed in the *CrissCross*[39] project for enrichment of the Relative Index of the German edition of the *Dewey Decimal Classification (DDC Deutsch)* by entries from the German *Schlagwortnormdatei (SWD)*. We will give a more detailed description of the underlying methodological considerations before illustrating the application by giving examples (Boteram & Hubrich 2010, Hubrich 2010, Hubrich 2011, Hubrich 2013).

The *degrees of determinacy* are numerical figures that add application-oriented content to the established equivalent intersystem relations connecting headings of the German subject headings authority file *Schlagwortnormdatei (SWD)* to numbers of the *Dewey Decimal Classification (DDC)*. They refer to (explicit or implicit) instance-class relations inherent in the *DDC* that are important for building complex *DDC* entities.

The invention and application of the degrees of determinacy must be seen in strong connection to the *DDC* instructions for number building. These instructions allow indexers to synthesize compound *DDC* entities and create built numbers only if the base subjects, with which the information resources deal, equal or at least approximate the full meaning of the modeled *DDC* classes. Class captions or terms listed in *class-here notes* make explicit such subjects[40]. Subjects that are thought to be less extensive in scope, having so-called *standing room* due to the fact that not a sufficient number of information resources deal with them to justify an own *DDC* class, cannot constitute base subjects for compound *DDC* entities[41]. In this case, number building is forbidden. Terms listed in *including notes* refer to respective example subjects[42].

The *CrissCross* degrees of determinacy make explicit in which respect the subjects that the *SWD* entities represent are included in the *DDC* classes, provided their meaning is thought in compliance with the *DDC* structure. There are four degrees that were specified for uni-directional connections between *SWD* headings and *DDC* numbers. Before applying them to our example, we will reproduce their definitional descriptions and give some examples:[43]

39 Cf. http://ixtrieve.fh-koeln.de/crisscross/index_en.html
40 Cf. http://www.oclc.org/support/documentation/glossary/dewey/default.htm#ClassHereNote
41 Cf. http://www.oclc.org/support/documentation/glossary/dewey/default.htm#StandingRoom
42 Cf. http://www.oclc.org/support/documentation/glossary/dewey/default.htm#IncludingNote
43 Cf. http://ixtrieve.fh-koeln.de/crisscross/degrees_of_determinacy_en.html

Degree of determinacy 4 (D4)
The connotation scope of the *SWD* heading is identical to the connotation scope of the topic emphasized in the *DDC* class heading, that is, it also has the same thematic context as the *DDC* class.

SWD	DDC		Det
Kriegsrecht <Völkerrecht>	341.6	Kriegsrecht Law of war	D4
Skunks	599.768	Mephitinae (Stinktiere) Syn.: Skunks	D4

Degree of determinacy 3 (D3)
The connotation scope of the *SWD* heading is identical or nearly identical to the connotation scope of a topic that approximates the whole of the assigned *DDC* class. According to *DDC* terms, topics that are nearly coextensive with the full meaning of a class or cover more than half of the content of the class approximate the whole of the *DDC* class. Topics in *class-here notes* are typical examples.

SWD	DDC		Det
Zarzuela	782.12	Operetten / Operettas Class here: Zarzuelas	D3

Degree of determinacy 2 (D2)
The connotation scope of the *SWD* heading is identical or nearly identical to the connotation scope of a topic that is logically part of the class but is less extensive in scope than the concept represented by the class number. Topics in *including notes* are typical examples.

SWD	DDC		Det
Cool Jazz	781.655	Modern Jazz Including: Bebop (Bop), Hardbop, Cool Jazz, Progressive Jazz	D2

Degree of determinacy 1 (D1)
The connotation scope of the *SWD* heading corresponds to a small part to the connotation scope of the assigned *DDC* class.

SWD	DDC		Det
Gleichaltrigkeit	303.327	Sozialisation durch Peergroups Including: Gruppenzwang Socialization by peer group	D1
Flugzeugwrack	363.124	Luft- und Weltraumverkehr Air and space transportation	D1

We can now illustrate the application of the degrees of determinacy for interoperability statements by coming back to the example given with the discussion of Figures 6.5 and 6.6 in Section 6.2.2. Different shapes of the edges of Figure 6.6 indicate a different type of relationship between *SWD* headings and *DDC* numbers that can be translated to one of the determinacy degrees.

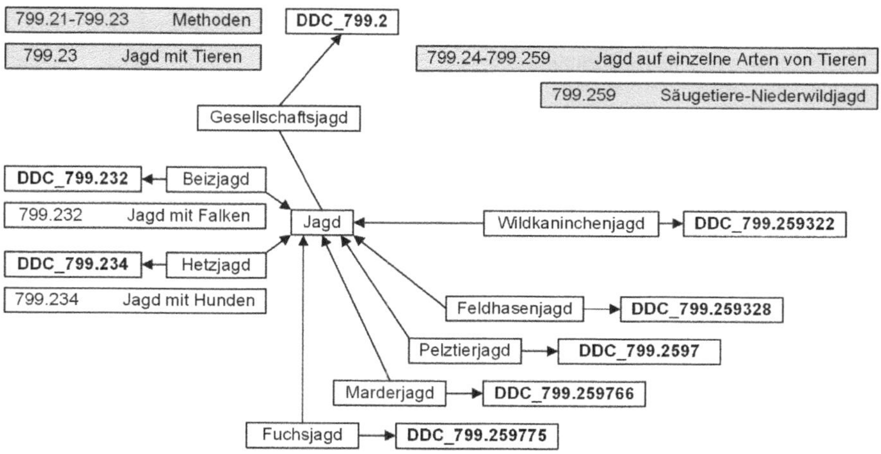

Fig. 6.7: Example for assembling relational enrichment and interoperability between *SWD* and *DDC*.

Figure 6.7 continues the presentation and focuses on the subject heading *Jagd*[44]. This is associated with three related terms (*Jäger – hunter, Jagdkunde – hunting, Tierfang – animal caught*).

44 Once more we provide a list with translations of the German headings: Jagd – hunt / chase, Jagd mit Tieren – hunting with animals, Jagd auf einzelne Arten von Tieren – hunt for individual

Three classes in the *DDC* can be seen as link points for the *SWD* heading *Jagd* (hunting):

799.2	*Jagd als Sport. Umfassende Werke über Jagd* *Hunting as a sport. Comprehensive works on hunting*
639.1	*Kommerzielle Jagd / Jagd in der Landwirtschaft* *Commercial hunting / hunting in agriculture*
179.3	*Jagd in der Ethik* *Hunting in ethics*

For the three *DDC* classes that are assigned to the not closer contextualized *SWD* heading *Jagd*, the following degrees of determinacy were chosen:

SWD	Det	DDC	
Jagd	D3	799.2	Jagd als Sport. Umfassende Werke über Jagd Hunting as a sport. Comprehensive works on hunting
Jagd	D3	639.1	Kommerzielle Jagd / Jagd in der Landwirtschaft Commercial hunting / hunting in agriculture
Jagd	D1	179.3	Jagd in der Ethik Hunting in ethics

We will discuss some details of our example from a more general point-of-view showing some features of the concept of determinacy degrees. In case of the degrees of determinacy *D4* and *D3*, the *SWD* headings refer to subjects that fully or at least approximately correspond to the meaning of the respective *DDC* classes. This implies that they can constitute base subjects for compound *DDC* indexates or that subordinate *DDC* classes may reflect concepts that are somehow subordinate to what is described by the *SWD* headings. The degree of determinacy *D4* differs from the degree of determinacy *D3* in that it implicitly also states that the subjects the *SWD* entities represent are fully included in the concept the *DDC* class describes. Thus, in a way it combines semantic and applicational information in contrast to the other degrees of determinacy that exhibit just applicational information. Whereas the latter may be valuable for issues of query expansion in respect to *DDC*-indexed information resources, the former makes it worthwhile not only to consider elementary *DDC* indexates but also compound *DDC* indexates within the frame of interoperability decisions.

---

species of animals, Niederwildjagd – Varmint hunting / small game hunting, Gesellschaftsjagd – hunting in society, Beizjagd – hawking, Jagd mit Falken – falconry, Hetzjagd – coursing, Jagd mit Hunden – hunting with dogs, Wildkaninchenjagd – abbit hunting, Feldhasenjagd – hare hunting, Pelztierjagd – fur hunting, Marderjagd – marten hunting, Fuchsjagd – fox hunting.

In case of the degree of determinacy *D2*, the *SWD* headings refer to subjects that are thought as being less extensive in scope than the respective *DDC* classes. This implies that the subjects do not constitute base subjects for any compound *DDC* indexates or that subordinate *DDC* classes never reflect subordinate subjects. Neither compound *DDC* indexates nor modeled subordinate *DDC* classes are likely to be associated with information resources that are relevant for the information need at hand (provided the SWD term used in initial query formulation adequately grasps this information need).

We will add some remarks that will be continued in Chapter 10 when discussing more general aspects of the benefit of conceptual interoperability for information retrieval. Figure 6.7 already shows some possibilities for assembling *relational enrichment* and interoperability. The subject heading *Jagd* from the *SWD* has been chosen as an example. The heading *Jagd* is associated with three related terms (*Jäger – hunter, Jagdkunde – hunting, Tierfang – animal caught*). It has 28 narrower terms that do not have any relations to further headings[45]. We cannot take them into account to full extent. To support cognitive conceptual searches, the headings can initially only be displayed in alphabetical order or in their incomplete hierarchical contexts. If connections to *DDC* are set up, by analyzing aspects one can derive descriptions of some relation types. For example, one part of the narrower terms refers to *hunting methods*, another part to *hunt for individual species of animals*. Among other things a more rapid estimate becomes possible concerning the relevance of the headings with regard to the search interest. We obtain a denser network of relations that is more suitable for supporting cognitive orientation operations. The suitability for supporting mechanical search processes will not be examined yet.

45 Cf. http://melvil.dnb.de/gnd/4027955-8

Part C
Vision – Ontology-based Indexing and Retrieval

7 Formalization in Indexing Languages

In Part A of this book, we have discussed the conceptual basics for organizing, representing, searching, and exploring knowledge. In Part B, examples for handling heterogeneity and identified problems with establishing semantic interoperability have been presented. The major objective of part C is to make suggestions for combining the properties of indexing languages with the methodological strength of formal knowledge representation languages in order to design retrieval solutions for hitherto unsolved or untackled problems. This chapter starts by summarizing the properties of indexing languages that can be seen as helpful for establishing connections to formal knowledge representation. Subsequent chapters will complement the considerations by discussing typed relations, inferences along their paths in knowledge representations and conceptual models on an aspect-oriented basis. All together this will constitute the basis for a proposal of an ontology-based indexing and retrieval concept.

7.1 Introduction and Objectives

In the following discussion, we will develop essential components of a model for indexing and retrieval that combines the strengths of the previous approaches for indexing of information resources with approaches of formal knowledge representation and reasoning. In particular, we will consider the relationships and interactions between indexing languages or other tools for representing semantic knowledge, the principles applied for indexing, and the resulting retrieval options.

Previous approaches using indexing languages for the retrieval of information resources have interpreted the components of indexing languages primarily or exclusively cognitively. The descriptors of thesauri or notations of classification systems were used for indexing according to predefined rules and for subsequent search processes. Relationships between the relevant entities are shown to varying degrees. The use of synonyms and hierarchical relations for automated retrieval processes has been well established but it has not yet become the accepted standard. Automatic inference is neither common nor is it supported by the concept of indexing languages. Focus on formal knowledge representation suggests to consider the relationships between the entities for machine evaluation to a greater extent. The previously observed quality of the relationships between the entities of indexing languages suggests to reflect on ways to improve their basic conceptual structure. Since indexing languages are tools with purpose limitation for document indexing, cross connections to the principles of the indexing process and the possibilities of a retrieval action need to be considered for knowledge modeling. Such a connection has to treat the question how enhanced forms of relations between the entities of a knowledge representation can be made available for searches. Therefore models must be specified, how the relationships can be connected to the documents for determining the hits for a search query.

By considering the ideas for the organization of a *Semantic Web*, we can add further aspects. Formal representation standards as expressed for example by the names *RDF*, *SKOS*, or *OWL*, give reason to hope that indexing and retrieval models do not have to be limited to proprietary systems. Rather, they may be related to the open and expanding document collections distributed over the web. It is necessary to make content-understood semantic compatibility to the object of interoperability. Existing indexing data could then lead to any improvement of the retrieval situation as are often directed as expectations for the rather naive linked data approaches. We will examine which contribution our model can provide for this.

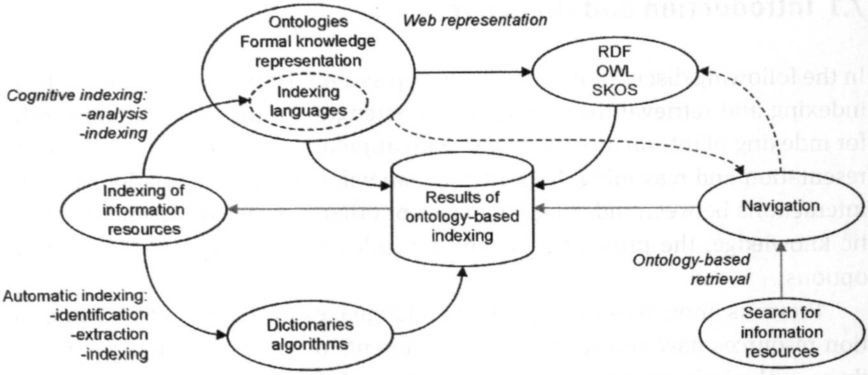

Fig. 7.1: Sketch of an ontology-based concept for indexing and retrieval of documents.

Figure 7.1 provides a graphical illustration of the ideas that are developed below. As a central idea can be considered that an attempt is made to connect the predominant cognitive understanding of indexing procedures with the principles of formal knowledge representation. This is intended especially for heterogeneous information environments by supporting retrieval options that make use of the possibilities of mechanical inferences. The resulting model will be summarized by the name ***ontology-based indexing and retrieval***. We refrain from presenting details already at this point. Most parts of the figure are almost self-explanatory for any indexing professional. The remaining components of the model as well as connections to questions of interoperability will be discussed subsequently in more detail.

But before going into details, we want to prepare our discussion by an example to illustrate the aims. Let us assume we want to perform a search for *illustrated books that show singing birds with roving spirit.*[46] What are the necessary prerequisites for representing the facts and knowledge supporting best possible an answer to this search interest by an information retrieval process?

In the usual model for indexing documents, index terms are assigned to documents or they are derived from the document description by machine processing. This connection between index terms and documents forms the basis for estimating the hits for a search query. In the case of intellectual indexing, it is ensured carefully to assign index terms only if they represent aspects of the document content, the *aboutness*. In our example, the term *migration pattern* (used as preferred term for the *roving spirit*) will only be used as an index term if the corresponding concept is treated as part of the document content and is not only seen as characteristic of a special species of singing birds. To support the combination of aspects for indexing and retrieval one would chose a faceted indexing language. Such a *faceted structure* would contain illustrated books as element of a form facet and singing birds as element of an animal facet. There are more animals with a roving spirit so it can be justified by an analogous consideration to see *migration pattern* as element of one facet with behavioral aspects and species of birds as elements of a zoological facet structured by taxonomic principles (Buchanan 1979).

Within the facets the descriptors are ordered in a hierarchical structure. For subsequent considerations on drawing inference, it is helpful to understand hierarchy not only as instance-based subordination but strictly based on the following principles:

- A sub-concept of a hierarchical concept system has all the features of the generic concept plus at least one further additional feature
- Polyhierarchies – i.e., a concept has more than one superordinated concept – are resolved in aspect-oriented facets, in which a term has only one generic term

46 We have chosen this example from the subject field of zoology, especially ornithology mainly by two reasons. First, almost anybody has a more than superficial knowledge about birds, their behavior and aspects considering them. A subject field more people are comparably familiar with, is hard to imagine. Secondly, a very well-structured and excellent written book about the construction of a faceted classification for zoology is part of the professional literature (Buchanan 1979).

For the given example of *singing birds with roving spirit*, this approach can be illustrated by Figure 7.2.

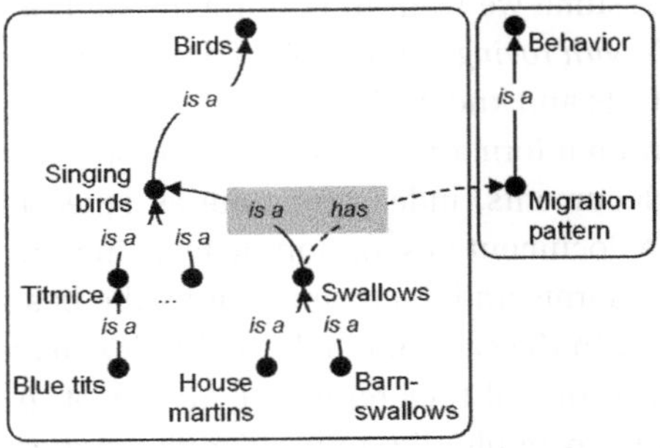

Fig. 7.2: Sketch of a faceted knowledge structure with aspect-dependent relations.

In regard to knowledge representations as structured repositories for representing concepts as entities with associated relationships one can draw first conclusions.

The use of aspect-dependent relationships between individual entities of a knowledge representation allows to express additional properties that may be important as knowledge about the represented entities for indexing and retrieval. In particular, the relations can be used to select the entities that are to be used for a specified search interest, in our example *singing birds with roving spirit*. This selection becomes possible without an entity having to be indexed. Indexing of an entity *migration pattern* might even be wrong in all cases in which it does not represent the document's aboutness. The feature of a kind of singing birds to be a bird with *roving spirit* does not justify to index a document about singing birds by an entity *migration pattern* as far as the aspect *roving spirit* is not treated itself. The aspect-dependent relation "has migration pattern" does not have to be expelled between all entities in the taxonomy facet and the behavioral facet, it is sufficient to connect to each at the highest hierarchical level respectively. Any expansion or drill-down to hierarchically subordinate entities – in our example, *house martins* and *barn swallows* – can be realized through an inference mechanism. We have thus given a first example of how relations between the entities of a knowledge representation can be used for a search process, even without the need to be specifically indexed.

The example discussed follows a general pattern. The desired feature for the search interest applies only in part to an entity's conceptual scope and the feature itself is not treated as contents of a document. Hence, the feature cannot be part of an indexing result. Such a situation cannot be solved by the usual indexing conventions. Any solution requires the presented combination of indexing by entities and structured knowledge in the knowledge representation. Therefore, it is obvious to deal with principles of knowledge representation and its use for indexing and information retrieval, if we want to solve problems of the mentioned type.

7.2 Common Characteristics and Differences between Indexing Languages and Formal Knowledge Representation

If ideas and methods of formal knowledge representation should be transferred for the purposes of indexing and retrieval, commonalities and differences between the two approaches should be analyzed and compared. It has become common to use the term *ontology* as a collective name for the results of formal knowledge representation without implying a sufficient discriminatory power for describing a specific meaning. One can find many different approaches that it can be difficult to understand which field of research the subject belongs to and how it can be useful. The various ontology-related approaches make it difficult to keep track of the different research directions and usage scenarios (Almeida et al. 2013). It is therefore necessary to provide an interpretation of this concept. Consulting *Wikipedia*, one can find the statement:

> In computer science and information science, an ontology formally represents knowledge as a set of concepts within a domain, and the relationships between pairs of concepts. It can be used to model a domain and support reasoning about concepts.[47]

A further widespread characterization reads:

> In theory, an ontology is a formal, explicit specification of a shared conceptualization.[48]

In this sense, an ontology describes a knowledge domain using a standardized terminology and relationships between the concepts defined. Additionally, inference rules can be used to derive knowledge statements not represented explicitly[49].

These statements establish a connection to ideas that are expressed in the model of the so-called *ontology* or *semantic stairway*. We give an illustration of this concept in Figure 7.3. This metaphor is often used to describe an ontology as an advanced form of knowledge representation with additional features compar-

---

47 Cf. http://en.wikipedia.org/wiki/Ontology_%28information_science%29

48 Cf. http://en.wikipedia.org/wiki/Ontology_%28information_science%29, cf. also: Gruber (1993).

49 Cf. http://www.gi.de/service/informatiklexikon/detailansicht/article/ontologien.html

ing it to a well-known indexing language.[50] This viewpoint can be judged as valid to some extent but it can be considered as insufficient, too.

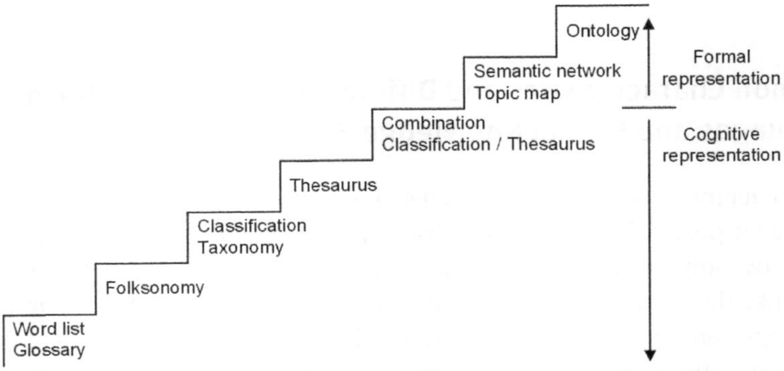

Fig. 7.3: Semantic stairway.

On the one hand, the illustration as a stairway seems to imply that every following stage shows an increase of semantic richness within the respective representation frame compared to the preceding one. This point of view can be supported by the specification of properties that we provide in the form of a table (Tab. 7.1).

Tab.7.1: Formal and content-related properties of the elements of the semantic stairway.

	Alphabetical order	Elimination of ambiguity	Systematic order	Core Semantic relations	Specified semantic relations	Inferences via relations
Word list Glossary	X	O	-	-	-	-
Folksonomy	-	O	X	O	-	-
Classification / Taxonomy	-	X	X	X	-	-
Thesaurus	X	X	O	X	-	-
Combination Classification / Thesaurus	O	X	X	X	-	-
Semantic network Topic Map	O	X	O	X	X	O
Word list Glossary	O	X	O	X	X	X

50 For simplicity of illustration, we followed this interpretation in Figure 7.1.

The symbols used are defined as follows:

X	=	constitutive feature of the concept and usually met
O	=	not a constitutive feature, but can be met
-	=	not a constitutive feature, cannot be met

On the other hand, however, it is suggested that on every higher stage the full sense of the concepts of the stages below can be presupposed. In particular, semantic nets and ontologies are considered as mere enlargements and improvements of indexing languages.

For example, this opinion is expressed in statements as the following:

> Topic Maps und Ontologien eignen sich zur Verbesserung von Suchsystemen, zur Navigation und zur Visualisierung. Ontologien erlauben zudem die Integration heterogener Datenquellen und gewährleisten Zukunftsfähigkeit, da sie die Fähigkeiten von Taxonomien, Thesauri und Topic Maps abdecken.[51]

However, this is not the case immediately. Rather, a change in the understanding of the concepts used is connected with the changing from one stage to the next. Particularly interesting for our considerations is the transition from the step thesaurus to the step ontology. This transition shows a kind of changing the paradigm for conceptual understanding. The cognitive interpretation of concepts is replaced by a formal specification to ensure machine processing. Knowledge about a concept as an entity of an ontology is only determined by a necessarily existing definition by specifying features of the concept. The formal definition including the information about relations to other entities is the basis for the inference processes, but not, however, for cognitive interpretations. This is particular evident in case of attempting to model associative relationships in the sense of indexing languages for the formal representation of knowledge. Any understanding of associative relationships is determined by human interpretation and withdraws itself from any direct formalization. This problem is shown to the full extent when trying to establish content-dependent interoperability between entities of different knowledge representations. We will come back to this problem in Chapter 10.

---

51 Cf.: http://wissensexploration.de/textmining-hintergrundwissen.php; Ullrich et al. (2003). – Translation by the authors: Topic maps and ontologies are suitable for the improvement of retrieval systems, for navigation and visualization. Ontologies also allow the integration of heterogeneous data sources and ensure sustainability, as they cover the power of taxonomies, thesauri and Topic maps.

Reasoning within the structure of a formal knowledge representation to derive true statements from the modeled knowledge has particular significance. A simple example should give an impression of such logical conclusions:

Deciduous trees have leaves
Fruit trees are deciduous trees
Apple trees are fruit trees
Fruit trees bear fruit
Apples are fruit
Golden delicious are apples

As a possible conclusion it can be derived:

Apples of the kind Golden delicious grow on fruit trees that have leaves

Such examples are catchy at first sight, but it is difficult to take them as orientation for building up consistent knowledge structures. Even the specification of characteristics for the production of generic hierarchies in the context of a formal modeling can be a difficult task. Examples of the following kind are given in many presentations about expert systems. The attempt to feature birds as *vertebrates that can fly* is refuted immediately by the example *penguins*. Exception clauses are needed in the formal modeling in order to avoid erroneous inferences (Bibel et al. 1993, 58–59).

The specified statement structures, modeled for example with tools of predicate logic, are successful especially as components of expert systems for dedicated application domains. They allow forms of reasoning based on the stored knowledge structure and additional inference rules that can be used in particular as diagnostic systems. Meanwhile they have been incorporated into the modeling concepts of general knowledge – examples are projects like *YAGO*[52] or *OpenCyC*[53], derived from the original *Cyc* project (Lenat 1995, Lenat & Guha 1990). *Doug Lenat*, the inventor of the *Cyc* project gives following examples:

> One can think of CYC as an expert system with a domain that spans all everyday objects and actions. For example:
> - You have to be awake to eat.
> - You can usually see people's noses, but not their hearts.
> - Given two professions, either one is a specialization of the other or else they are likely to be independent of one another.
> - You cannot remember events that have not happened yet.

52 Cf. http://www.mpi-inf.mpg.de/yago-naga/yago/
53 Cf. http://www.cyc.com/platform/opencyc

- If you cut a lump of peanut butter in half, each half is also a lump of peanut butter; but if you cut a table in half, neither half is a table.[54]

Such attempts have to overcome many difficulties before they can meet the demands of modeling real-world needs statements. For example, it is said that *OpenCyc* is able to infer the statement "the person is wet" from the modeled clauses "Peter swims in the sea and the sea consists largely of water".[55] The workload involved is however considerable and the benefit – at least for the tasks of indexing and retrieval – disputed.

We must draw attention to a further fundamental difference if we want to make analogies to expert systems for our approach. In expert systems or other systems of formal knowledge representation, the entire interpretation of the concept meaning is projected onto the properties of the relationships which are defined between the entities. Entities of an expert system are not interpreted cognitively and used to research document content. If we want to employ techniques of formal knowledge representation for document indexing and retrieval, we need to establish a support of machine processing with cognitive interpretation of the entities and the relationships established between them.

For this purpose, it has to be clarified how the knowledge structure can be made available for a retrieval process (Köhler et al. 2006). Usually, the results of indexing provide linkages between indexing languages and the documents. The documents can be searched by using the assigned index terms but not by the relationships established between the entities, neither in the sense of *a priori* relationships established in the indexing language itself nor in the sense of *a posteriori* relationships between assigned index terms representing a single topic of a document. Thus, questions arise such as:

- Does the distinction between coordinate and syntactical indexing have any significance for the connection of knowledge representation with information retrieval?
- Can benefits for a full-text retrieval or retrieval on the results of automatic indexing be drawn from the semantic structure of a knowledge representation?

We will come back to these questions in course of our discussion.

So far, no immediate proposal for the transfer of specific approaches to knowledge representation and drawing conclusions to the purpose of indexing and retrieval while maintaining a cognitive interpretation of entities has been

54 Cf. Lenat & Guha (1990).

55 Cf. http://de.wikipedia.org/wiki/Cyc

given. It shall be the special object of the present discussion to develop ideas for such a transfer.

Approaches from formal knowledge representation may not be a suitable role model for the tasks of document indexing. But they can provide ideas of how knowledge should be represented in order to take advantage for generating search results in the process of information retrieval.

7.3 Prerequisites for an Ontology-based Indexing

Subsequently, we present a model for structuring semantic content that combines the knowledge stored in a knowledge representation with the possibilities of indexing for retrieval operations. This means that it should be possible to cognitively interpret the entities as elements of a knowledge representation. Particular attention is paid to the possibilities and processes to generate result sets that do not only use the entities as search terms, but perform conclusions based on the stored relations. To ensure best possible terminological consistency, we will use the term *inference* for all these forms of conclusions. We do not want to raise the claim of reasoning in a formalized logical understanding.

Important attributes of the model are illustrated in Figure 7.4. These attributes include some terminological agreements. Figure 7.4 is a continuation of Figure 2.13 and completes the visualizations explaining the respective parts of the indexing languages reference framework. So we do not need to explain all details of the figure but can restrict explanations to the new elements. Also for the sake of terminological simplicity, we decided not to distinguish between the usual types of indexing languages (classifications, thesauri) and their building elements (notations, descriptors) phenomenologically. Instead, we generally speak of *knowledge representations* and *entities*. For these and other terminological agreements we refer to the systematic glossary in the appendix.

We summarize the characteristics of the approach. The basic assumption is the separation into an area *world* (in Fig. 7.4 on the upper left side) with concepts, relationships between them, and statements about phenomena in the world that use the concepts and relationships. For the task of indexing, a task-related section is selected from this reservoir. By known rules, the concepts and relationships are used to define them as entities and relations in the context of a knowledge representation (upper right area of Fig. 7.4).[56]

56 Details on this methodological approach were already presented elsewhere and will not be repeated here (Gödert 2010a, Gödert 2010b).

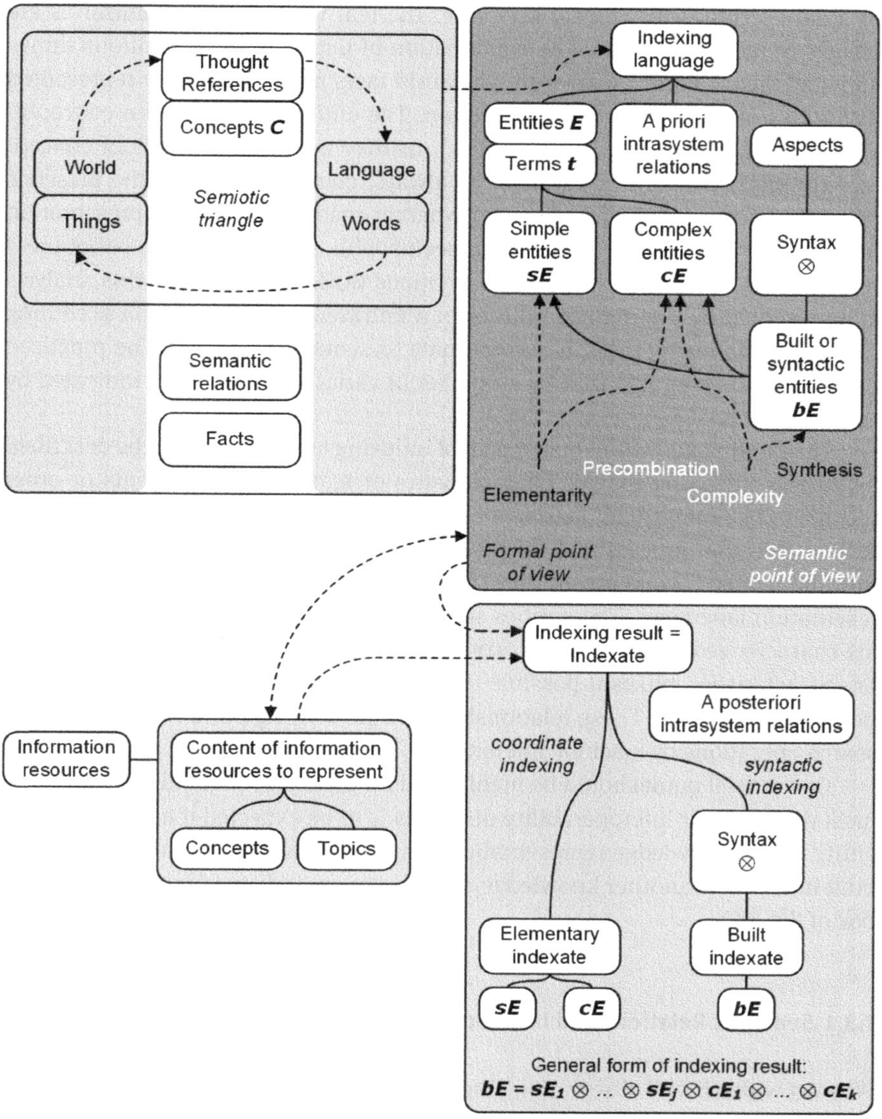

Fig. 7.4: Entity model for structuring semantic content in knowledge representations.

For a complete understanding of all requirements associated with indexing tasks it is important to bear in mind that entities and their relations do not only refer to a world of real objects or phenomena but also to *fictitious* ones. The reference-object for indexing is always a meta-object, e.g., a document, an image, a data set, or a data record. Only in very rare cases the real world objects themselves are objects of indexing efforts. The combination of fictitious facts (fictitious things and statements about them) with real world facts must be likewise represented as entities of a knowledge representation. The entities might be of a conceptually elementary nature (simple entities) or they might show forms of conceptual complexity (complex entities). As always, complexity means the presence of more than one conceptual aspect whether made explicit by representation in terms or symbols or not. Indexing begins with an analysis of the aboutness regardless is binding to the real or a fictitious world. The result of this analysis is represented by pre-defined entities of a knowledge representation according to specified indexing rules, e.g. coordinate or syntactic indexing. The practiced procedures are characterized by a number of variations, which are indicated by the complexity of Figure 7.4.

The familiar viewpoint on a model of indexing and retrieval can be described as follows. Indexing assigns characteristics or features to documents or other records to be represented. Retrieval uses the assigned characteristics or features for the selection process and for determining the numbers of hits. We assume that the indexed terms are entities from indexing languages or knowledge representation languages. The entities stand for objects or concepts, which in turn are characterized by characteristics or features. The common presence of features or characteristics makes it possible to establish different forms of relationships between the entities. These relationships are the starting point for the design of search operations by machine inferences.

One crucial point should be highlighted for our subsequent discussions. The most difficulty for interoperability decisions is to be expected if a pre-combined entity of one knowledge representation has to be conceptually compared with a built indexate of another knowledge representation (indicated in the upper right box of Fig. 7.4).

7.3.1 Semantic Relations and Inferred Document Sets

We start with a trivial observation. The retrieval operation provides access to documents through the connection between entities of indexing languages and documents to generate result sets, as shown by Figure 7.5.

We consider it important that this generation of a result set can be described as an inference process (Glossay F). The conclusion is drawn from the relationships between entities and documents on the basis of previous indexing. Therefore, the use of retrieval tools (e.g. truncation, Boolean operators, proximity operators) for generating result sets can be seen as an inference act (see Fig. 7.6).

For an abridged description we want to refer to this process as *induced inference* (Glossay C3.3). It certainly appears at first unusual to describe the formation of a result set as an inference process. Later on, we will discuss what benefits can be drawn from this point of view.

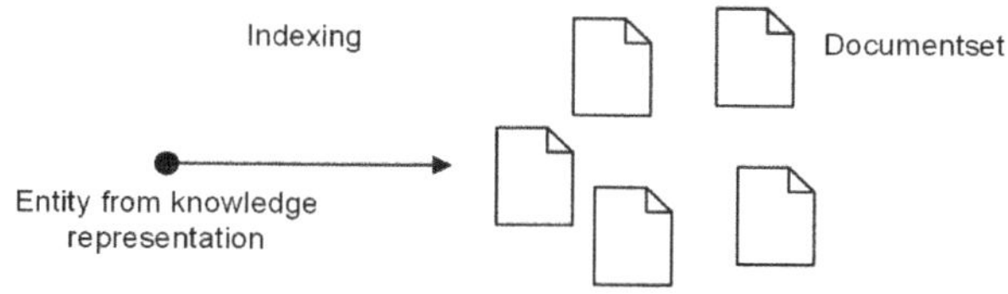

Fig. 7.5: Inferred document set for an indexed entity.

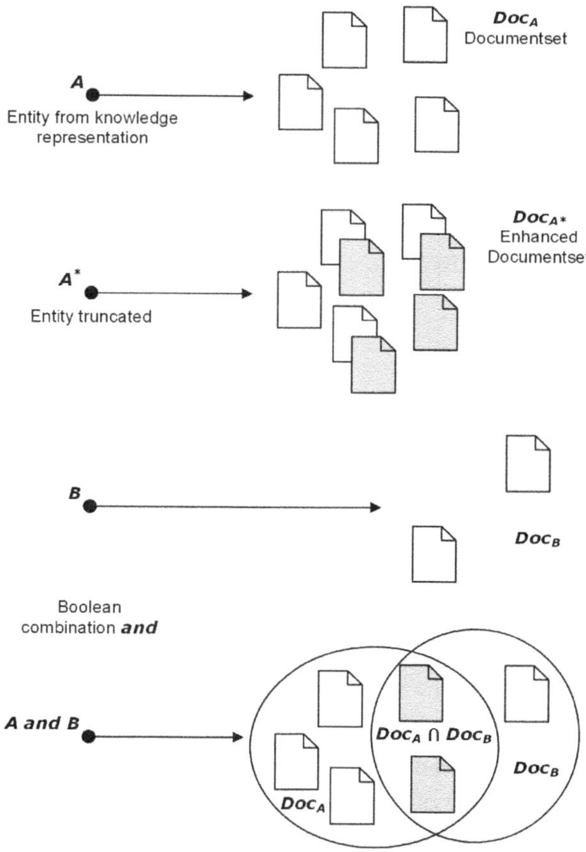

Fig. 7.6: Retrieval tools as inference operations.

By means of this concept, we will now describe the relationships between the entities of a knowledge representation and have a first look at their inference properties. It is particularly obvious to consider first the *hierarchical relationship.*

It is commonly expected that the hierarchical relation supports inference procedures, but in fact we need to clarify how hierarchy must be defined formally, so that inference properties can be ensured.

As a further type of relations between entities we can mention all forms of *associative relationships* between concepts. Usually they are expressed without differentiation as *Related Term* or in the form of *See also references* in familiar indexing languages.

It is not equally obvious whether the different types of associative relationships can be used for inference processes. We need to look at this question again later. If one combines the drawing of inferences along the hierarchy paths of a knowledge representation with the idea of generating result sets illustrated by Figure 7.6, the idea of generating document sets represented in Figure 7.7 comes up. Starting from an upper hierarchy level, all subordinate entities are considered for the formation of a result set. This form of search is well-known as *Search-down, Drill-down, Expand* or *Explode.* Nowadays, it is a standard part of a thesaurus-based information retrieval. We want to distinguish the inference along the edges of hierarchically related entities from the process to derive the documents associated with a node, the *induced inference.*

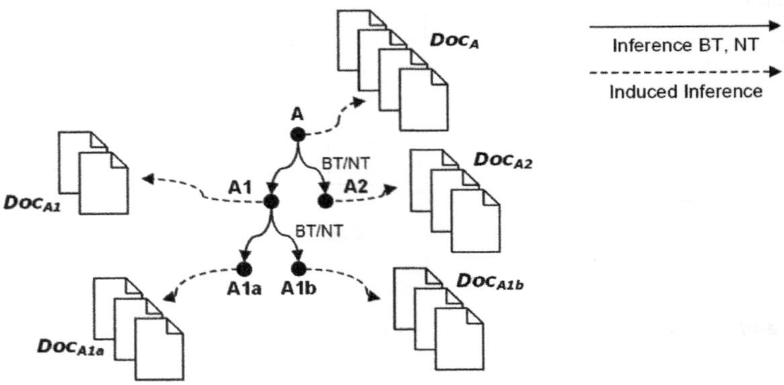

Fig. 7.7: Induced inference.

By using the concept of induced inference we can introduce the concept of a transitive closure C_{NT} *(A).* At this point our considerations are motivated by the processes for generating document sets on the basis of knowledge structures like thesauri or structured vocabularies. In Section 8 we will return to these issues considering them from a more formal point of view.

The *transitive closure C* (Glossary C3.4) of a relation is the set of all documents that can be generated formally by inference processes along the edges of the relation specified and by including the induced inferences for the assigned nodes. Figure 7.8 shows an example of the transitive closure of a hierarchical relation for the entity *A*:

$$C_{NT}(A) = \{Doc_A, Doc_{A1}, Doc_{A2}, Doc_{A1a}, Doc_{A1b}\}$$

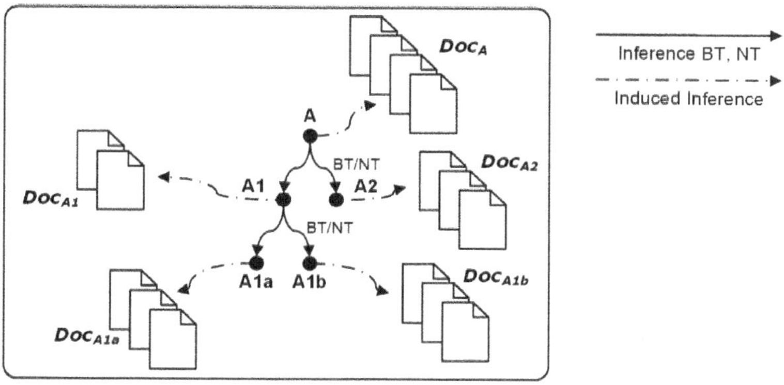

Fig. 7.8: Transitive closure of a hierarchical relation.

Establishing a conceptually valid hierarchy, one can regard the transitive closure $C_{NT}(A)$ as a useful extension of the set Doc_A. At this point of our discussion, it is not necessary to presuppose a formal description of transitivity, as it has already been given in Section 2.1.2. Later on, we will make use of such a formal definition.

On the other hand, it has to be recognized that the induced transitivity is tied to the indexing process and its underlying indexing principles. Therefore, the induced transitivity is influenced by the structure of the indexing language and likewise by the indexing process. Consequently, transitivity as a formal property of a relation in the indexing language is not sufficient to guarantee thematically consistent enhancements for the resulting document sets. Two points-of-view require special attention for the connection between the entities of an indexing language and the – possibly multiple – topics of a document established by the indexing process:

1. The possibility of transitive extension of a search query within a retrieval environment. If this extension is available, the indexing process must be carried out according to other rules than if this option was not available.
2. The connection to forms of syntactic indexing of complex and multiple topics of a document with explicit designation of *a posteriori* relations in the indexing results.

In the following, we will provide some examples to illustrate our considerations.

Example 1

We are looking for an *illustrated book showing European songbirds.*

An answer requires the ability to formulate a query by combining some parts in the form:

Entity for songbirds (S) plus narrower terms in Boolean combination with other entities describing geographical (G) and formal (F) aspects. In more abstract formulation, the $ sign stands for an appropriate conceptual, not a mere formal term truncation. The + sign stands for the Boolean operator *AND*:

$$S\$ + G\$ + F\$$$

Example 2a

We are looking for a document about the *behavior of finch parents while feeding their fledglings.*

An answer requires the ability to formulate a query by combining some parts in the form:

Entities (*S1*, ... , *S4*) in Boolean combination with other entities (possibly including truncation) and a directed relation (->) to other entities. In more abstract formulation:

$$S1 + S2 + S3 \rightarrow S4$$

Example 2b

We are looking for a document about the *behavior of finch fledglings while feeded by their parents.*

As before, an answer requires the ability to formulate a query by combining some parts in the form: Entities in Boolean combination with other entities (possibly including truncation) and an oppositely directed relation (<-) to other entities. In more abstract formulation:

$$S1 + S2 + S3 \leftarrow S4$$

In addition to the hierarchical relationship, the associative relationship between entities is well-known from indexing languages. An extension of the notion of a *transitive closure* to the associative relationship $C_{RT}(A)$ is visualized by Figure 7.9. The process of forming a transitive closure is formally transferred to the edges of an associative relation without considering any content-related plausibility.

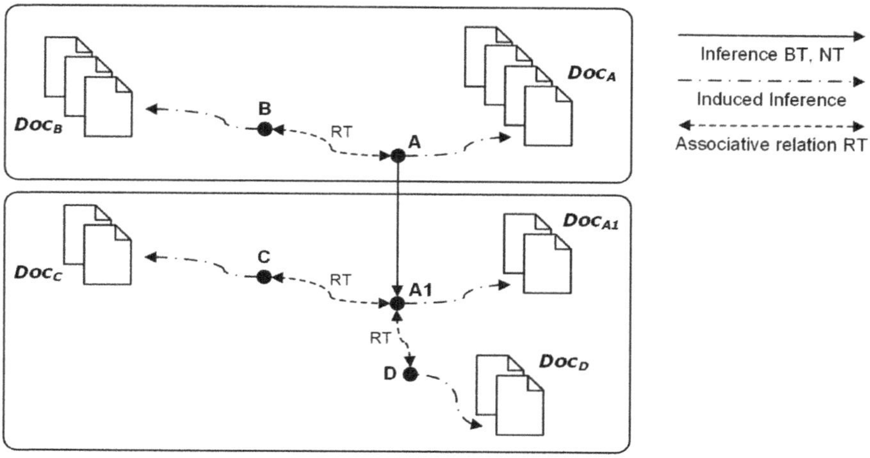

Fig. 7.9: Formally built transitive closure for associative relationships without content-oriented justification.

Formally, the transitive closures C_{RT} *(A)* and C_{RT} *(A1)* can be characterized by the following sets of documents:

$$C_{RT}(A) = \{Doc_A, Doc_B,\}$$
$$C_{RT}(A1) = \{Doc_{A1}, Doc_C, Doc_D\}$$

It remains to be clarified whether C_{RT} *(A)* and C_{RT} *(A1)* can be taken as content meaningful enlargements of Doc_A. Numerous examples generating documents sets using related descriptors from existing thesauri show that generally it cannot be expected that the process of forming a transitive closure over all paths emanating from an entity will lead to a meaningful extension of the document set. We will later come back to the question of how inferences can be made possible through this type of relationship.

If the formation of a transitive closure for a relation is carried out over several stages – for the hierarchy relation this is already indicated in Figure 7.8 with 2 stages – the content-dependent success of the process depends mainly on the property of transitivity of the relation involved. Transitivity as a formal property of a relation ~ means that from $a \sim b$ and $b \sim c$ follows that $a \sim c$ is valid. The ideally constructed hierarchical relation with generic broader and narrower concepts satisfies the condition of transitivity. It can be said that the narrower concept at the eighth level has all the properties of the initial concept and – at least eight – additional features.

Existing thesauri and classification systems show that this ideal description is not always valid. Broader and narrower terms or classes are not always connected by relations that permit transitive inferences. An example of this well-known fact has been given in Section 2.1.2, presenting a short excerpt from the *DDC*. Normally, no attribute is defined for justifying the validity of the established relation. This can be attributed to the fact that conceptual order created in these systems traditionally has been done only for cognitive interpretation and not for machine processing. It was not seen as a disadvantage that the knowledge structure was not described by a formal logic structure. The basic ideas of faceted structures have not been fully exploited yet.

This aspect becomes even clearer in case of considering the formal qualities of associative relations. This type of relationship is traditionally oriented at the cognitive interpretation of similarity or kinship by humans. Basically the naming gives strong hints for this observation. In general it must be assumed that a transitive continuation of closure formation cannot be made if content-meaningful results are expected.

By summarizing the formal properties of the relations considered so far, we obtain:

- The *hierarchical relation* with its entity pairs *broader Term / narrower Term* as nodes of the corresponding edges is obviously not symmetric. It may be transitive by choosing suitable criteria for establishing the hierarchy. Accordingly, the process of closure formation can be carried out formally over the entire transitive hierarchy path.
- The *associative relation* with *related Terms* as entity pairs is symmetric by definition, but not necessarily transitive. The closure formation cannot be justified in general. Any transitive continuation along the paths of the relation is not guaranteed.

From this perspective, questions can be derived which will be illustrated by Figures 7.10 and 7.11.

Question 1: Can conditions be specified giving a content-oriented justification for valid transitive continuation of closure formation for the associative relation (cf. Fig. 7.10)?

Question 2: Can conditions be specified giving a content-oriented justification for valid transitive continuation of closure formation for combinations of hierarchical and associative relations (cf. Fig. 7.11)?

Let us consider first the formal result of a closure formation for the combination of different types of relations, as shown in Figure 7.10.

The formally built closure consists of the document set:

$$C_{NT,RT}(A) = \{Doc_A, Doc_B, Doc_{A1}, Doc_{A2}, Doc_{A1a}, Doc_{A1b}, Doc_C, Doc_D\}$$
$$= \{Doc_A, Doc_{A1}, Doc_{A2}, Doc_{A1a}, Doc_{A1b}\} \cup \{Doc_B, Doc_C, Doc_D,\}$$

No statement is made so far whether $C_{NT,RT}(A)$ can be seen as a meaningful extension of Doc_A by considering content-oriented arguments.

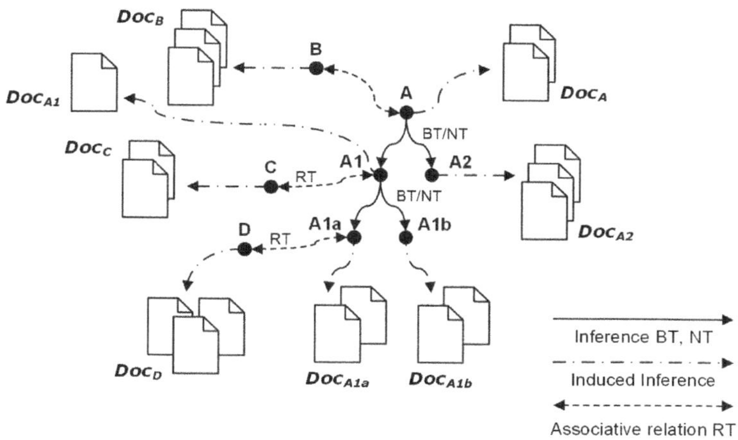

Fig. 7.10: Formally built transitive closure for the combination of different types of relations without content-oriented justification.

A further enlargement of the process of closure formation to more than one associative relation is shown in Figure 7.11.

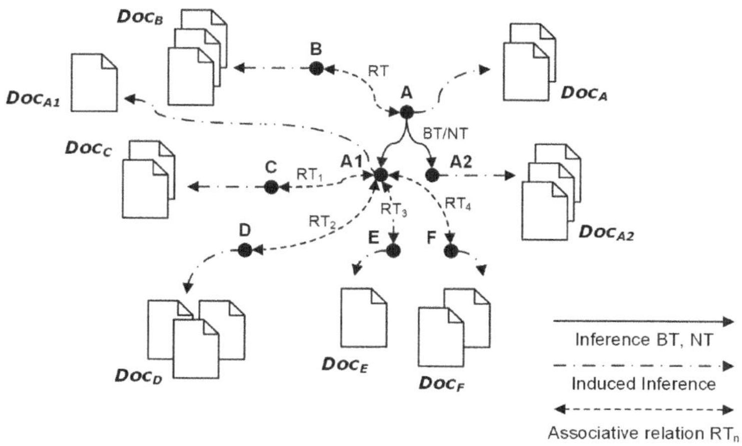

Fig. 7.11: Formally built transitive closure for the combination of different types of associative relations without content-oriented justification.

The entire closure formally consists of the following document sets:

$$C_{RT1}(A1) = \{Doc_{A1}, Doc_C\}$$
$$C_{RT2}(A1) = \{Doc_{A1}, Doc_D\}$$
$$C_{RT3}(A1) = \{Doc_{A1}, Doc_E\}$$
$$C_{RT4}(A1) = \{Doc_{A1}, Doc_F\}$$

$$C_{RT}(A1) = C_{RT1}(A1) \cup C_{RT2}(A1) \cup C_{RT3}(A1) \cup C_{RT4}(A1) = \{Doc_{A1}, Doc_C, Doc_D, Doc_E, Doc_F\}$$

$$C_{NT,RT1}(A) = \{Doc_A, Doc_B, Doc_{A1}, Doc_{A2}, Doc_{A1a}, Doc_{A1b}, Doc_C\} = \{Doc_A, Doc_B, Doc_{A1}, Doc_{A2}, Doc_{A1a}, Doc_{A1b}\} \cup \{Doc_C\}$$

$$C_{NT,RT}(A) = \{Doc_A, Doc_B, Doc_{A1}, Doc_{A2}, Doc_{A1a}, Doc_{A1b}, Doc_C, Doc_D, Doc_E, Doc_F\} = \{Doc_A, Doc_B, Doc_{A1}, Doc_{A2}, Doc_{A1a}, Doc_{A1b}\} \cup \{Doc_C, Doc_D, Doc_E, Doc_F\}$$

In the case of further associative relationships existing between the entities, a form of structure results resembling the visualization of Figure 7.12.

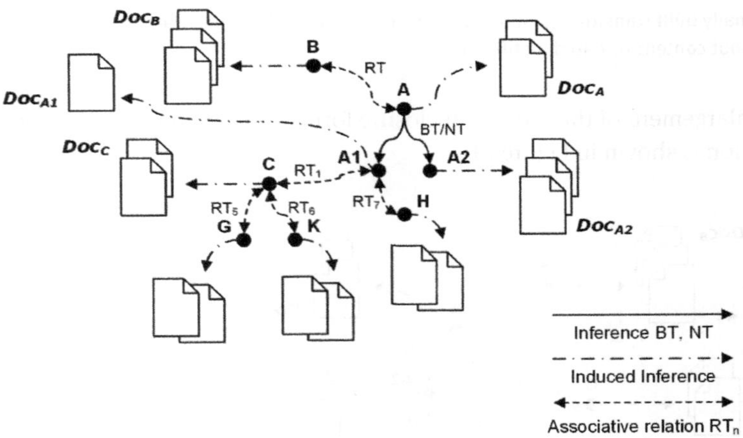

Fig. 7.12: General situation of associative relationships between entities.

Without statements about the content-related justifications, the following closures can formally be specified for different associative relations:

$$C_{RT1}(A1) = \{Doc_{A1}, Doc_C\}$$
$$C_{RT6}(A1) = \{Doc_{A1}, Doc_H\}$$
$$C_{RT}(A1) = \{Doc_{A1}, Doc_C, Doc_G, Doc_H, Doc_K\}$$

We will come to this back later on and consider questions of drawing inferences for associative relations when we have introduced the concept of typed relations. Before doing so, we need to put together some details about faceted concept systems.

7.3.2 Facets and Inferences

We will consider the case that the content of a document consists of *topics* with a form of conceptual complexity that cannot be represented only by elementary indexates. Instead, the complexity should be indexed by forms of built indexates, that is, combinations of several entities from a knowledge representation, instead. It makes sense to do this within the framework of faceted structures. The basic form of such a structure is outlined in Figure 7.13. For ease of presentation, we choose concepts of the subject areas *animals* and *places on earth*.

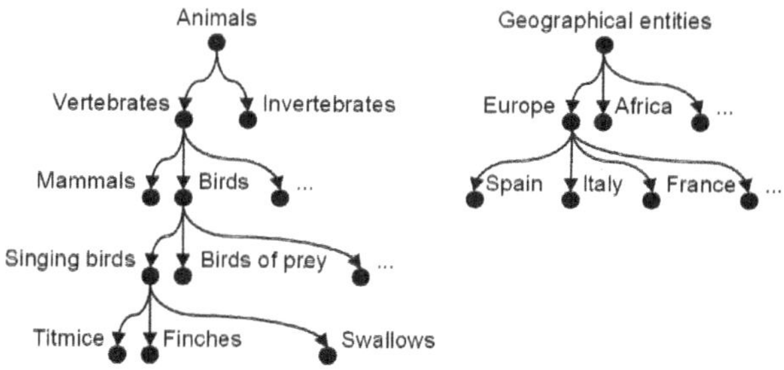

Fig. 7.13: Knowledge structure with general facets.

A structure that is suitable for a search on *illustrated books of European songbirds* is shown in Figure 7.14.

The construction of *built indexates* for complex topics and the need for establishing a proper hierarchy with transitive inheritance of properties leads to the need of a subfaceted structure of certain subject areas (Buchanan 1979). Many concepts are to be characterized by more than one aspect. If all entities of a knowledge representation are ordered within the frame of only one facet, the corresponding entities can be assigned by different paths to more than one superordinate node. Commonly, this situation is characterized as a polyhierarchy. We already discussed the need of avoiding those polyhierarchical structures, when proper hierarchies shall be established. In fact, a concept like *migratory bird* must not be seen as a single or better elementary concept that can be ordered within a taxonomic facet. Instead, it must be seen as a composed concept with conceptual parts. One part is *bird* (refering to a taxonomic aspect) and a second *roving spirit* (refering to a behavioral facet). Such aspect views characteristically contain aspects exhibiting relations to many entities of another facet, in our example the entities of the behavior facet are related to many entities (representing species) of the animal facet. Figure 7.15 indicates a corresponding structuring with one taxonomic and three additional subfacets.

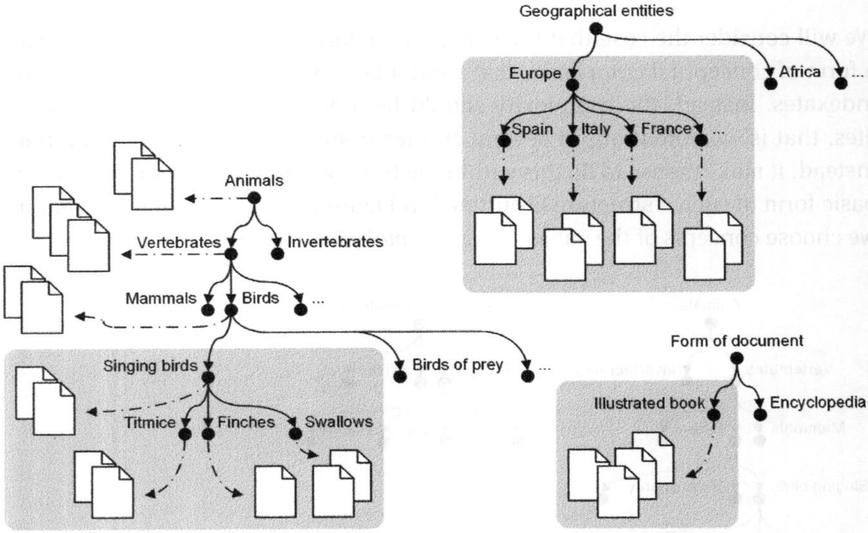

Fig. 7.14: Knowledge structure with general facets and associated documents.

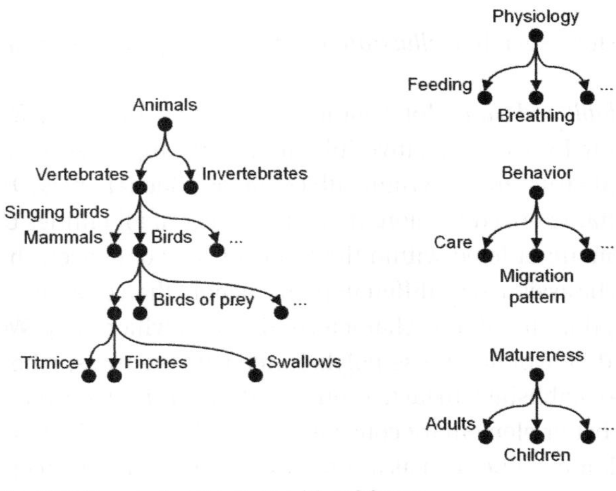

Fig. 7.15: Knowledge structure with subfacets.

Applying the structure from Figure 7.15 to the topic *behavior of singing birds while feeding their fledglings*, the inferred documents can be determined as shown in Figure 7.16.

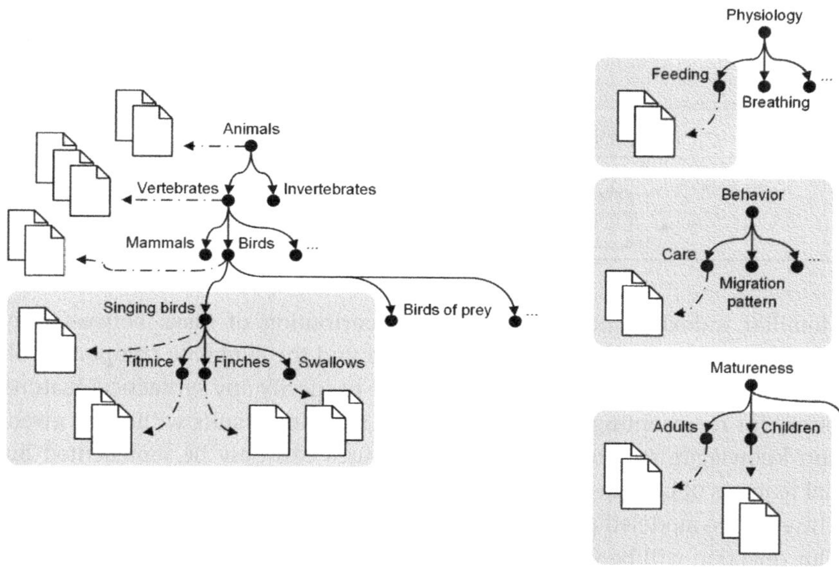

Fig. 7.16: Knowledge structure with subfacets and inferred documents.

In this example, a directed relation occurs – entity *A* feeds entity *B*. We can represent this by assigning roles to the entities, one role might be an agent of the action, the other an object, to which the action is directed. Alternatively, one can distinguish two relations, one for each direction. Figure 7.17 expresses this fact in principle, yet without showing concrete suggestions for modeling this situation.

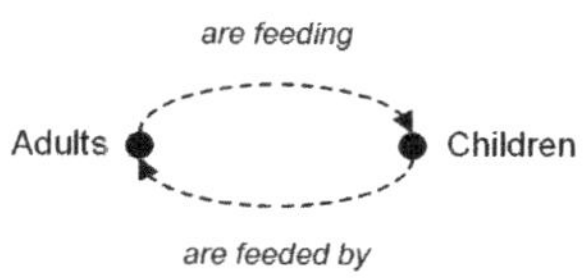

Fig. 7.17: Directed relationships.

Within the context of familiar indexing models, such a distinction is treated by applying methods of *syntactical indexing*. Generating a set of documents cannot be limited in considering the specified entites, but must also include their syntactical roles, in our example this would be the direction of the action relation. Common tools for expressing the syntactical role are *role operators* or other syntax connectors. Generating the result set requires not only the entities to be indexed but also an analysis and choice of the relations involved. Figure 7.18 indicates the situation in principle.

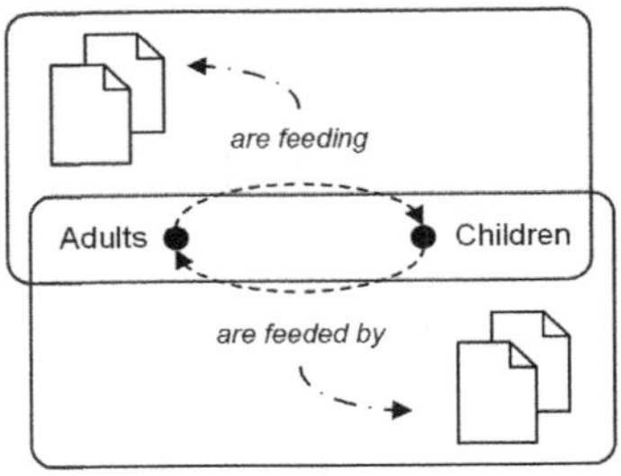

Fig. 7.18: Directed relationships treated within the context of syntactical indexing.

The familiar indexing models comprise a distribution of tasks between the semantic component of the indexing language and the syntactic component of the indexing result. Therefore, it is not possible to specify any syntactical feature necessary for representing a complex topic by indexing results within the given *a priori* knowlegde structure. Syntactical features can only be represented by special features of built indexates. However, a relation within a given knowledge structure can be modeled as bi-directional.

Our question will be whether this situation can be changed by using typed relations instead of symmetric associative relations. Typed relations between entities provide the opportunity to specify their directions and thereby the roles of the entities. The question remains whether such kinds of relations can achieve a particular contribution for syntactical context of indexing results even if they are no built indexates. Let us have a look at Figure 7.19.

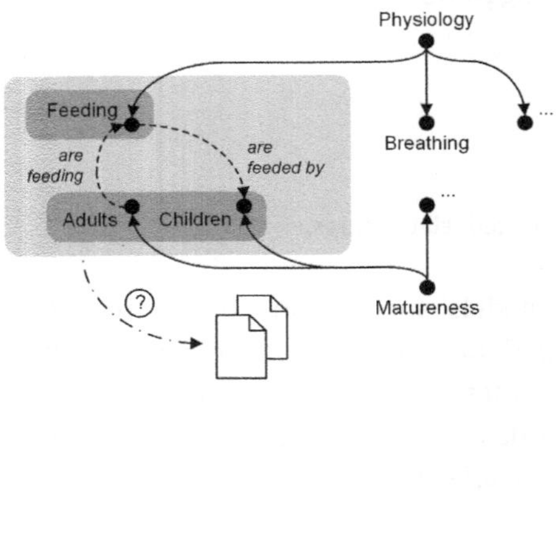

Fig. 7.19: Directed relationships and inferred document sets (1).

It is immediately obvious that the structure represented in Figure 7.19 is not sufficient to distinguish the direction of any relationship contained in the context of the document. Only the entities have discriminating characteristics for selecting corresponding documents. As already indicated, in such cases it is necessary to represent complex document topics by built indexates using syntactical devices. A specific document reference can be expressed only using materials in the indexing process and represented as indexing result. Only if the direction of the relationship is part of the indexing result, a corresponding differentiated formation of document sets becomes possible. We give a respective illustration in Figure 7.20.

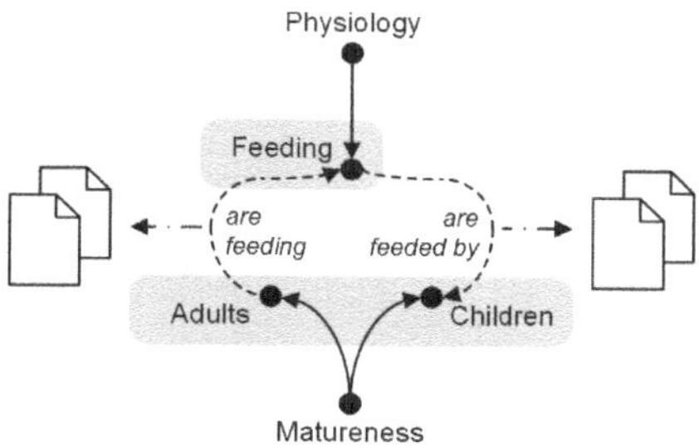

Fig. 7.20: Directed relationships and inferred document sets (2).

To demonstrate it once more regarding our example, the two indexing results

Singing birds – Adults – Feeding (are feeding) – Children
Singing birds – Adults – Feeding (are feeded by) – Children

have identical entities as parts, but are characterized by different directions of a relation. Different sets of documents should be inferred by selecting the appropriate relation for a specified search query.

We can draw the conclusion that syntactically formed indexing results keep on being necessary when looking for most precise search results, including directed relations or other syntactical discrimination features.

It is also advisable to retain the familiar distinction between *a priori* and *a posteriori*. By *a priori* we denote the knowledge modeled by entities and relations of a knowledge representation. It is available as an element for the formation of indexing results, no matter whether by principles of coordinate or syntactical indexing. *A posteriori* stands for a knowledge context generated by document topics. Whether this form of knowledge refers to real world or fictional phenomena, is insignificant. It has to be represented in the form of built indexates. Adequate retrieval features have to be defined for ensuring the generation of appropriate document sets.

On the other hand, our example of *songbirds with roving spirit* has shown that with the use of the modeled knowledge it will be possible to formulate restrictions on search queries without these restrictions being part of the indexing result itself. Key to this approach was a suitable structure of the knowledge representation with typed relations between the entities. By an inference process over the edges of the appropriate relation one could select all entities being necessary for the search process. We now want to examine the conditions for this procedure a little more closely.

Figure 7.21 shows an example of a knowledge structure in which each entity has been connected to each of its relational attribute nodes, regardless of any hierarchical subordination.

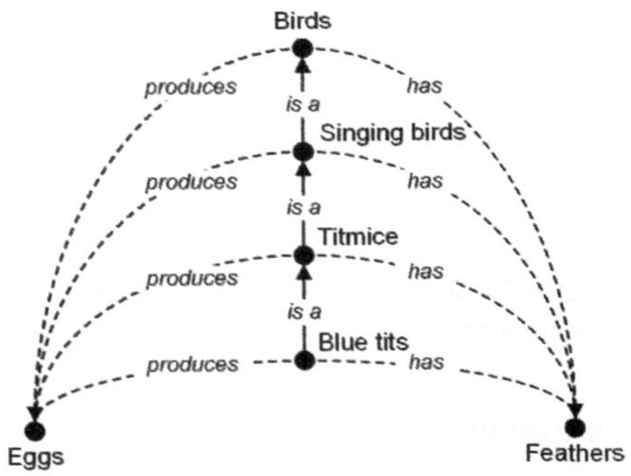

Fig. 7.21: Knowledge structure with redundant property declarations.

An essential characteristic of any formal knowledge representation is to not express every property of an entity explicitly. Whenever it is possible, properties are derived by inference from the properties of other entities. If we look at Figure 7.21, we see that the properties *have feathers* and *lay eggs* were modeled redundantly for the entities *singing birds*, *titmice* and *blue tits*. They can be derived for all entities from the characteristics of the entity *birds*. Such a possibility to derive properties by inference mechanisms simplifies the network structure of entities and relations significantly. Figure 7.22 gives a visualization for the general setting.

The following rules for the derivation can be specified:

A_n *is a (generic)* A_{n-1},
is a (generic) is a relation with the property to be transitive,
A_1 *has* property C.

We can infer the conclusion

=> A_n *has* property C.

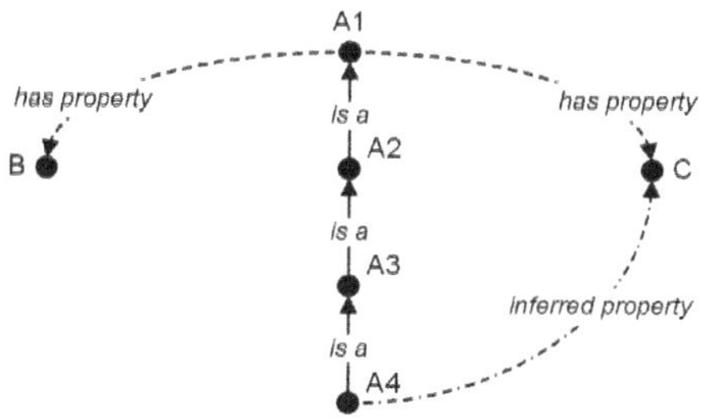

Fig. 7.22: Knowledge structure with inferred properties.

Let us consider next the task of integrating an entity *migratory birds* to our knowledge structure shown in Figure 7.13. Figure 7.23 shows an initial proposal.

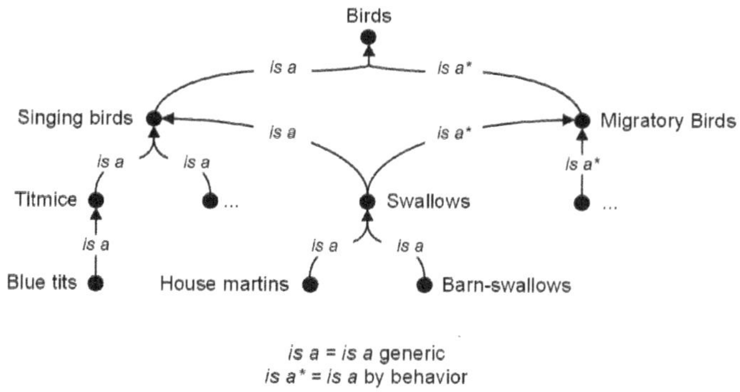

Fig. 7.23: Knowledge structure with aspect-oriented polyhierarchy.

It is characteristic for this proposal that the entity *swallows* is subordinate to two other entities, *singing birds* and *migratory birds*. We have already recommended to avoid such an aspect-oriented polyhierarchical structure. At first glance, such an approach seems advantageous, so we will summarize the disadvantages. If the suggested approach was generalized to all modeled aspects, this would lead to a confusing, frequently pre-combined conceptual structure. This can be seen immediately from our example. Migratory birds are only one example of animals with a roving spirit, there are a lot of bird species and other animals to be ordered at different taxonomic domains with this behavioral feature. All of them need to be connected to at least one node for their taxonomic place and another node for characterizing them as a member of a family with roving spirit.

It is therefore advisable to split up the aspects of polyhierarchical relations into a faceted order with only one superordination for any node in the frame of a facet. This is shown in Figure 7.24.

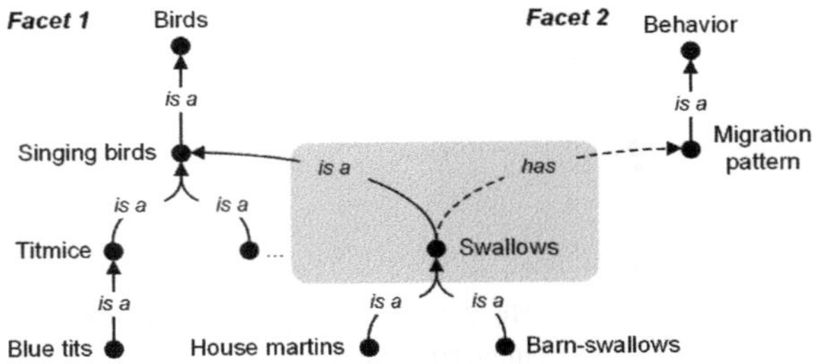

Fig. 7.24: Aspect-oriented knowledge structure with faceting and typed relations.

The aspect-oriented polyhierarchy is dissolved in a faceted structure. The aspects are available via typed relations to other areas. One relation is modeled as intra-faceted connection, the other as inter-faceted. Each relation can subsequently be used as a selection feature for search interests. It is important to note that the entities can be selectively equipped with exactly the typed relations which have the necessary property. In our example this means that not all songbirds have a roving spirit. Therefore, no relation

Singing birds – has – migration pattern

should be established. This relation can only be associated with the entity of the highest possible level in the hierarchical structure, in our example:

Swallows – has – migration pattern

For the entities of hierarchically lower levels, in our example, *house martins, barn swallows*, these properties can be derived through inference.

The reasoning presented here bears resemblance to the exception clauses which are required for some items in the context of formal knowledge representations to model real world matters correctly. We have already indicated this by giving the example of birds – *vertebrates that can fly* and the counterexample *penguins*. Our approach helps avoiding the necessity of exception clauses. Instead, one has to choose the suitable hierarchical place for connecting the entities by a relation that allows to derive the correct inferences.

We want to come back to the already mentioned benefit of inferences for the structuring of the facets. We have discussed this aspect by considering Figures 7.21 and 7.22. Now let us have a look at Figure 7.25. In this illustration, the entities are separated into facets, but no options for intra-faceted inferences have been scheduled.

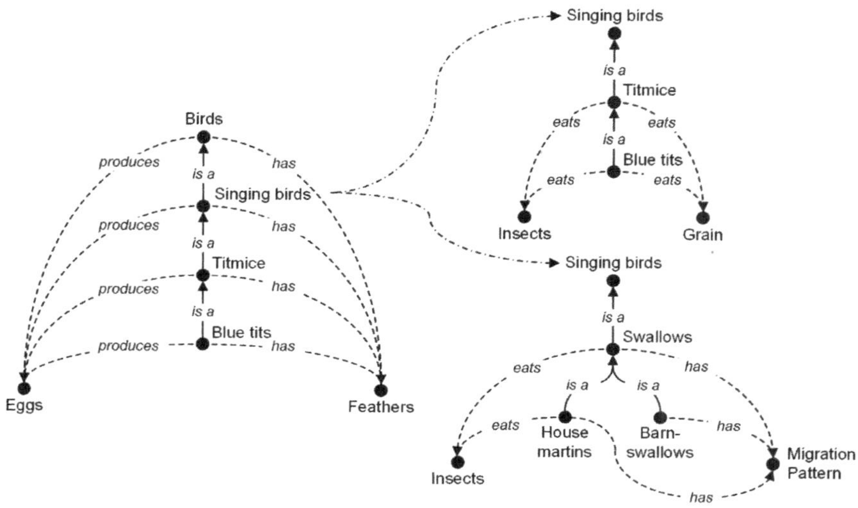

Fig. 7.25: Aspect-oriented knowledge structure with facets and typed relations without inferences.

Taking both the faceting and the possibilities for making inferences via the hierarchical structure into account, we obtain the representation of Figure 7.26 with the same assurance as in Figure 7.25.

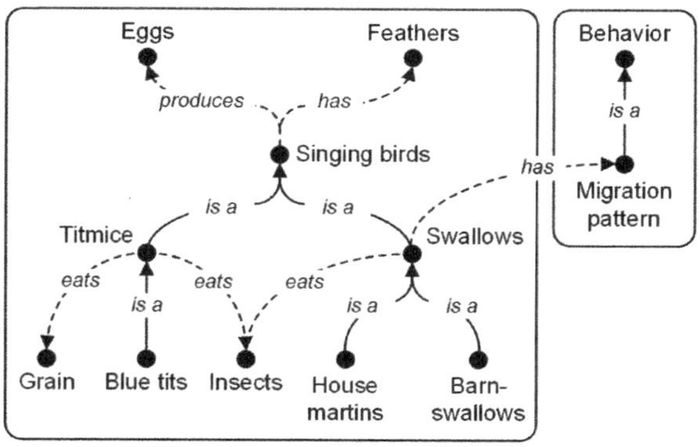

Fig. 7.26: Aspect-oriented knowledge structure with facets, typed relations and inferences.

The following statements can be derived – in free verbal formulation – from the structures represented in each of the figures:

Blue tits have feathers, lay eggs and eat both seeds and insects
Martins are migratory birds with feathers that eat insects
Barn swallows are migratory birds with feathers that eat insects

In general, the possibility of making inferences is a considerable gain in structural simplicity of the knowledge representation with constant expression-strength.

We have already stressed the importance to choose the right location in the hierarchical structure for connecting the entities of one facet to an attribute expressing node of another facet for supporting conclusions along the edges. We want to support this with another example and consider for this purpose Figure 7.27.

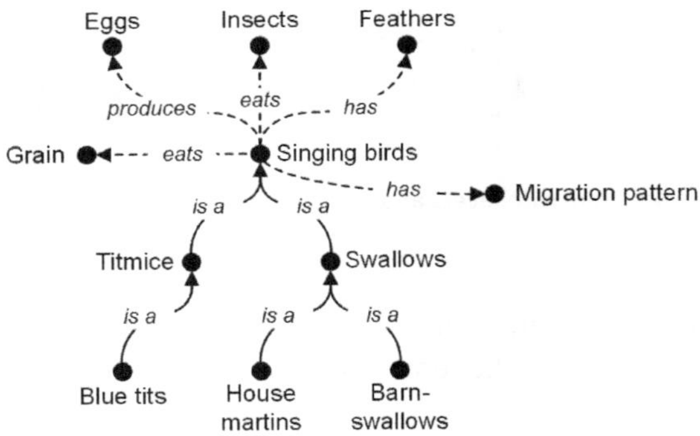

Fig. 7.27: Knowledge structure with incorrect connection of typed relations.

In this illustration, the connection between *singing birds* and *grain* and likewise the connection between *singing birds* and *migration pattern* is wrong. By using these connections it would be possible to infer for example:

Blue tits are migratory birds with feathers that put eggs
House martins have feathers and eat insects as well as grain

Both inferences are not supported by real world phenomena. Blue tits do not have a roving spirit and house martins do not eat grain. Therefore, the connections should not be modeled in our knowledge representation. For modeling the entities' context in a correct fashion, we have to constitute connections at a deeper hierarchical level.

With this last consideration we have paved the way to connect our previously developed concept of induced inferences for generating document sets with the concept of conceptual filtering along the edges of the relationships contained in the knowledge structure. We will discuss this using the following examples. At first, we are looking for:

Documents about all types of songbirds with feathers that lay eggs

Figure 7.28 shows a suitable corresponding knowledge structure where we have omitted to show connection to any documents. To indicate the difference to Figure 7.26 the lines upward from *singing birds* are drawn in a different shade of gray.

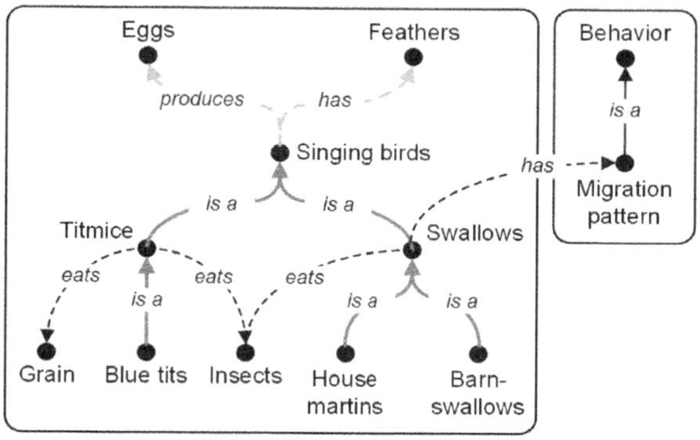

Fig. 7.28: Inferring document sets by inferences about the relations of the knowledge structure.

We want to specify the inference chain and the type of the derivation principle used in each step.

Step 1: Transitive inferences about the stored hierarchical relations

Blue tits are titmice are *singing birds*
House martins are *swallows* are *singing birds*
Barn swallows are *swallows* are *singing birds*

As result, we get the set of entities {*singing birds, titmice, blue tits, swallows, house martins, barn swallows*} that is used for inferring the corresponding document set.

Step 2: Inferences about direct relations between entities

Singing birds have *feathers*
Singing birds lay *eggs*

No restriction is required, the hits remain at the result of step 1.

The next example is supposed to include a question that combines different aspects. Processing an answer requires the combination of entities ordered in different facets. We are looking for:

Documents about all kinds of songbirds with roving spirit that eat insects

Figure 7.29 gives an illustration of a suitable knowledge structure. To indicate the differences to Figures 7.26 and 7.28 two lines starting at *swallows* are drawn in a dashed form.

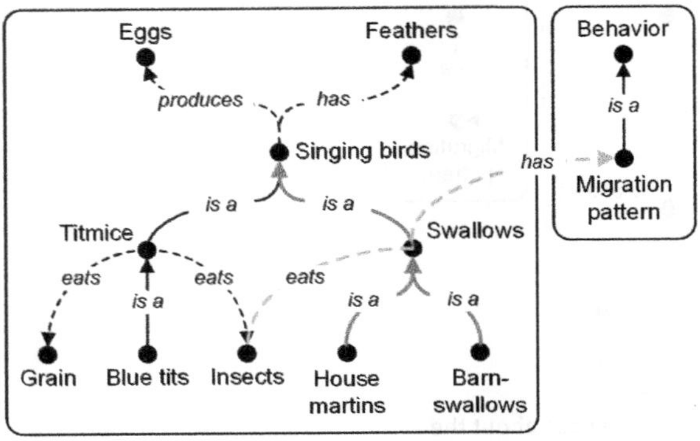

Fig. 7.29: Inferring document sets by inferences about the relations of the knowledge structure with more than one facet.

Once more, we specify the inference chain for generating the document set:

Step 1: Transitive inferences about the stored hierarchical relations

House martins are *swallows* are *singing birds*
Barn swallows are *swallows* are *singing birds*

Step 2: Restrictions on stored relations between the facets

In general, not all species of songbirds do have a roving spirit. It is therefore not appropriate to use the entity *singing birds* for generating the document set.

Step 3: Inferences about direct relations between entities

Swallows have *migration pattern*

Step 4: Combination of the abovementioned types of inferences

> *House martins* are *swallows* have *migration pattern*
> *Barn swallows* are *swallows* have *migration pattern*

The set of entities used for generating a document set comprises {*swallows, house martins, barn swallows*}.

Step 5: Inferences about direct relations between entities

> *Swallows* eat *insects*

No further restriction is necessary, the hits remain at the result of step 4.

With this derivation, we have discussed once more the example already addressed at the beginning of this section. But now the discussion was filled with more details so that the method of using relations between facets and drawing conclusions about the edges of the knowledge structure should have been explained more transparently.

As a special feature of the presented example one could think of modeling the inter-faceted relations depending on certain conditions, so that these conditions would have to be met for entities being considered in a search result. Thereby, an important difference to the pure Boolean combination of search terms would have been described. These restrictions would affect the formation of numbers of hits even if the corresponding entities are not themselves part of the document-associated indexing results.

By discussing our examples, we learned about several examples of typed relations which were employed to avoid polyhierarchical or aspect-oriented connections. The application of typed relations is a characteristic feature of knowledge representations with benefits such as selection and specification tools for the processing of search interests which goes beyond the benefits of non-specific associative relationships in the familiar thesaurus structure. Non-specific associative relations are more likely to support navigation and information functions, but not automatic search processes.

We will have to consider the typed relations as tools for building knowledge structures in more detail in the following sections. In particular, the question will arise whether the different types can be brought into a beneficial order or even a beneficial system. A lot of different types arise in different fields of application. Each relation can be of special benefit for its respective application domain. From the viewpoint of general knowledge structures it is important whether there are patterns that allow a clustering of typed relations for general application. Once more we give some examples of modeling for different subject areas.

8 Typification of Semantic Relations

Based on appropriate examples, this chapter discusses the potential of specified, logically valid semantic data being interpretable both for cognitive and machine-supported information retrieval processes. Special attention is devoted to the crucial task of enriching and restructuring existing indexing languages viz. refining the relational inventory by means of abstraction and generalization.

If one wants to connect entities of a knowledge representation by typed relations, an inventory of relations is needed. Ideally, this inventory should be characterized by universality and domain-indepent applicability. Such properties would ensure its usability as broad and independent as possible from a specific domain knowledge. Proving its sufficiency in granularity has to be thought of as a separate step.

Each application domain usually has a specific spectrum of relationships that can be established between its concepts. An illustrative example of the domain-specific range of possible relations are properties and roles that can be taken by individuals and that can lead to relationships to other entities of a knowledge representation (Meyer 2013). Without claim of completeness the following list can be indication for that:

born in
married to
divorced from
child of
parent of
learned profession
studied discipline
employed at
professional activity
influenced by
has an impact on
works / collaborates with
is / was the owner of the function / position
is / was a member of
is the author of
was awarded the prize
excellence award
exercise of artistic activity
playing the instrument
discipline from sports practice
is the winner at occasion
is a victim of

By specification of the context (personal data and personal career, leisure and hobbies, family, professional field, political field, artistic or scientific producing) the list can be differentiated and expanded in many ways. In a general use case it is presumably not probable to apply an inventory designed for a special application domain. It can be expected that the total amount of relations would exceed any vision of a manageable measure. So a clear demand for decreasing the number of relations appears.

8.1 Inventories of Typed relations

We have to combine our search for an inventory of relations with modelling tasks supporting the indexing and retrieval of documents in a way that the aboutness of a document is represented and made available best possible for retrieval purposes. For a more precise determination we have already noted in Chapter 1 that this task does not include the representation of document-independent general knowledge. Instead, we see the goal of our approach in the structuring of knowledge, which is necessary for representing the aboutness of a document, its relevant topics and content statements. To represent a document aboutness, it is necessary to remember the distinction between two fundamentally different forms of relationships between concepts:

1. Relationships between concepts that are independent of any reference to documents. We can interpret them as parts of world knowledge and have already introduced them as *a priori* relationships. We model them as different types of relations between entities within the knowledge representation.
2. Relationships between concepts that are given only by the aboutness of the document. By this aspect, they exist independently from any relation to world knowledge. They can also be given by reference to fictional knowledge. Examples are offered by all forms of fictional literature, e.g., attempts to refute the theory of relativity or giving proofs for squaring the circle. We have introduced such document-dependent relationships between concepts as *a posteriori* relationships. They are modeled in the context of syntactical indexing by dedicated syntax devices.

It will be considered in more detail whether there are interactions between *a priori* and *a posteriori* relationships that should be taken into account for the modeling of knowledge representations. At first, we limit our discussion to the type of *a priori* relations.

It would be desirable if the plurality of domain-specific inventories could be overcome by modeling a domain-independent core inventory, providing domain-independent validity as well as the potential of differentation within a particular domain. For reasons of consistency, the inventory has to be considered as obligatory in the context of a single application. For the development of such an inventory, different procedures can be considered.

Frequently, the task of creating an inventory of typed relations is limited to a particular object field or domain of knowledge, as shown prototypically by the creation of expert systems. In this application environment the benefit of typed relations is undisputed and they are used successfully. So far, it seems obvious to make use of the methods for our purposes, too. The use would be based on developing specific properties of objects and inventories of highly specific significance for the respective field of application. Such an approach can be described as a bottom-up approach. It must be seen as serious drawback that domain-specific requirements are hardly transferable to the needs of another application field.

Additionally, the entire consideration of a content-related meaning is projected onto the properties of the relations between the entities. Entities of an expert system are not cognitively interpreted and are not used to search for document content. We cannot follow this way completely, as we want to develop relational inventories for document indexing and retrieval and provide them for effective use. We can only choose a path in which the cognitive interpretation of entities is not excluded and which also supports the automated interpretation of relations' paths.

Therefore, we have to tread another path to develop relational inventories – correspondingly characterizable as a top-down approach. We take the methods for deriving faceted structures by analyzing general aspects or categories as a prototypical procedure. This procedure implies a cognitive interpretation. It is not necessary to abandon domain-specific aspects, as they must be specified only within the general framework.

Treading such an approach is not new, however, we must take note of a constraint. Different approaches have been undertaken to create such an inventory of typed relations. However, so far there is still no agreement about a generally accepted inventory. A series of studies was devoted to purely analytic objectives and provides valuable results with suggestions for further research (Perreault 1994, Bean 2001, Green & Bean 2006, ISO 25964-1 2011). Other studies put forward proposals of typed inventories with orientation to practical work. We want to present the objectives and proposals of two studies in more detail.

The first of these studies intends to provide a differentiated inventory of semantic relations. The objective was to support enhancements of content-related access points in information retrieval processes (Michel 1997).

In the study, various sources were evaluated and an inventory of semantic relations was compiled on this basis. Additionally, subject headings of the *Library of Congress Subject Headings (LCSH)* list were analyzed for their *see-also references*. Similar relationships were identified using the previously created inventory. The analysis showed a wide variety of semantic relationships. The final inventory comprises 165 relations which we reproduce subsequently (Tab. 8.1) in its condensed form (Michel 1997):

Tab. 8.1: Inventory of relationships from the *ALCTS Final Report*.

Equivalence
lexical variants
singular/plural (e.g. Tooth/Teeth)
hyphens (e.g. On-line/Online)
inversions (e.g. Architecture, Domestic/Domestic architecture)
acronyms (e.g. Information retrieval/IR)
spelling variants (e.g. Color/Colour)
technical/popular (e.g. Currency/Money)
language variations
regional (e.g. Soda/Pop)
national (e.g. Elevators/Lifts)
absolute synonyms (e.g. Dwellings/Residences)
Hierarchical
part/whole (e.g. Basements/Buildings)
genus/species (e.g. Dwellings/Igloos)
class/instance (e.g. Mountains/Mount Rushmore)
Associative
field of study/object of study (e.g. Botany/Plants)
field of study/practitioner (e.g. Medicine/Physicians)
agent/process (e.g. Brain/Perception)
causal relationships (e.g. Plant diseases/Crop losses)
position in time and space (e.g. Meteors/Meteorites)
frequently interchangeable/near synonyms (e.g. Dwellings/Houses)

The second study is based on case studies. It analyzes associative relations found in various thesauri and discusses possible extensions and differentiations under consideration of suspected effects on information retrieval (Tudhope et al. 2001). Explicitly the question is asked: “Is an extended core set of associative relationships possible?”[57]

Based on the example of the *Getty Art and Architecture Thesaurus (AAT)*[58], rules for defining associative relationships are reported, compared with other studies and expanded so that a typification of associative relationships can be carried out in the form of a fixed inventory. The proposal results in a domain-in-

57 Cf. Tudhope et al. (2001), 9.

58 Cf. http://www.getty.edu/research/tools/vocabularies/aat/

dependent inventory of eleven types of associative relations[59]. We show the list in Table 8.2:

Tab. 8.2: Inventory of associative relationships from a study by *D. Tudhope.*

RT (Plain) for undifferentiated associative relationships
Meaning connection
Meaning overlap
Distinguished from
Antonym
Conjuncted terms
Causal (taken broadly – many inter-facet relationships might fit here)
Dependency/requires
Uses
Product
Patient
and possibly Spatial and Temporal connections
Partitive (taken broadly)
Constituent parts
Aggregate groups
Property/attribute

The study emphasizes the use of typed associative relations in thesauri as a tool for information retrieval. The advantage of an extension of the general thesaurus relation *Related Term* by a limited set of specified associative relations is seen in strict separation of the semantics of the relation and of the semantics of the associated descriptors. Negative effects on information retrieval processes, especially the uncontrolled increase of query terms and a loss of precision, are not expected.

We can summarize that the development of an inventory of typed relations as a substitute for the non-specific associative thesaurus relation remains a desideratum. Even the accessibility of the aims cannot be taken for granted methodologically. Especially when creating interoperable information environments this issue will remain of relevance. As mentioned earlier, this situation resembles the search for a standard citation order of a universal faceted classification[60].

59 Cf. Tudhope et al. (2001), 10.
60 Cf. http://www.miskatonic.org/library/facet-web-howto.html

Because of the fundamental importance for our purposes we want draw attention on this historical topic.

As a historical starting point, we will mention the development of the *Colon Classification* by *S.R. Ranganathan* (Ranganathan 1987). This system contains five top level facets shown in Table 8.3. Each of them can be specified in the context of particular subject fields. For the sake of brevity, the specifications are indicated here only by additions in brackets.

Tab. 8.3: Facet structure of the *Colon Classification.*

Personality (the something in question, e.g. a person or event in a classification of history, or an animal in a classification of zoology)
Matter (what something is made of)
Energy (how something changes, is processed, evolves)
Space (where something is)
Time (when it happens)

We are now coming back to the question of a *citation order* being determined by the given sequence of facets. This citation order is used to form a coextensive expression for syntactic representation of complex document contents. The facets are supplemented by so-called *phase relations* as a means of syntactic refinement of the indexing result, we show them in tabular form in Table 8.4. Principles of application and examples can be found in the *Colon Classification*[61]. For our purposes, it is not decisive which codes were chosen for expressing a specific meaning. It is only of interest what types are available.

Tab. 8.4: Phase relations of the *Colon Classification.*

Intra-Array	Intra-Facet	Inter-Subject	Kind of Phase relation
t	j	a	General
u	k	b	Bias
v	m	c	Comparison
w	n	d	Difference
x	p	e	Tool
y	r	g	Influencing
t	j	a	General

61 Cf. Ranganathan et al. (1987), 106.

The method of the *Colon Classification* has found various historical continuations. We will mention here only the *Bliss Classification. 2nd edition (BC)* (BC2 1992) as the methodological successor of the research work of the *Classification Research Group (CRG)* (Austin 1969a, Austin 1969b, Austin 1976a, Classification Research Group 1969, Coates 1969, Foskett 1970). We reproduce in Table 8.5 the facet structure in sequence of the citation order[62]:

Tab. 8.5: Facet structure of the *Bliss Classification, 2nd ed.*

thing/entity
kind
part
property
material
process
operation
patient
product
by-product
agent
space
time

Vanda Broughton, one of the editors of *BC2*, states:

> These fundamental thirteen categories have been found to be sufficient for the analysis of vocabulary in almost all areas of knowledge. It is however quite likely that other general categories exist; it is certainly the case that there are some domain specific categories, such as those of form and genre in the field of literature.[63]

Combining the various approaches discussed so far, we have developed an inventory of typed relations that is shown in Table 8.6.

62 Cf. Broughton (2001), 79.
63 Cf. Broughton (2001), 79–80.

Tab. 8.6: Proposal for an inventory of typed relations.

Equivalence
Synonym
Hierarchy
Abstraction, generic context
Whole / Part
Earlier / Later, chronological context
Association
Raw material / product
Causality (cause – effect)
Person as actor / action
Institution as actor / action
Person as actor / product
Institution as actor / product
Action/ product

This inventory will be used in subsequent discussions as a proposal for a replacement of the unspecified associative relationship. We will come back to this inventory in Section 9.3 when we deal with the question of how the properties of relations can be used for machine processing.

In addition to the development of relation types according to a content-oriented perspective one can think of other forms, especially forms based on a numerical differentiation. Such a form of typing was already introduced as so-called *degrees of determinacy*. We will come back to this approach in more detail in Section 8.3.3 and once more in Section 10.2.2. For our present discussion it is sufficient to mention the benefit of such an approach for the design of ranking algorithms. Of course, the combination of both approaches to define inventories of typed relations is conceivable.

8.2 Typed Relations and their Benefit for Indexing and Retrieval

In the following, we have to combine the preceding considerations with our core task. This task consists of producing indexing results for document contents and making them available for optimized retrieval purposes. In general, document contents must be seen as a sum of one or more complex topics. In any case, an indexing result for a complex topic requires more than one individual entity of a knowledge representation. Most often, even a pure sequence of entities is not sufficient for a coextensive representation of a complex topic. Finding appropriate methods for a coextensive representation of each of these topics by indexing results is the challenging task to be faced.

In general, an indexing result is formed from the individual entities of an indexing language. We summarize the following cases that have already been distinguished by former discussions:

1. The document content is represented by an elementary indexate or by a built indexate, an additive sequence of individual entities. This corresponds to the well-known indexing principle of coordinate indexing. Boolean retrieval can be seen as its counterpart in retrieving. It is comparatively easy to argue for a benefit of a filter function by using typed relations. We will still illustrate this by examples. However, a limitation arises in the case that complex issues should be represented coextensively by the indexing result.
2. The document content as a whole or sub-topics as parts should be represented coextensively as indexing results. In this case, syntactic indexing methods must be applied. These methods express the aspect orientation of concepts by facets with *a priori* relations between the entities. Entities from different facets can be synthesized by means of a citation order with respect to the document-oriented *a posteriori* relations. Role operators or other syntactical devices are used for specifying directed relationships[64]. In this case, too, is the result a syntactic phrase whose sequential ordering is determined by a citation order. The citation order will allow to arrange the individual aspects by a predetermined importance of the aspects. It allows to form a phrase for each sub-topic.

The *citation order* of the *BC2* can serve as an example of how to build syntactical phrases as indexing results[65]:

> *thing/entity > kind > part > property > material > process > operation > patient > product > by-product > agent > space > time*

A further prominent historical example with an elaborated citation order is given by the verbal indexing system *PRECIS* (*PREserved Context Index System*). (Austin 1987, Austin 1984). The system was built on the work of the *Classification Research Group*. It has worked out in a special manner a separation between the *a priori* structuring of entities in a standardized vocabulary and a syntax for rep-

64 Cf. Figures 7.17 and 7.18 in Section in 7.3.1.

65 Cf. Bliss Bibliographic Classification – BC2 (1992); http://www.blissclassification.org.uk

resenting conceptual *a posteriori* correlations in an indexing result. The aim of a coextensive representation of topics or even sub-topics was supported by a highly differentiated citation order. Entities could as well be characterized by *a priori* defined aspects as by roles corresponding to *a posteriori* relationships originating from the document context (Austin 1976b).

We show the *scheme of role operators* in Table 8.7. We will not discuss further details of their interpretation and application, but refer to the literature (Austin 1984). Our only interest is focused on the analogy of the approaches.

Tab. 8.7: Scheme of *PRECIS* operators.

Primary operators		
Environment of core concepts	0	Location
	1	Key system; Thing when action is not present; Thing towards which an action is directed, e.g. object of transitive action, agent of intransitive action
	2	Action; Effect of action
	3	Performer of transitive action; "Intake"
	4	Viewpoint-as-form
	5	Selected instance, *e.g. study region, sample population*
	6	Form of document; Target user
Secondary operators		
Coordinate concepts	f	"Bound" coordinate concept
	g	Standard coordinate concept
Dependent elements	p	Part; Property
	q	Member of quasi-generic group
	r	Assembly
Special classes of action	s	Role definer; Directional property
	t	Author-attributed association
Primary codes		
Theme interlinks	$x	1st concept in coordinate theme
	$y	2nd / subsequent concept in theme
	$z	Common concept
	$a	Common noun
	$c	Proper noun (class-of-one)
	$d	Place name

Secondary codes		
Preceding differences (*3 characters*)	*1st and 2nd characters:*	
	$0	Non-lead, space generating
	$1	Non-lead, close-up
	$2	Lead, space generating
	$3	Lead, close-up
	3rd character = number in the range 1 – 9 indicating level of difference	
Date as a difference	$d	
Connectives	$v	Downward reading connective
	$w	Upward reading connective

A special feature of the system was its orientation towards natural language. A coextensive indexing is particularly successful under these circumstances because the indexing language – the terminological definitions of the entities and their *a priori* relationships – and indexing processes can be adjusted together.

In our days, the semantic component of the method no longer seems particularly progressive. At the time *PRECIS* was invented, there was no influence on terminological structuring by methods of formal knowledge representation. The specification of relationships between entities in the *PRECIS* thesaurus was limited to the well-known relations from other thesauri. Only synonymy, hierarchy and non-specific associations were modeled as *a priori* relations.

Syntactic indexing results, such as *PRECIS* strings, synthesized *DDC* numbers or other forms of built indexates, are characterized by a high content-related expressiveness and a high degree of differentiation capacity. Since they represent the topics of documents searched for, they would be desired objects for executing thematic searches. On the other hand, due to their formal shape they do not have any favorable qualities for the integration in navigation and search operations. Even their alphabetical arrangement led to complicated sorting methods, which sooner or later have contributed to the abolition of the entire procedure. Such a process can best be seen by redesigning the methods used for producing the alphabetical subject indexes of the *British National Bibliography*. At first, *PRECIS* was introduced to increase the expressiveness of the entries compared with its predecessor method *chain indexing*. Afterwards, *PRECIS* was substituted by *COMPASS*, a method inferior by regarding its contents' expressiveness. A further decrease of expressive power came with the launch of the *Library of Congress Subject Headings (LCSH)*. The last substitution even includes the reinvention of an indexing method with pre-combined indexates (Austin 2009).

From evaluating this process by methodological aspects, we can draw the following conclusion. There was a dependency of the indexing language on documents with a high requirement for a dynamic update. This prevented the creation of desirable navigation environments, tapping the full potential of the syntactical phrases. Thus, the navigation was limited to the level of the indexing language. An added value of the syntactic indexing result could be obtained at most by looking into an alphabetical index or by recognizing its display in the document description. Both aspects could not convince in the long run compared to combinations of coordinate indexing with Boolean retrieval.

Full benefit from the results of syntactic indexing can only be drawn when they are offered within a specially designed retrieval environment. The necessary development expense, however, was usually spared. Retrieval environments were mostly restricted to a Boolean access to the individual components of a built indexate so that no benefit could be drawn from the syntactic value. Often it was not even possible to access sub-topics expressed by different indexates.

In all these examples, an allocation of tasks between the structured entities within the knowledge representation and the expressions of complex document content through a syntactic phrase is visible. The retrieval function is usually supplemented by a navigation facility for the entities and their conceptual relationships. The possibilities for exploring conceptual relationships are thereby limited. Hierarchical relationships can be tapped only in one aspect. Aspect-crossing correlations are represented only by the non-specific associative relation. Correlations between document-specific topics, which are formed as indexates by synthesizing entities from different areas according to *a posteriori* aspects, cannot be made the subject of navigation, although they are the ultimate goal of search interests. The distribution of tasks between an entitiy structure and syntactic indexing results thus did not lead to convincing solutions.

It was found, moreover, that even in the context of elaborated indexing principles as used for *PRECIS*, it is difficult to make a clean demarcation between the *a priori* and the *a posteriori* view. One could find the sequence *thing* > *kind* or *thing* > *part* as syntactic expression in the citation order as well as constituting relations for relationships of the entities within the respective knowledge representation. Another example is the process/product relationship, which on the one hand can be seen as a typed relation. On the other hand it is part of the citation order of *BC2* for building syntactic indexates on the basis of *a posteriori* relations.

We are therefore interested especially in possible connections between typed relations and the syntactical features of a citation order. Nowadays, it is a widespread opinion that a citation order only plays a role in the organization of the indexed material and not likewise for the purposes of information retrieval[66]. We do not share this position. Rather, we consider the citation order as an important tool for coextensive and consistent formulation of complex document issues. We want to suggest ways in which such a connection could be used for the preparation of indexing results made so far by using syntactic indexing. High significance is accorded to the opportunities to draw inferences about the paths of typed relations that are modeled between the entities of the knowledge representation.

The following factors show why the development of such an indexing and retrieval model is beneficial:

- Knowledge representations that organize their entities in facets with hierarchical relations, intra-faceted typed relations and synonyms as types of *a priori* relationships may be used for conceptual navigation or exploration (hierarchy and intra-faceted specified association), and for query expansion (synonyms) within a conceptual aspect.
- Document-specific topics are represented by means of *a posteriori* relations between entities by built indexates in the form of syntactical phrases. These phrases offer no well-suited preconditions for a content-oriented navigation task. Especially, no restriction on the *a posteriori* relations is usually possible. It is therefore understandable that makeshift knowledge structures were constructed using pre-combined elements. Examples are given by the *DDC* or the *LCSH*. However, the result of such an approach is the replacement of a transitive hierarchy through a case-based subordination. The latter violates the principle of inheritance, whenever the criteria for structuring the pre-combined topics are changed. An automated inference about the relation paths of subordinate entities is no longer possible.
- The use of an inventory of typed relations and the connection of entities placed in different facets by typed relations offers the possibility to use the properties of entities as selection criteria for a search process without the entities needing to be indexed. Thus, it is possible to make document-specific topics searchable without the prerequisite of syntactical indexing methods.

However, we must note that the complexity of the task is increased by considering not only closed information enviroments with principally known inventory of resources but by considering additionally heterogeneous and distributed information environments. So far, we do not have reliable test-scenarios for certifying any efforts made. The benefit of an inventory of typed relations for retrieval processes can be presented only by methodological considerations and exemplary

66 Cf. Denton, issue 2.3.5.

search environments. Results of any retrieval test within the framework of concrete information systems are not known.

Before presenting further details of our indexing and retrieval model in Section 10.3 we want to present some examples. They should give an idea of how typed relations can be used in order to achieve a ballast-neutral refinement of the results, both for navigating the content of the knowledge representation and for the search and finding process.

8.3 Examples of the Benefit of Typed Relations for the Retrieval Process

Subsequently, we introduce different examples, each using its own relation inventory for the respective object and fields of application. At the present time, these examples can only underline the potential of the methodology, a real application is not combined with that yet. But it should become clear how to implement such applications. They may also provide a contribution to the production of interoperable knowledge representations for heterogeneous information systems using the semantic data representation approaches by *RDF* triples.

8.3.1 Example 1: Aspect-oriented Specification of the Generic Hierarchy Relation

We start with an example whose inventory of relation types was derived by differentiation of the hierarchy relationship according to different aspects. The example is taken from the domain *theatre* and the entities were assembled by selecting the subheadings for the subject heading *Theater* in a general controlled vocabulary, the German *Schlagwortnormdatei (SWD)* (Boteram 2008). Figure 8.1 shows a visualization of the concepts with all associated subconcepts modeled as a knowledge structure.

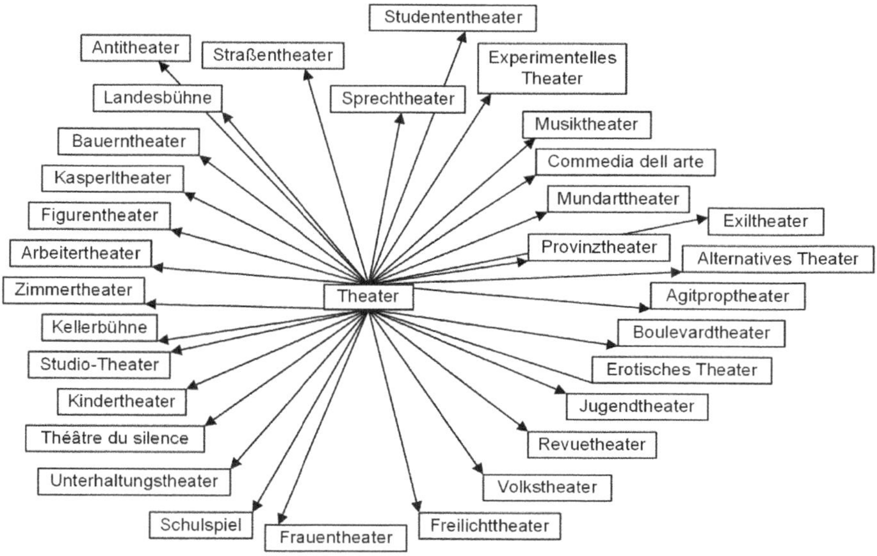

Fig. 8.1: The *SWD* heading *Theater* with all typed subheadings.

A more precise analysis of each relationship shows that the subconcept formation was performed according to various criteria. This becomes apparent by the following examples[67]:

> *theater > street theater, room theater, open-air theater, ...*
> *theater > speaking theater, music theater, dialect theater, ...*
> *theater > youth theater, children's theater, folk theater, ...*

As we mentioned repeatedly, this approach has some drawbacks. The transitive closure of the heading *Theater* would include all specific terms, no selection of individual aspects is allowed. Such a differentiation is possible only by providing a more detailed specification of the subconcepts. Therefore, a stage model was used, which is reproduced in Table 8.8.

67 The translations of the subject headings are given by the autors, they are not part of the *SWD* and should only be seen as hints for understanding the German headings.

Tab. 8.8: Graded model of the generic relation *BTG* for the sample *Theater*.

1st level	2nd level	3rd level	4th level
BT			
	BTG		
		BTG : Participant	
			BTG : Participant: Actor
			BTG : Participant: Audience
		BTG : Function	
		BTG : Form	
			BTG : Form : Genre
			BTG : Form : Tradition
		BTG : Local reference	
		BTG : Method	
		BTG : Institution	

From this differentiation, an inventory of relations can be derived whose relationships connect the concepts in accordance with a specified characterization. As an example, the Figure 8.2 shows only the connections for *generic relation according to genre (NTG)*, the Figure 8.3 shows the connections for *generic relation according to actor (NTA)*.

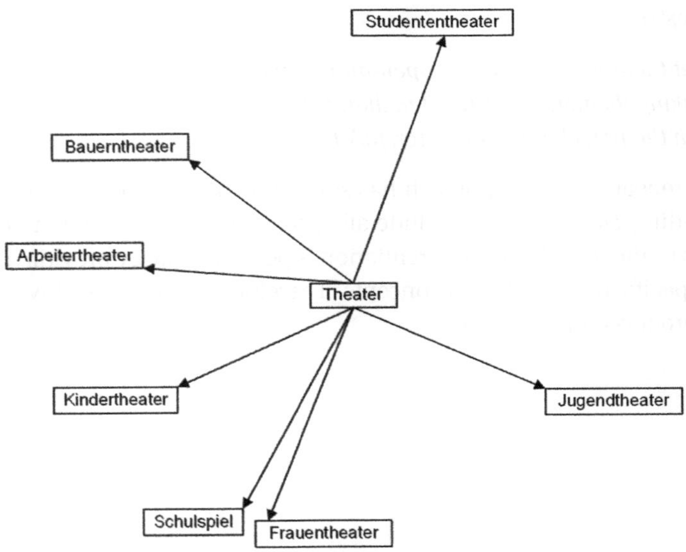

Fig. 8.2: Reduced network containing only the *generic relation according to genre (NTG)* for *Theater*.

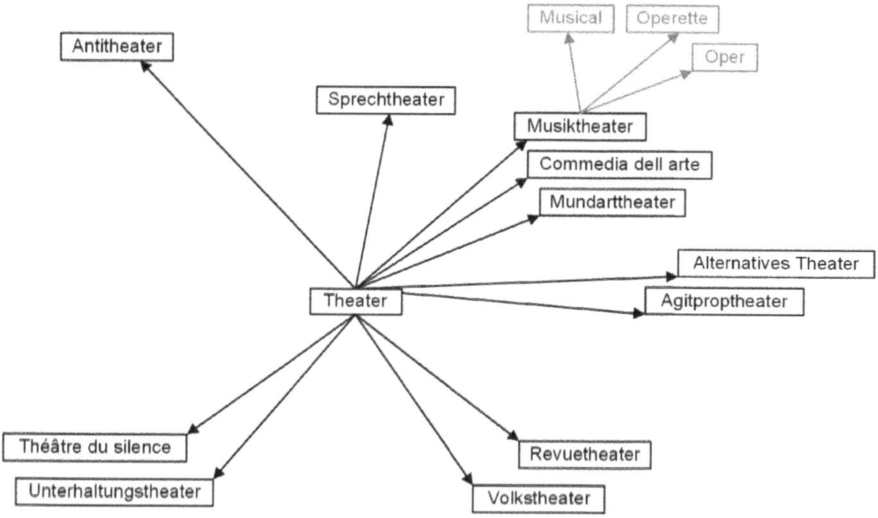

Fig. 8.3: Reduced network containing only the *generic relation according to actor (NTA)* for *Theater.*

As an important contrast to the classical approach, it can be noted that the concepts of Figures 8.2 and 8.3 do not need to be examined individually in an intellectual analysis to perform a search operation. Rather, they are provided through an automated selection process after selecting the corresponding type of relations.

8.3.2 Example 2: Typed Relations of a Topic Map built from the ASIST Thesaurus

For the following example, selected descriptors of the section *indexing and retrieval* of the *ASIST Thesaurus* (ASIST Thesaurus 2005) were extracted. In a next step a set of typed relations were used for an extended differentiation of the thesaurus associative relationship, while the thesaurus descriptors were modeled as entities of a Topic Map (Park 2003, ISO 13250 1999, Pepper et al. 2001, Garshol 2002, Garshol 2005). In addition, a database was set up, whose documents were indexed by the descriptors of the *ASIST Thesaurus*. Both systems, the Topic Map and the database, were connected via a Web interface with each other, which allows conceptual navigation and search using the extended relational inventory.

Starting point of the modeling was the network of relationships present in the *ASIST Thesaurus*. For a first example we have chosen the descriptor *index languages*. Figure 8.4 shows the hierarchical context.

- language (*facet*)
  - language
  - language types
    - command languages
      - common command languages
    - data definition languages
    - human language
      - English language
      - idioms
      - jargon
      - non English languages
        - Chinese language
      - index languages
        - classification schemes
          - Bliss Bibliographic Classification
          - Colon Classification
          - Dewey Classification
          - International Patent Classification
          - Library of Congress Classification
          - Universal Decimal Classification
        - controlled vocabularies
          - ontologies
          - subject heading lists
            - Library of Congress Subject Headings
            - Sears Subject Headings
          - switching languages

Fig. 8.4: Hierarchical context of the descriptor *index languages* in the *ASIST Thesaurus.*

Figure 8.5 shows the descriptor entry for the descriptor *index languages* and its corresponding thesaural relations.

DE index languages
TP language (Facette)
BT language types
NT classification schemes
NT controlled vocabularies
UF indexing languages
UF indexing vocabularies
UF retrieval languages
UF search languages
RT index language construction
RT index terms
RT indexing
RT indexing term links
RT information retrieval
RT information retrieval indexes
RT role indicators
RT subject indexing

Fig. 8.5: Descriptor entry with thesaural relations of *index languages* in the *ASIST Thesaurus.*

As shown in Figure 8.5, eight related terms were assigned to the descriptor *index languages*. The corresponding network of relations is visualized in Figure 8.6. It can be seen that there are associative relations between *index languages* and the eight related terms as well as between some of the related terms. This observation gives first hints for possible distinctions of the meaning of an individual relation and a subsequent typing for distinguishing the meaning.

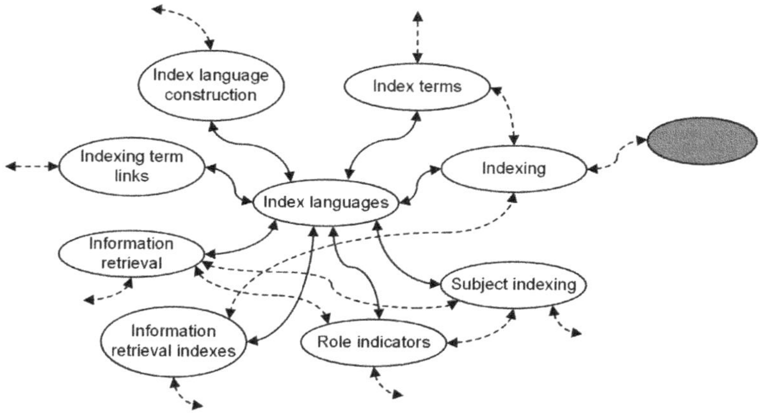

Fig. 8.6: Visualization of the associative relationships for the descriptor *index languages* in the *ASIST Thesaurus*.

The open edges in Figure 8.6 indicate that a related term has even further descriptors assigned as related terms. In Table 8.9 we give three examples, the descriptors *index languages*, *indexing*, and *index terms*. The descriptor *indexing* has 12 other descriptors associated as related terms. We show them at first only as a list:

- *abstracting and indexing service bureaus*
- *authority files*
- *classification*
- *classification schemes*
- *facet analysis*
- *index terms*
- *indexer consistency*
- *indexing exhaustivity*
- *indexing specifity*
- *information retrieval indexes*
- *literary warrant*
- *weighting*

A content-related analysis of those terms that are connected through more than one stage of the associative relation confirms the expectation very clearly that one generally cannot expect to produce thematically coherent clusters or even substantive inferences about the relational paths of a nonspecific association relation.

As the entire net of all related terms cannot be represented here, we confine ourselves to reproduce a selective trail about seven stages, originating from the descriptor *index languages*:

> *Index languages* RT *indexing* RT *authority files* RT *personal names* RT *pseudonyms* RT *proper names* RT *name indexing* RT *corporate names*

In the next step of our modeling, the nonspecific association relationship was replaced by an inventory of typed relations. The inventory used was based on the list shown in Table 8.6. For a thorough theoretical consideration of this approach, we refer to Section 9.2.3. We give three examples in Table 8.9.

Tab. 8.9: Related terms of descriptor *index languages* assigned to typed relations.

Index languages			
Production	Component / condition	Method	Application (Product)
Index language construction	Role indicators	Indexing	Information retrieval indexes
		Information retrieval	Indexing term links
		Subject indexing	Index terms

Indexing				
Method	Application (Tool)	Application (Product)	User (Institution)	Properties
Weighting	Classification schemes	Authority files	Abstracting and indexing service bureaus	Literary warrant
Facet analysis		Information retrieval indexes		Indexer consistency
Classification		Index terms		Indexing exhaustivity
				Indexing specifiy

Index terms			
Component / condition	Method	Application (Tool)	Application (Product)
Concepts Citation order	Weighting Classification	Thesauri	Subject indexes Headings Search terms

The result of the assignment of related terms to the types of the inventory provides a different picture on cluster building, without giving immediate evidence that such an assignment ensures the drawing of conclusions. Compare for example the entity clusters:

Method
Index languages – Indexing – Weighting, Facet analysis, Classification

Application (Product)
Index languages – Index terms – Subject indexes, Headings, Search terms

In any case, the use of typed relations as a filter criterion to increase the precision of a search result is motivated by these examples.

With the help of the Open Source software *Ontopia*[68], a knowledge representation in the form of a Topic Map was modeled from the descriptors and additionally stipulated typed relations.

Figure 8.7 shows an excerpt of our Topic Map for the entity *index languages* with its typed relations to other entities.

68 Cf. http://www.ontopia.net

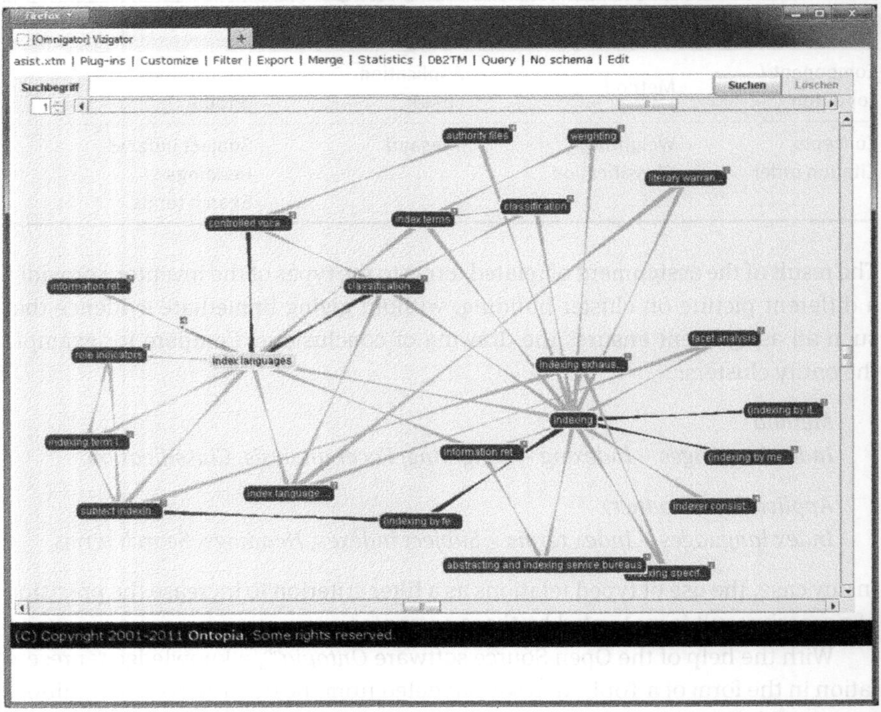

Fig. 8.7: Topic Map for an excerpt from the *ASIST Thesaurus* with additional typed relations (generated by Ontopia).

The modeling carried out is based on the relations as they exist in the *ASIST Thesaurus*. As evidence we show the following preamble formulated in the *XTM* format[69]:

```
<?xml version="1.0" encoding="ISO-8859-1"?>

<topicMap xmlns="http://www.topicmaps.org/xtm/1.0/"
xmlns:xlink="http://www.w3.org/1999/xlink">

  <!-- Präambel 1: Definition of the thesaural elements -->

  <topic id="Descriptor">
    <baseName>
      <baseNameString>Descriptor</baseNameString>
    </baseName>
  </topic>
  <topic id="Synonym">
```

69 For a specification of *XTM* cf.: Pepper et al. (2001). Cf. also the introduction in Section 3.2.1.

```
    <baseName>
      <baseNameString>Synonym</baseNameString>
    </baseName>
  </topic>
  <topic id="HierarchicalRelation">
    <baseName>
      <baseNameString>Hierarchical Relation</baseNameString>
    </baseName>
  </topic>
  <topic id="HierarchicalRelationMember">
    <baseName>
      <baseNameString>Member of Hierarchical Relation</
baseNameString>
    </baseName>
  </topic>
  <topic id="SynonymousRelation">
    <baseName>
      <baseNameString>Synonymous Relation</baseNameString>
    </baseName>
  </topic>
  <topic id="SynonymousRelationMember">
    <baseName>
      <baseNameString>Member of Synonymous Relation</
baseNameString>
    </baseName>
  </topic>
  <topic id="ScopeNote">
    <baseName>
      <baseNameString>Scope Note</baseNameString>
    </baseName>
  </topic>
  <topic id="Document">
    <baseName>
      <baseNameString>Related Documents</baseNameString>
    </baseName>
  </topic>
  <topic id="AssociativeRelation">
    <baseName>
      <baseNameString>Associative Relation</baseNameString>
    </baseName>
  </topic>
  <topic id="AssociativeRelationMember">
    <baseName>
      <baseNameString>Member of Associative Relation</
baseNameString>
    </baseName>
  </topic>
```

The *XTM* format allows to create subtypes of the associative relation by modeling them as instances of *AssociativeRelation*. The particular roles, which are assigned to a topic within such a relation are represented by the respective role pairs of *role 1* and *role 2*. For the relation *Methodology* this is encoded as:

```
<!-- Präambel 1-A: Typed associative relations -->
<!-- Relation -->
<topic id="Methodology">
  <baseName>
    <instanceOf>
      <topicRef xlink:href="#AssociativeRelation"/>
    </instanceOf>
    <baseNameString>Associative Relation (Methodology)</
baseNameString>
  </baseName>
</topic>

<!-- role 1 -->

<topic id="isMethodOf">
  <baseName>
    <instanceOf>
      <topicRef xlink:href="#MethodologyRelationMember"/>
    </instanceOf>
    <baseNameString>is method of</baseNameString>
  </baseName>
</topic>

<!-- role 2 -->

<topic id="isAdopting">
  <baseName>
    <instanceOf>
      <topicRef xlink:href="#MethodologyRelationMember"/>
    </instanceOf>
    <baseNameString>is adopting</baseNameString>
  </baseName>
</topic>
```

The connection between two entities – *indexing* and *abstracting_and_indexing_service_bureaus* by the relation *Methodology* with the role pair *isAdopting* and *isMethodOf* then looks as follows:

```
<!-- Präambel 2: Definition of entity roles of typed relations -->
  <association>
    <instanceOf>
```

```
        <topicRef xlink:href="#Methodology"/>
      </instanceOf>
      <member>
        <roleSpec>
          <topicRef xlink:href="#isAdopting"/>
        </roleSpec>
        <topicRef xlink:href"#abstracting_and_indexing_service_
bureaus"/>
      </member>
      <member>
        <roleSpec>
          <topicRef xlink:href="#isMethodOf"/>
        </roleSpec>
        <topicRef xlink:href="#indexing"/>
      </member>
    </association>
```

We refrain from specifying further modeling details of this Topic Map example.

To simulate a web-based information environment, the Topic Map was linked via a Web interface to a document collection of about 14,000 documents so that the use of the *XTM*-encoded entities and relations was no longer limited to navigation purposes, but also allowed us the retrieval over the document collection via a search form[70].

Figure 8.8 shows the interface by which the search statements can be entered[71]. The *Ontopia* specific query language *tolog* (Garshol, Tolog language tutorial 2007) not only allows querying the names of the topics, but also to use the modeled relationships between the topics as selection criteria. After performing a request with *tolog*, the topics are displayed that meet the conditions of the request. These topics are the basis for generating the set of documents that appear as a result of the search.

---

70 Special thanks to *Jens Wille* who set up the search environment and thus allows performing the first experiments as well as verifying our statements.

71 Cf. http://ixtrieve.fh-koeln.de/ghn/

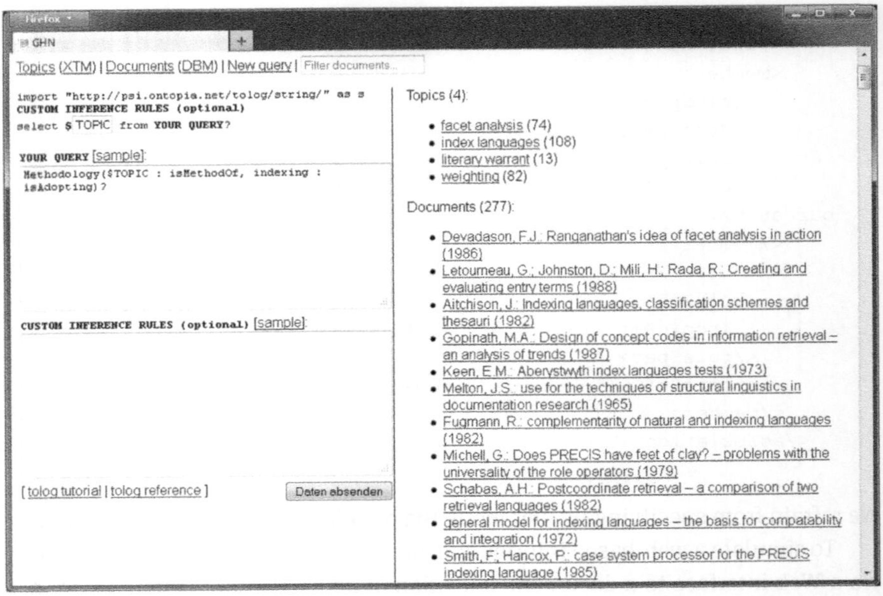

Fig. 8.8: Web interface for searching the *ASIST* Topic Map and corresponding documents.

We give two examples of querying for different relations of the entity *indexing* and discuss them in some more detail for better comprehension of our approach. Figure 8.8 shows a request for documents that the entity *indexing* considers as *methodic procedure*. The selection of the topics reads as *tolog* input (left side of Fig. 8.8):

```
Methodology($TOPIC : isMethodOf, indexing : isAdopting)?
```

The related topics are displayed in Figure 8.8 below the heading *Topics* (upper right side). For our search query we receive four topics:

- *facet analysis*
- *index languages*
- *literary warrant*
- *weighting*

This corresponds to the modeling approach using typed relations in our *ASIST* Topic Map for the topic *indexing*, namely the relation *Methodology*, as is shown in Figure 8.9.

- Associative Relation (*Characterization*)
  - is characterizing
    - indexer consistency
    - indexing exhaustivity
    - indexing specificity
- Associative Relation (*Methodology*)
  - is adopting
    - facet analysis
    - index languages
    - literary warrant
    - weighting
  - is method of
    - abstracting and indexing service bureaus
- Associative Relation (*Production*)
  - is producing
    - information retrieval indexes
- Associative Relation (*Usage*)
  - is using
    - authority files
    - classification
    - classification schemes
    - index terms
- Hierarchical Relation
  - Broader Term
    - (indexing by feature indexed)
    - (indexing by item indexed)
    - (indexing by method used)

Fig. 8.9: Typed relations for the topic *indexing* modeled in the *ASIST* Topic Map.

Under the heading *Documents* twelve documents are displayed that have been indexed with one of the four topics (lower right side of Fig. 8.8), we show them here once again as a separate list:

- Devadason, F.J.: Ranganathan's idea of facet analysis in action (1986)
- Coetzee, P.C.: Theory of logistic facet analysis (1968)
- Broughton, V.: Faceted classification as a basis for knowledge organization in a digital environment – the Bliss Bibliographic Classification as a model for vocabulary management and the creation of multi-dimensional knowledge structures (2001)
- Kim, M.; Kang, S.; Lim, J.: Automatic user preference learning for personalized electronic program guide applications (2007)
- Bonnici, L.J.; Kim , J.; Burnett, K.; Miksa, S.D.: Development of a facet analysis system to identify and measure the dimensions of interaction in online learning (2007)
- Beghtol, C.: Facet concept as a universal principle of subdivision (2006)
- Small, H.; Zitt, M.: Modifying the journal impact factor by fractional citation weighting – the audience factor (2008)
- LaBarre, K.: Facets, search and discovery in next generation catalogs – informing the future by revisiting past understanding

- Facets: a fruitful notion in many domains – special issue on facet analysis (2008)
- Skare, R.: Complementarity – a concept for document analysis? (2009)
- Kumar, V.; Neelameghan, A.; Deokattey, S.: method for developing a domain ontology – a case study for a multidisciplinary subject (2010)
- LaBarre, K.: Facet analysis (2010)

Our second example asks for documents about *instruments* of the topic *indexing*. The *tolog* input reads:

```
Usage($TOPIC : isInstrumentOf, indexing : isUsing)?
```

The relevant topics in this case are:
- *authority files*
- *classification*
- *classification schemes*
- *index terms*

They correspond to the modeling of the relation *Usage* for the topic *indexing* (cf. the box with dashed lines in Fig. 8.9). The determined document set in this case consists of 565 documents, which we do not want to show here[72].

Evaluating the results of both queries, we will at first repeat that the requests were directed against a set of about 14,000 documents. The indexing of documents with descriptors of the *ASIST Thesaurus* was carried out partly on the basis of an automatic indexing process using the software *Lingo*[73] (Lepsky & Vorhauer 2006). The indexing quality therefore may be suboptimal in some cases compared to an intellectual indexing process. Our aim was to illustrate the basic procedure and, in particular, to demonstrate the potential of typed relations as a selection filter. Although in both cases the topic *indexing* was used as starting point of the requests, their connections via the typed relations *Methodology* and *Usage* leads to different topics and thus to different result sets.

With the specification of the following examples we want to emphasize even more how the formation of result sets may be affected by the use of typed relations and how inferences via the typed relations can be linked with inferences along the hierarchical paths. In order to achieve this we limited the *tolog* queries by so-called *custom inference rules*.

Controlled vocabulary can adopt the role of a product when its creation is considered. But it can also play the role of a resource when it is used for index-

72 The search can be performed by using the interface: http://ixtrieve.fh-koeln.de/ghn/
73 Cf. http://lex-lingo.blogspot.com

ing. In our Topic Map the topic *controlled_vocabularies* can therefore occur on both sides of the relationship *Production.* As in the case of syntactic indexing the modeling of this relationship is indicated by a directional dependance. This directionality can be specified by the query language. We obtain the following results for each direction:

Direction 1 (isProducing)

```
Production($TOPIC : isProducing, controlled_vocabularies :
isProductOf)?
```

The request can be interpreted to mean that such topics are searched that represent *requirements* for the topic *controlled_vocabularies* in the understanding of the modeled relation *Production.* Only one topic is found:

vocabulary control (41)

The corresponding result set includes 41 documents and will not be shown here.

Direction 2 (isProductOf):

```
Production($TOPIC : isProductOf, controlled_vocabularies :
isProducing)?
```

The request can be interpreted to mean that such topics are searched that represent *products* for the topic *controlled_vocabularies* in the understanding of the modeled relation *Production.* One topic is found that is associated with 140 documents:

authority files (140)

We will now include all narrower terms for a search on the topic *controlled_vocabularies.* In this case, a hierarchical expansion has to be performed and the query needs to be supplemented by inference rules, so-called *custom inference rules.* Our query interface provides a separate input box for this purpose, which is shown in Figure 8.10 down left.

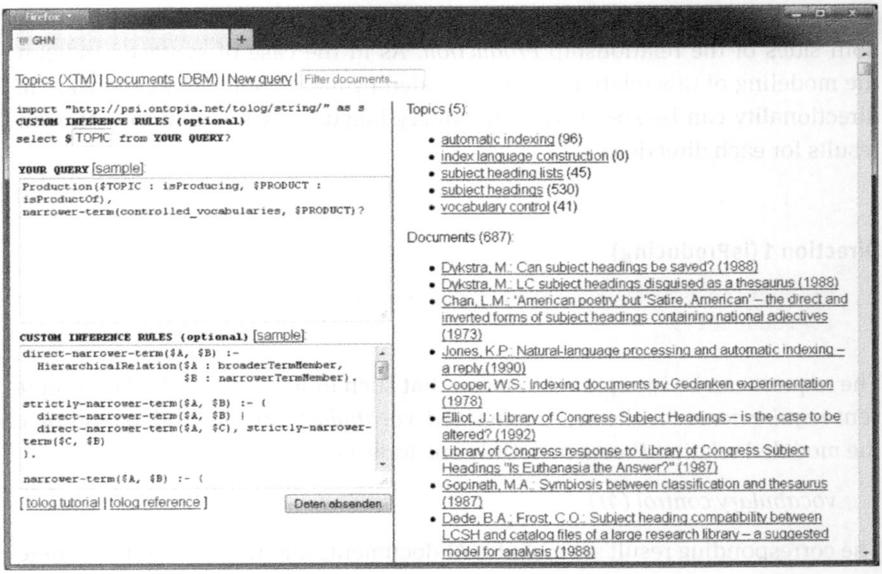

Fig. 8.10: Web interface for searching the *ASIST* Topic Map including *custom inference rules.*

Predefined are the following rules. They can be activated by the link *"sample"*. If desired, they may be substituted with own rules.

```
direct-narrower-term($A, $B) :-
  HierarchicalRelation($A : broaderTermMember,
                       $B : narrowerTermMember).

strictly-narrower-term($A, $B) :- {
  direct-narrower-term($A, $B) |
  direct-narrower-term($A, $C), strictly-narrower-term($C, $B)
}.

narrower-term($A, $B) :- {
  $A = $B | strictly-narrower-term($A, $B)
}.

narrower-term-1($A, $B) :- {
  $A = $B | direct-narrower-term($A, $B)
}.

narrower-term-2($A, $B) :- {
  narrower-term-1($A, $B) |
  narrower-term-1($A, $C), narrower-term-1($C, $B)
}.
```

```
narrower-term-3($A, $B) :- {
  narrower-term-2($A, $B) |
  narrower-term-2($A, $C), narrower-term-1($C, $B)
}.

direct-broader-term($A, $B) :-
  direct-narrower-term($B, $A).

strictly-broader-term($A, $B) :-
  strictly-narrower-term($B, $A).

broader-term($A, $B) :-
  narrower-term($B, $A).

broader-term-1($A, $B) :-
  narrower-term-1($B, $A).

broader-term-2($A, $B) :-
  narrower-term-2($B, $A).
broader-term-3($A, $B) :-
  narrower-term-3($B, $A).
```

With the initial request, a search for topics should be possible that represent *requirements* in the sense of the modeled relation *Production* for producing *controlled_vocabularies* regardless of their special type.

The *tolog* input for the query reads:

```
Production($TOPIC : isProducing, $PRODUCT : isProductOf),
narrower-term(controlled_vocabularies, $PRODUCT)?
```

Five topics are found that are associated with 687 documents:

- automatic indexing (96)
- index language construction (0)
- subject heading lists (45)
- subject headings (530)
- vocabulary control (41)

The second query

```
Production($TOPIC : isProductOf, $PRODUCT : isProducing),
narrower-term(controlled_vocabularies, $PRODUCT)?
```

is used for all products that are produced with the help of *controlled_vocabularies* (including all narrower concepts). Two topics are found with 502 associated documents:

- *authority files (140)*
- *thesauri (372)*

In the next step the result of a search is to be specified by an additional condition. We are looking for all kinds of controlled vocabularies (topic: controlled_vocabularies), that are using methods of the subject field lexicography (topic: lexicography) for producing the products:

```
Production($TOPIC : isProductOf, $PRODUCT : isProducing),
narrower-term(controlled_vocabularies, $PRODUCT),
Methodology($TOPIC : isAdopting, lexicography : isMethodOf)?
```

The query leads to one topic associated with 372 documents:

thesauri (372)

Finally, we want to supplement the impressions of the options of our approach by a rather artificial example. The additional constraint should consist of a negation. The query is directed towards products based on all forms of controlled vocabularies but the products themselves should not apply vocabulary control. The *tolog* input reads:

```
Production($TOPIC : isProductOf, $PRODUCT : isProducing),
narrower-term(index_languages, $PRODUCT),
not(Methodology($TOPIC : isAdopting, vocabulary_control :
isMethodOf))?
```

The result comprises three topics associated with 140 documents:
- *authority files (140)*
- *indexing term links (0)*
- *information retrieval indexes (0)*

With these examples, the basic way is sketched of how a knowledge representation under the conditions of the technical data representation can be used for an interoperable Web retrieval. This also shows how typed relations can be used as a filter for the specification of queries without using methods of syntactic indexing. However, we need to emphasize the exemplary character of our examples to demonstrate the methodological approach. More precise statements about the potential and the qualitative properties of the procedure require further research, including the development of appropriate test scenarios.

8.3.3 Example 3: Degrees of Determinacy

We will now come back to the concept of *degrees of determinacy* as methodological approach for characterizing the conceptual strength of a uni-directional mapping between entities of different indexing languages by numerical figures.

We will enhance the discussion given in Section 6.2.5 dealing with entity-based conceptual exploration by aspects of establishing conceptual interoperability in heterogeneous information environments.

Therefore, we would like to refer once again to the assertion that the combination of entities of various knowledge representations implies a great potential for query expansion. On the one hand, this can be done by adding further entities that can be taken as a hierarchical enlargement within the second knowledge representation for an entity of the initial representation. Secondly, however, this can also be done in the context of a relational extension if the knowledge representations have varying differentiation of their relational structure. This should be the case very often. Attention must be paid to the question of which entities are connected to each other, so that the objective of a content-related interoperability remains preserved.

Our example in Section 6.2.5 (cf. Fig. 6.5, 6.6, and 6.7) has shown that from a methodological perspective a critical issue has to be considered. If connections are set up between the entities of different knowledge representations, one expects a statement about a content-related equivalence of the associated entities. Analyses show that in general the relationships between the entities show different forms of contextual similarity. The spectrum ranges from complete equivalence to forms of weak resemblance. In the example given next, there are three classes in the *DDC* that can be seen as link points for the *SWD* heading *Jagd* (hunting):

799.2 *Jagd als Sport. Umfassende Werke über Jagd*
Hunting as a sport. Comprehensive works on hunting
639.1 *Kommerzielle Jagd / Jagd in der Landwirtschaft*
Commercial hunting / hunting in agriculture
179.3 *Jagd in der Ethik*
Hunting in ethics

The classes can be distinguished by aspect viewpoints and all three viewpoints give rise to a connection of the respective class to a heading *Jagd*. This is especially the case if the heading itself does not have a contextual disambiguation. However, one will not consider these three connections as equally strict in content. Because of the different aspect viewpoints, complete conceptual equality cannot be assumed. In order to deal with this, the following degrees of determinacy have be assigned:

SWD	Det	DDC	
Jagd	D3	799.2	Jagd als Sport. Umfassende Werke über Jagd Hunting as a sport. Comprehensive works on hunting
Jagd	D3	639.1	Kommerzielle Jagd / Jagd in der Landwirtschaft Commercial hunting / hunting in agriculture
Jagd	D1	179.3	Jagd in der Ethik Hunting in ethics

The degrees of determinacy can be viewed methodologically as another example for the typing of relationships. In particular, they can serve as a replacement or at least as a complement for those forms of uni-directional mappings between the entities of different knowledge representations that are typed by content-oriented criteria. By intellectual allocation, the context of the entities can be considered and a scaled indication of the conceptual equivalence can be assigned. As scaled indication they become an instrument for the design of search options or for ranking algorithms. We will come back to this aspects when we deal specifically with the requirements of a content-related semantic interoperability.

As an important consequence for any further discussions concerning conceptual interoperability, connections between entities of different knowledge representations should generally be understood as uni-directional mappings.

Figure 6.7 in Section 6.2.5 shows some possibilities for assembling relational enrichment and interoperability. Again, the subject heading *Jagd* from the *SWD* serves as an example. We have already shown that the heading is associated with three related terms and has 28 narrower terms without any relations to further headings. Now we can conclude that, supporting cognitive conceptual searches, the headings can initially only be displayed in alphabetical order or in their incomplete hierarchical contexts. If connections to *DDC* are set up, descriptions of some relation types can be derived by analyzing the different contextual aspects. For example, one part of the narrower terms refers to *hunting methods*, another part to *hunt for individual species of animals*. Among other things, a more rapid estimate becomes possible concerning the relevance of the headings with regard to the search interest. We obtain a denser network of relations that is more suitable for supporting cognitive orientation operations. The suitability for supporting mechanical search processes will be examined in the next chapter.

9 Inferences in Retrieval Processes

As part of the treatment of prerequisites for an ontology-based model of indexing and retrieval in Section 7.3 and by discussing our examples in the previous section, we have already implicitly asked the question of the usefulness of inferences for retrieval processes. In this section we want to carry out a more systematic treatment of the question of which formal structures of knowledge representations are particularly well-suited to support an automatic derivation of result sets. Formally, this should be done by building a transitive closure as introduced in Section 7.3.1. Furthermore, it must be done with respect to content-related requirements when evaluating the result set. Pursuing the aim of a self-contained presentation, it cannot be avoided repeating some arguments given already in course of this book. However, the reasoning will emphasize formal aspects more strongly than content-oriented aspects.

At first, we will clarify our understanding of inference which cannot be limited to a formal logical understanding, as we are looking for a connection between the content interpretation and the benefit for machine processing. We give a summary of types of inferences that should be looked at in detail and orient ourselves to the well-known types of semantic relations and to the already given interpretation of induced inferences, cf. Section 7.3.1. Special attention is given to the combination of different types of relationships. A first list of inferences is given by a content characterization:

1. Synonyms
2. Inference by hierarchy relations within facets
3. Typed cross faceted relations for filtering (formulation of constraints) of entities
4. Inferences about relations of different type
5. Induced inferences for generating document sets
6. Inferences by connecting the entities of different indexing languages or knowledge representations (interoperability)

We will further distinguish the inferences more formally by level in the sense of numbers of edges between the corresponding nodes. In the following, we will present the resulting types and discuss them in detail. It may be necessary to repeat some of the statements already given in previous sections (especially Section 7.3) to enable a self-contained presentation. The order of our presentation differs from the sequence given above.

9.1 Inferences of Level 1

An *inference of level 1* implies that entities of a knowledge representation (as nodes of a network intended) are collected additionally for a search formulation, being connected by an edge of the length of 1 to the originating entity.

9.1.1 Hierarchical Relationships

In order to derive general statements about inferential properties of hierarchical relationships they need to be distinguished by different types. As first type we will consider the *is-a* relationship.

In formal knowledge representation, a hierarchical relationship between concepts is represented by an *is-a* relation, cf. Figure 9.1. This relation serves as prototype for deriving inferences.

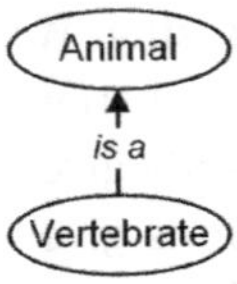

Fig. 9.1: Hierarchy as *is-a* relation.

In the context of the indexing languages, the *is-a* relation corresponds to the *generic relation* as a representative of the hierarchical relationships as it is established already by classification systems and thesauri. The hierarchy between the broader and the narrower term can then be read as a narrower term *is-a* broader term with respect to the contents represented and the shared set of properties. The narrower concept must be characterized by at least one additional property. This relationship is not reversible, therefore the *is-a* relation is not symmetric.

An inference of level 1 allows to build result sets by collecting all documents via induced inferences that were indexed with a certain entity or any narrower entities of level 1. This process is shown in Figure 9.2 by omitting the symbols for documents.

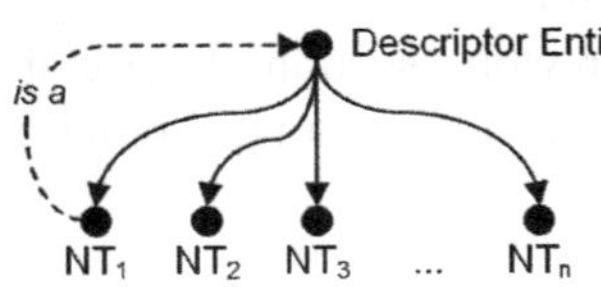

Fig. 9.2: Hierarchy as relation between broader and narrower terms in indexing languages.

The second well-known member of the hierarchical relationships in the context of indexing languages is the *whole-part* relationship. An example is shown in Figure 9.3. The arguments given so far can be transferred to this issue. An important use case for this type of relationship is described by the task of developing a systematic structure for geographical concepts. The relation can also be applied successfully for objects of the material world.

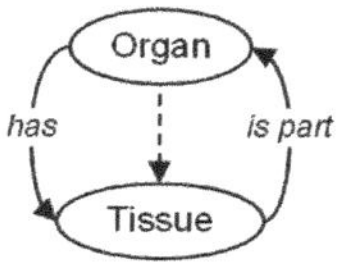

Fig. 9.3: Whole-part relationship.

Depending on the direction, the relation can be read as *has part* or *is part of.*

In traditional indexing languages it is not very often distinguished between the two types of hierarchical relationships, although the distinction is an integral part of the corresponding standards (ISO 25964-1 2011).

Sometimes the *instance* relation is specified as a further type of hierarchical relationships (ISO 25964-1 2011). From a structural point of view there is no need to distinguish them from the mentioned types. Therefore, we refrain from further consideration.

Another kind of relationship in the context of hierarchical relations is given by the *chronological* or *temporal* relationship. In indexing languages, this relation is expressed by statements as *former – later* or *later – former.* A special case is given by the *genetic* or *descent* relation, sometimes seen as an associative relationship depending on the type of lineage. Taking the periods next to points in time into account, a time hierarchy is not only established by the time line, but can also be established by nested periods. We do not consider it necessary to address these issues in more detail or to illustrate them graphically. It is sufficient to note that relations of this type allow us to draw inferences, too.

9.1.2 Associative Relationships

We already remarked repeatedly that the associative relationships of indexing languages present special problems for a more precise description of their inference qualities[74]. One reason for this is that it is a definitional feature of this type of relations to be characterizable by content considerations exclusively. In index-

74 Cf. discussion in Section 7.2.2.

ing languages a not nearer definable number of related terms can be associated to an entity without being related by explicitely stated criteria. The connection of entities really may be a matter of association. The property of symmetry is a special quality of these associative relations. The cognitive interpretation of the similarity or association of two concepts cannot be distinguished in its direction, as far as association is not characterized by criteria, cf. Figure 9.4.

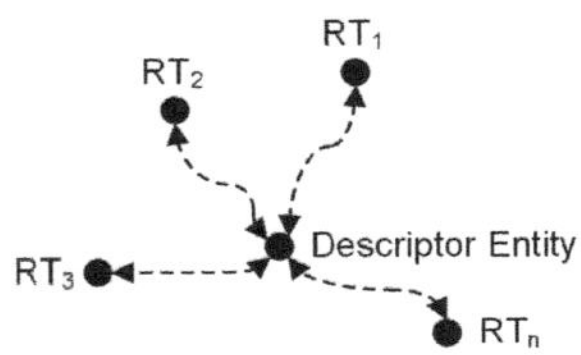

Fig. 9.4: Associative relationships in indexing languages.

For a further illustration, we give some additional examples from the *ASIST Thesaurus* (ASIST Thesaurus 2005).

- Index languages RT {Index terms, Indexing, Subject indexing, Role indicators, Information retrieval indexes, Information retrieval, Indexing term links, Index language construction}
- Automatic indexing RT {Automatic classification, Computational linguistics, Content based indexing, Information processing, Machine aided indexing, Natural language processing}

9.1.3 Typification of the Synonymy / Equivalence Relationship

Our approach of typing associative relationships proceeds in several stages. First, the synonyms of indexing languages should be subjected to a closer examination (Gödert 1987). The agreement of synonyms is based on two conditions:

- The words under consideration are different linguistic representations of a concept (true synonyms). The most suitable linguistic representation becomes the preferred term in the context of the indexing language, the other ones are declared as access or reference terms.
- By decision a synonymy setting was made for near synonyms. This means that one does not want to express the actually existing context-dependent differences in meaning by two different entities for the purposes of the indexing language.

In natural language, we can often find the phenomenon of context-dependent interchangeability of words. This phenomenon is well-known by the term *near synonyms*. In an impressive way such cases are put together in synonym dictionaries. The individual words have distinct meanings, therefore they do not meet the strict requirements of the full conceptual identity for true synonyms in the context of indexing languages. However, they can be used for one another in a given context.

Figure 9.5 illustrates the problem of near synonyms in more detail (Gödert, Lepsky & Nagelschmidt 2011, 31–35)[75].

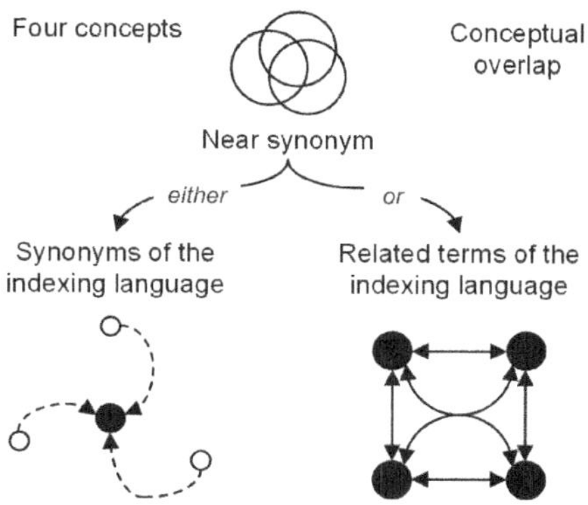

Fig. 9.5: Treatment of near synonyms in indexing languages.

Compare the examples from the *ASIST Thesaurus* in Table 9.1

Tab. 9.1: Examples of declared synonyms in the *ASIST Thesaurus*.

Interfaces		**Managers**	
UF	Human computer interfaces	UF	Library administrators
Publications		**Archives**	
UF	Information products	UF	Historical records
Education		**Faculty**	
UF	Instruction	UF	Deans
	Teaching		Professors
			Teachers

Looking at the above example, it immediately becomes obvious

75 Cf. also discussion in Section 2.1.1 illustrated by Figure 2.3.

- that there are by no means only true synonyms in the sense of conceptually identical entities, but also near synonyms which provide an independent conceptual meaning outside the controlled vocabulary;
- that the notion of transitivity as a defining property of an equivalence relation is not present within the synonym sets (compare the examples *education* and *faculty*).

In any case, a consideration of synonyms for inference processes requires a more detailed analysis, especially if interested in the property of transitivity. If necessary the synonym relationship has to be converted into a hierarchical or a typed association relation.

Let us have a look at an example consisting of three German natural language nouns: *Lärm – Krach – Streit*. Translating the words in English, e.g. *noise – quarrel – dispute* – shows that the example is not transferable[76]. Different from the corresponding English words, both pairs of words

Lärm – Krach
Krach – Streit

can be interpreted as synonyms. In German, the word *Krach* is a homonym. *Lärm* and *Streit* are by no means synonyms. Figure 9.6 illustrates the interrelations.

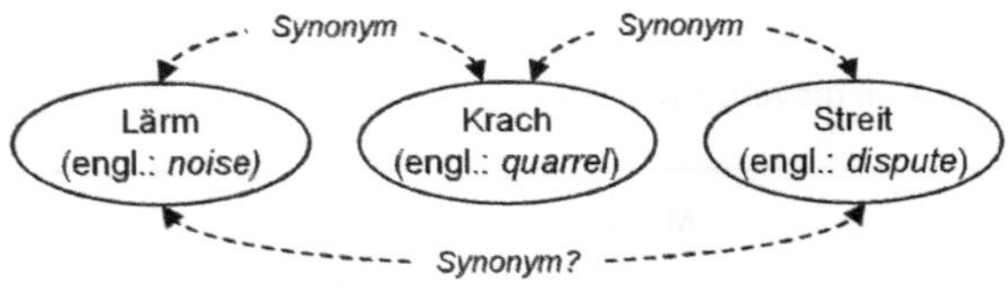

Fig. 9.6: Lack of transitivity for near synonyms: an example.

This example shows very clearly that synonyms do not own the property of inheritance. An even more striking example shows possible consequences of this deficiency. The following sequence of words consists of a trail of synonyms

authentic -> believable -> probable -> ostensible -> pretended -> spurious -> unauthentic

The endpoint of this synonym trail from six levels is an antonym compared with the word at the beginning (Murphy 2008, 158).

For a clear and consistent formation of document sets as hits for search queries, it is not conducive to preserve ambiguity. Therefore, near synonyms are

76 A comparable example with English words is given by: *dive – header – topline.*

removed from indexing languages and treated alternatively either as synonyms or as related terms. Usually, the best linguistic representation to deal with synonyms becomes the preferred term, meaning that the other ones are declared as reference terms – in our present consideration these are viewed to be semantically interoperable. This case is shown in Figure 9.7. The result is a strong semantic normalization. The terms of the access vocabulary are not entities and therefore cannot be connected to any other entities.

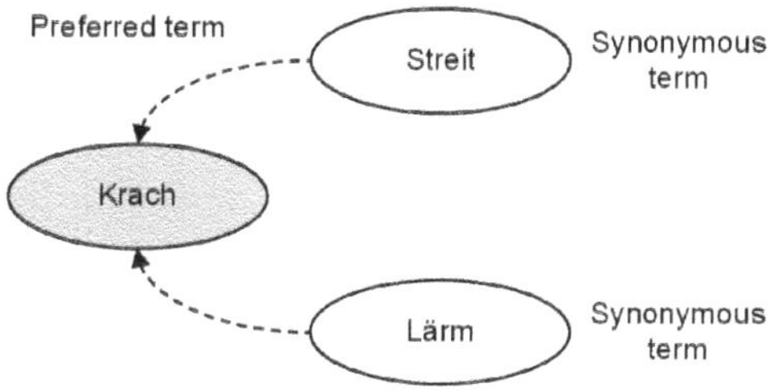

Fig. 9.7: Treatment of near synonyms as preferred term with access vocabulary.

An alternative approach is to treat the terms of a near synonym as related terms. Any related term remains as an entity in the indexing language provided with an independent conceptual meaning, and hence it cannot be replaced by another entity. These terms are modeled as entities of the knowledge representation and can be connected to other entities by relations of the inventory used. The result may be an unclear semantic differentiation and we cannot speak of interoperability between the related terms. Their common use for a search query may be useful, but they are not semantically interchangeable.

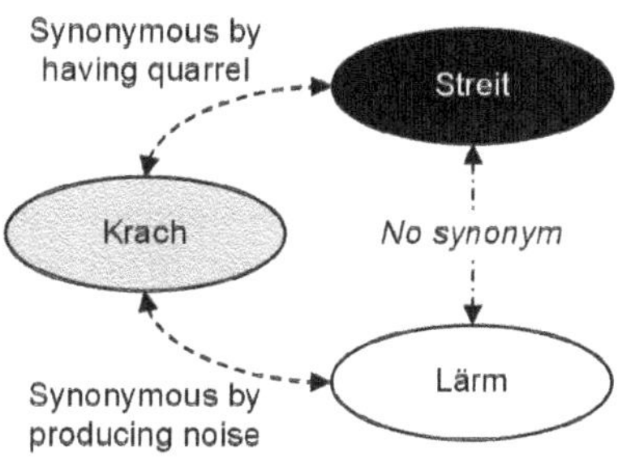

Fig. 9.8: Treatment of near synonyms by typed relations: Initial situation.

In our model we recommend the treatment of near synonyms either as hierarchical or as typed associative relations. This allows a better support for both the conceptual structure within a knowledge representation and the implementation of inference rules. We again illustrate the initial semantic situation of our example in Figure 9.8.

A modeling of this distinction would create two separate entities with the conceptual meanings of *Krach (by having quarrel)* and *Krach (by producing noise)*. Both have to be represented in an appropriate form as entities of the knowledge representation. It is desirable to provide access links for the well-known words of the common language. Figure 9.9 illustrates how this can be achieved.

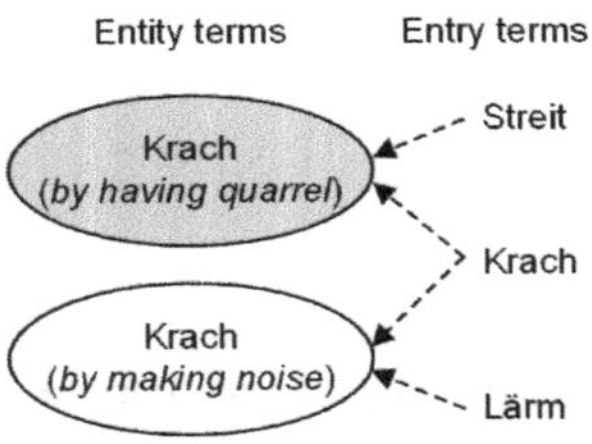

Fig. 9.9: Disambiguation of a near synonym.

It deserves attention that the usual models for ontologies and other forms of knowledge representation provide no preferred terms in the sense of indexing languages. All synonyms are modeled as independent entities. They are related by synonymy relationships to the same concept and represent it equivalently[77].

9.2 Inferences of Level 2 and of Higher Levels, Transitivity

Inferences of level 2 and of higher levels, are to be understood as the inclusion of entities that can be achieved in the conceptual network through a path consisting of two or more consecutive edges. In such cases the formal property of *transitivity* is indispensable. We have already mentioned the property several times and will now repeat only its formal definition. A relation ~ is said to be transitive if the following conclusion is true: $a \sim b$, $b \sim c$ then $a \sim c$ is true also. In this statement, *a*, *b*, *c* stand for entities or nodes and ~ for a relation of the semantic net. In Section 7.3.1 we have called the result of collecting all nodes of a knowledge structure by transitivity along the edges as transitive closure.

77 This can be seen for example by the property *owl:sameAs* in the ontology language *OWL*.

9.2.1 Hierarchical Relationships

We continue the considerations carried out in Section 9.1.1. Figure 9.10 gives a visualization of a hierarchy in indexing languages over several stages.

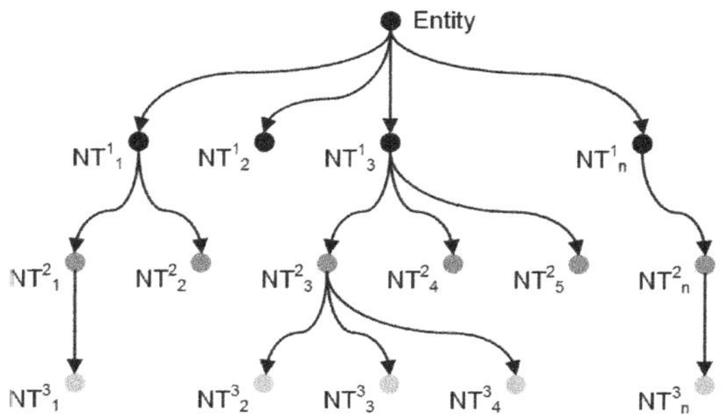

Fig. 9.10: Hierarchical paths in indexing languages.

To ensure transitivity in hierarchical relationships it is of utmost importance to follow two essential requirements:

1. Any narrower concept must provide all characteristical features of the respective broader concept and at least one more.
2. When moving from one hierarchical level to the next lower level within the same hierarchy trail, the characteristical features of the respective entities must belong to the same conceptual facet.

Only if these requirements are fulfilled, inferences can be drawn about all levels of a hierarchy trail. Performing the process of generating a transitive closure as described in Section 7.3.1 then is best supported both formal and in terms of content-orientation. If necessary, a formal statement has to be made ensuring the inference process. If the requirements are not fulfilled, a formal statement should be made to prevent the inference act and to exclude entities from the generation of a conceptual closure. To ensure mechanical inferences, it is not sufficient to rely on a cognitive interpretation of the relations.

We start our discussion once more by considering the generic type of the hierarchical relationship. Continuing the example of Figure 9.1, we give an example for an inference of more than two levels for the generic relationship in Figure 9.11.

We have indicated the respective derivations by different types of arrows, as they are listed in the legend of Figure 9.11. Overall, the inference *Blue tit is-a animal* is a valid statement.

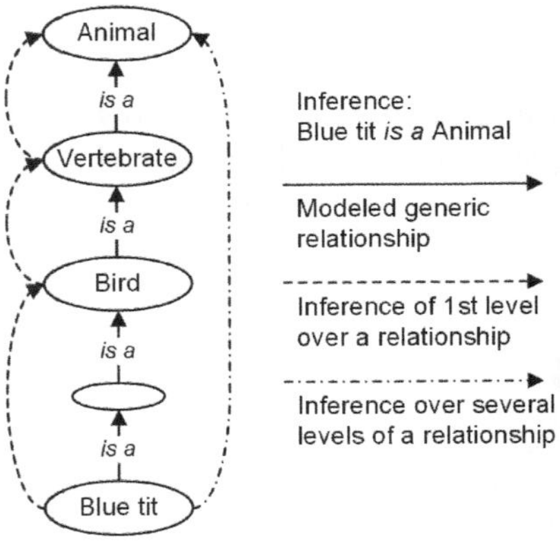

Fig. 9.11: Drawing inferences along hierarchical paths of generic relationships.

As stated previously, we do not want to treat the relationship between a general concept and an *instance* as a special type of hierarchical relationship. An instance is always the last node of a trail and no continuation to a further level of hierarchy is possible. Examples are objects with unique individuality, e.g., people, works of art, or concrete products. It is important to note that a general term may comprise a very large number of instances. Conversely, an instance can have relations with several general concepts, a form of appearance already discussed as polyhierarchy. Both reasons suggest that it should be carefully balanced whether instances should be set in relation to general concepts.

For the second type of hierarchical relationships, the whole-part relationship, no new description is required, a continuation of the example given in Figure 9.3 is given in Figure 9.12.

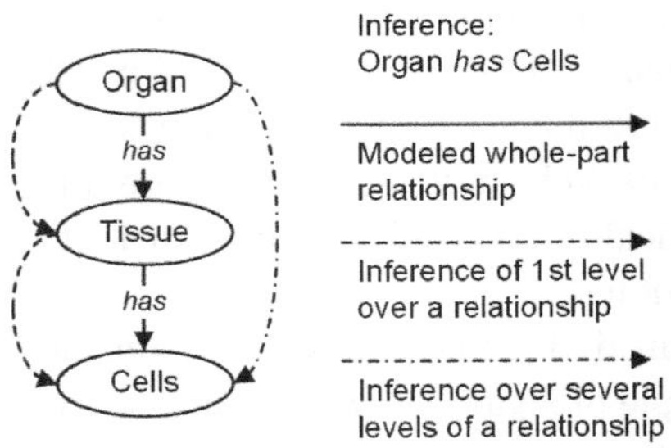

Fig. 9.12: Drawing inferences along hierarchical paths of whole-part relationships.

Again, we have indicated the respective derivations by different types of arrows, as they are listed in the legend of Figure 9.12. Overall, the inference *organ* has *cells* is valid.

The next step considers inferences along relational paths by combinations of generic and whole-part relationships. We look at an example in which the following statements are modeled:

- *A blue tit is a bird*
- *An animal has a heart*
- *A bird is an animal*
- *An organ has tissues*
- *A heart is an organ*
- *Tissue has cells*

A modeling could have the appearance as shown in Figure 9.13:

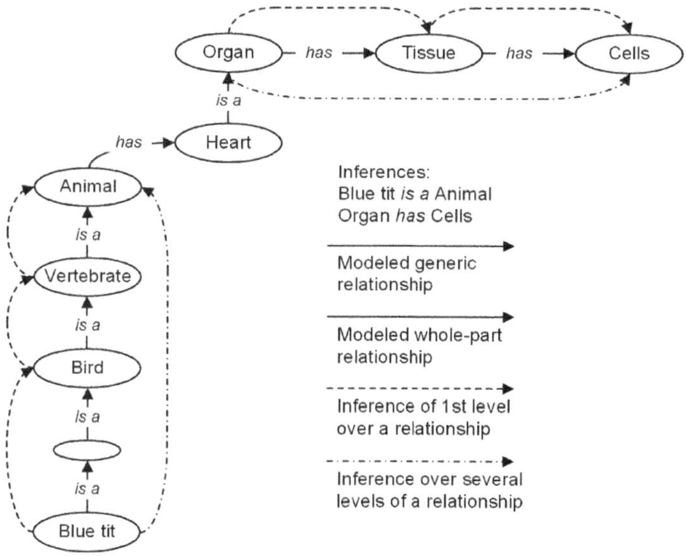

Fig. 9.13: Combining inferences for different types of hierarchical relations (1).

The meanings of the relations are defined in the legend of Figure 9.13. The modeling uses the two hierarchical relations already used in the examples before:

- *is a (abstraction)*
- *has (whole-part)*

Both types of relations are transitive. As a result of our previous discussion we can derive the statements:

- *Blue tit* is a *animal*
- *organ* has *cells*

The property of transitivity can be continued to the combination of the two types of relationships. As an overall result, we obtain the conclusion:
– *Blue tit* has *cells*

Figure 9.14 shows the corresponding visualization.

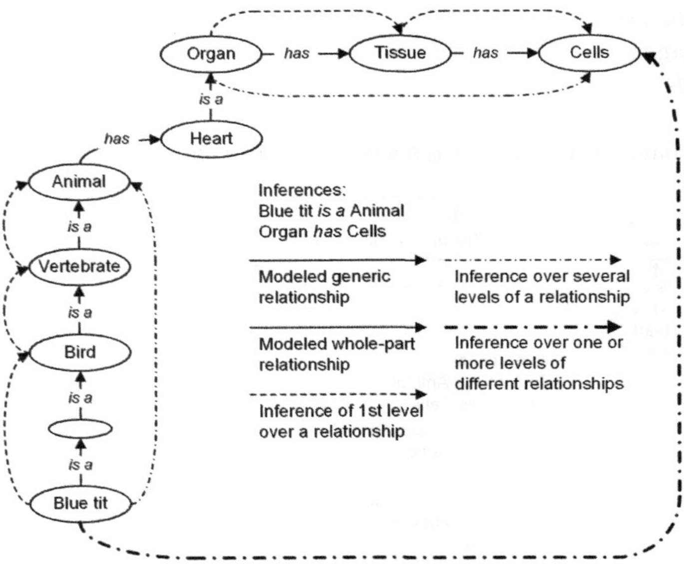

Fig. 9.14: Combining inferences for different types of hierarchical relations (2).

9.2.2 Unspecific Associative Relationships

In the case of *unspecific associative relationships*, all nodes of the network would be considered for drawing the inference that can be accessed via pathways of associative relationships having a length of two or more levels seen from the initial node. Figure 9.15 shows an example.

In the previous sections we have already stressed that examples taken from the classical thesaurus environment show that a blanket application of the inference process on associative relationships over several levels is not possible. In the following, we want support this statement by discussing two examples.

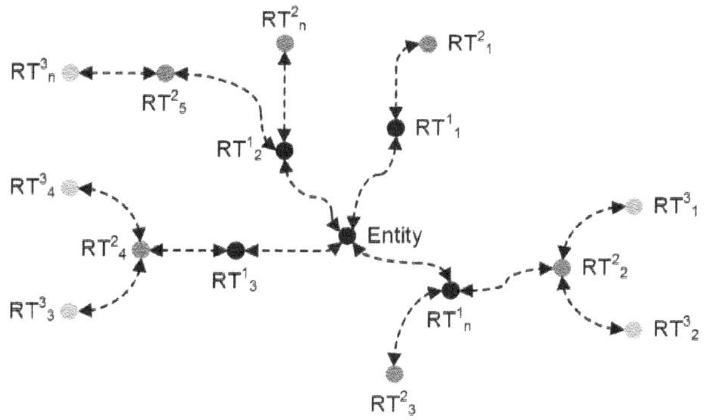

Fig. 9.15: Net of entities with associative paths of greater length.

Example 1: ASIST Thesaurus

Tab. 9.2: Paths of associative relations from the *ASIST Thesaurus*.

Automatic indexing		
RT of path length 1	RT of path length 2	RT of path length 3
Automatic classification	Automatic categorization	Categories
Computational linguistics	Cluster analysis	Classification
Content based indexing	Computational lexicography	Co-occurence analysis
Information processing	Full text searching	Cognitive science
Machine aided indexing	Image indexing	Computer science
Natural language processing	Information science	Cybernetics
	Knowledge representation	Data presentation
	Natural language interfaces	Domain analysis
	Probabilistic indexing	Image analysis
	Relevance ranking	Image databases
	Text processing	Image retrieval
		Images
		Information retrieval
		Information science education
		Information scientists
		Information technology
		Librarianship
		Linguistics
		Ontologies
		...

For the first example we choose again the *ASIST Thesaurus* with its thematical focus on information science and technology (ASIST Thesaurus 2005). The initial entity should be the descriptor *Automatic indexing*. Table 9.2 shows descriptors that are associated to *Automatic indexing* as related terms (RT) by varying path length.

For example, a trail of associative terms beginning with *Automatic indexing* and ending with *Images* or *Cognitive science* cannot be seen as suitable for creating thematic clusters with a sharp conceptual border.

Example 2: INFODATA Thesaurus

Tab. 9.3: Paths of associative relations from the *INFODATA-Thesaurus*.

Dokumentationssprache				
RT of path length 1	**RT of path length 2**	**RT of path length 3**	**RT of path length 4**	**RT of path length 5**
Ordnungssystem	Anordnungstechnik	Datenanordnung	Dateiaufbau	Benutzerführung
	Hierarchie	Permutation	Datenbankaufbau	Browsing
		Relation	Datenstruktur	Datei
			Hypertext	Datenfeld
			KWIC	Datenverknüpfung
			KWOC	Elektronisches Publizieren
			Registererstellung	Entity-Relationship
				Erstellung
				Formatierung, Index, Indexierungsverfahren, Kategorienschema, Maschinelle Registererstellung, Metadaten, Multimedial, Objekt-orientiert, Register, Relational, Struktur, Volltextspeicherung, Wörterbucherstellung

The second example is taken from the German thesaurus *INFODATA* (INFODATA Thesaurus 2000) with a thematic spectrum similar to the *ASIST Thesaurus*. As initial entity, the descriptor *Dokumentationssprache*[78] was chosen. Table 9.3 shows the corresponding related terms by varying path length.

Once more, it can be argued by chosing descriptor trails that generally no conceptual clusters with sharp borders can be formed.

Such compositions of related terms with higher edge length could be specified for each thesaurus, while the main statement would not be affected. Associative trails are to be interpreted cognitively. With increasing length of the path the conceptual relationship between the entities becomes random. This arbitrariness cannot be reconciled with the notion of a transitive inference.

9.2.3 Typification of Associative Relationships

From the arguments given above we can conclude that inferences along associative paths of level 2 or more require a formal characterization of each edge to be usable for such a process. It may be helpful to base this formal designation on a content property that leads to a typing of associative relationships. In this way, we obtain a formal argument to replace the non-specific associative relationships by an inventory of typed relations. As a consequence of such an approach it can already be stated that the typed relations have a directionality and can formally no longer be regarded as symmetrical.

It has been mentioned that each field of application allows to derive a spectrum of typed relationships. Accordingly, it is necessary to develop an inventory that contains a limited number of types and that is as independent as possible from the respective field of application. In Section 8.1, a proposal for such an inventory was introduced, cf. Table 8.6.

Let us take a closer look at the above example of associative relationships in the *ASIST Thesaurus*. By applying the inventory of our proposal we have derived a spectrum of relations:

- *Component / condition*
- *Method*
- *Application (Activity)*
- *Application (Automatic process)*
- *Application (Tool)*
- *Application (Product)*
- *User (Person)*

---

78 This descriptor corresponds to *index language, indexing language, documentation language* or *documentary language*. To preserve the authenticity of the example, we present the descriptors only in their German form.

- *User (Institution)*
- *Subject field, area of application, reference range*

We have limited our approach to such relationships that center around cognitively interpreted factual aspects of the concepts involved. We are not primarily interested in relationships that can be established by time or statistical coincidences between persons, institutions, events, and subject matters. Arranging the related terms according to this spectrum, we get the compilation of Table 9.4. Through analysis of existing relationships, however, still visible context in the thesaurus cannot be reproduced in our compilation. For example, *Classification* is understood in the compilation as an activity and not as a product or resource, *Image databases* is understood as a prerequisite and not as product, *Automatic classification* is understood as a method rather than automatic process. These contextual references must be specified differently where appropriate.

Tab. 9.4: Assignment of descriptors of the *ASIST Thesaurus* to typed relations.

Component / condition	Categories Images Image databases Data presentation
Method	Automatic classification Cluster analysis Co-occurence analysis Automatic categorization Image analysis Computational linguistics Computational lexicography Knowledge representation Domain analysis Information retrieval Relevance ranking Probabilistic indexing
Application (Activity)	Content based indexing Image indexing Classification

Application (Automatic process)	Image retrieval Machine aided indexing Information processing Information technology Natural language processing Full text searching Text processing
Application (Tool)	Ontologies
Application (Product)	Natural language interfaces
User (Person)	Information scientists
User (Institution)	Information science education
Subject field, area of application, reference range	Information science Cognitive science Computer science Cybernetics Librarianship Linguistics

This approach was the basis of our discussion in Section 8.3.2. Generally, it will be of interest whether this approach is suitable for a transitive inference along the paths of typed relationships. An answer cannot be given yet, as it requires more studies and experiments.

9.3 Inferences by Combining Different Types of Relationships

Let us now consider the case that the paths of differently typed relations are composed for drawing inferences. In general, one cannot expect that transitive inferences are possible in this case. Thus we have to distinguish individual cases from each other.

9.3.1 Synonymy Relation with Hierarchical Relationships

What is interesting is the case of transition from synonymy to hierarchical relationships. Only in this case, the special function of the access vocabulary can be considered. A reverse connection is not feasible in the case of classical indexing languages, as descriptors may not be associated with non-descriptors. It can be assumed that the combination between synonymy and any form of hierarchical relationships will be transitive if our considerations for the definition of synonyms in Section 9.1.3 are observed. The aforementioned practice of formal knowledge representation to regard synonyms as equivalent entities (cf. our remarks at the end of Section 9.1.3) should not be considered further at this point.

9.3.2 Chronological Relation with Hierarchical Relationships

For the transitions from a chronological structure into a hierarchical structure, transitive inheritances are given because of the transitive initial situation of both types of relationships. Precondition here is that the participating chronological structures have an identical direction of the time arrow.

9.3.3 Transitions from Associative Relationships to a Hierarchical Structure

With Figure 9.16, let us consider that a transition from an associative relationship to a hierarchical structure takes place.

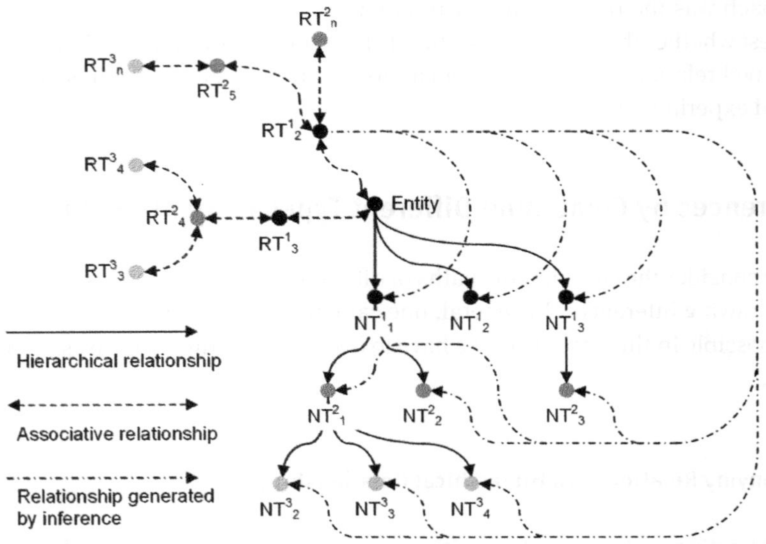

Fig. 9.16: Transition from associative relationships to a hierarchical structure.

Since the transitive inheritance is given for the hierarchical structure, the process of closure formation can be extended from the initial associative relation to the hierarchical structure. Therefore, the entities of the initial associative relation have to be connected in a reasonable conceptual context.

9.3.4 Transitions from a Hierarchical Structure to Associative Relationships

Figure 9.17 shows the reverse case, i.e., the transition from a hierarchical structure to associative relationships.

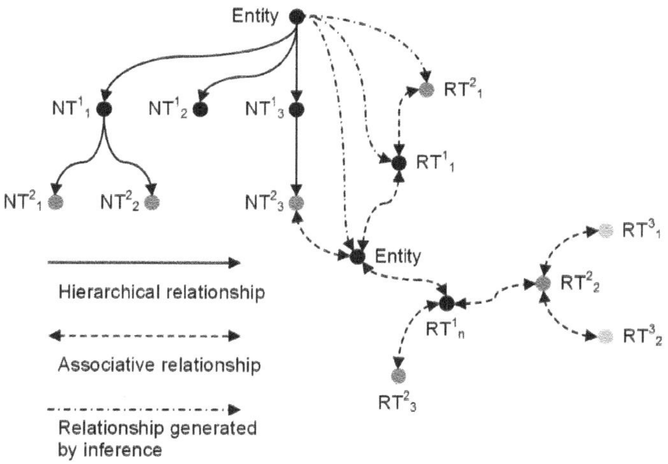

Fig. 9.17: Transitions from a hierarchical structure to associative relationships.

In general, no inheritance can be expected for this transition from the hierarchical structure to the relationships of an unspecified associative structure. It must be left open for the time being whether this statement can be modified by replacing the unspecific associative relationships with typed ones.

We summarize our previous considerations in tabular form[79]. As a means for structured representation we use the inventory of relations proposed in Table 8.6 in Section 8.1. The result is shown in Table 9.5 for the case of combining the same type of relations and in Table 9.6 for the case of combining different types of hierarchical relationships. We refrain from giving examples for each case. Such examples can easily be derived from the given or other material.

---

79 For this analysis and compilation we used some additional references: Cruse (2002), Pribbenow (2002), Weller & Peters (2008).

Tab. 9.5: Transitivity in case of same type of relations.

Type of relation	Relation 1	Relation 2	Transitivity
Equivalence	Synonym	Synonym	O
Hierarchy	Abstraction, generic context	Abstraction, generic context	+
	Whole / Part	Whole / Part	+
	Abstraction, generic context	Whole / Part	-
	Whole / Part	Abstraction, generic context	-
Chronological context	Earlier / Later	Earlier / Later	+
	Later / Earlier	Later / Earlier	+
	Earlier / Later	Later / Earlier	-
	Later / Earlier	Earlier / Later	-
Association	Unspecific assoziation	Unspecific assoziation	-
	Raw material / product	Raw material / product	+
	Causality (cause – effect)	Causality (cause – effect)	+
	Person as actor / action	Person as actor / action	-
	Institution as actor / action	Institution as actor / action	-
	Person as actor / product	Person as actor / product	-
	Institution as actor / product	Institution as actor / product	-
	Action/ product	Action/ product	-

+: Transitivity is given
-: Transitivity cannot be expected
O: Not allowed for classical indexing languages

Tab. 9.6: Transitivity in case of different types of hierarchical relationships.

Type of relation	Relation 1	Relation 2	Transitivity
Hierarchy	Synonym	Abstraction, generic context	+
	Synonym	Whole / Part	+
	Abstraction, generic context	Synonym	O
	Whole / Part	Synonym	O
Chronological context	Synonym	Earlier / Later	+
	Synonym	Later / Earlier	+
	Earlier / Later	Synonym	O
	Later / Earlier	Synonym	O
	Abstraction, generic context	Earlier / Later	+
	Abstraction, generic context	Later / Earlier	+
	Earlier / Later	Abstraction, generic context	+
	Later / Earlier	Abstraction, generic context	+
	Whole / Part	Earlier / Later	+
	Whole / Part	Later / Earlier	+
	Earlier / Later	Whole / Part	+
	Later / Earlier	Whole / Part	+

+: Transitivity is given
-: Transitivity cannot be expected
O: Not allowed for classical indexing languages

9.3.5 Transitivity for Combinations of Typed Associative Relationships

As mentioned before, in general, no inheritance of transitivity can be expected for combinations of unspecified associative structures. We also left the statement open whether this proposition can be modified by replacing the unspecific associative relationships by typed ones. We can say, however, that inference statements are possible for the combination of typed relations with hierarchical relationships. Table 9.7 presents a survey of the combinations of types of relations allowing a transitive inheritance. We have compiled only those cases that yield a positive statement for transitive continuation. There may be additional cases that would complete the list.

Tab. 9.7: Transitivity for combinations of typed associative relationships.

Type of relation	Relation 1	Relation 2	Transitivity
Association	Unspecific assoziation	Abstraction, generic context	+
	Unspecific assoziation	Whole / Part	+
	Unspecific assoziation	Earlier / Later	+
	Raw material / product	Abstraction, generic context	+
	Raw material / product	Whole / Part	+
	Raw material / product	Earlier / Later	+
	Action/ product	Abstraction, generic context	+
	Action/ product	Whole / Part	+
	Action/ product	Earlier / Later	+
	Person as actor / action	Abstraction, generic context	+
	Person as actor / action	Whole / Part	+
	Person as actor / action	Earlier / Later	+
	Institution as actor / action	Abstraction, generic context	+
	Institution as actor / action	Whole / Part	+
	Institution as actor / action	Earlier / Later	+
	Causality (cause – effect)	Abstraction, generic context	+
	Causality (cause – effect)	Whole / Part	+
	Causality (cause – effect)	Earlier / Later	+
	Person as actor / product	Abstraction, generic context	+
	Person as actor / product	Whole / Part	+
	Person as actor / product	Earlier / Later	+
	Institution as actor / product	Abstraction, generic context	+
	Institution as actor / product	Whole / Part	+
	Institution as actor / product	Earlier / Later	+

If for special use cases or by other conditions the formal properties of entities and relations are known in detail, results could be derived that may not be regarded as generally valid. This should be the subject of appropriate investigations.

We can state as an evaluation that there are more cases of transitivity along paths of conceptual relationships than only along the hierarchical relation. This could be a sufficient stimulus for increasing the use of formal modeling techniques for the design documentation of languages. On the basis of the current state of knowledge, we cannot provide a complete list of transitivity properties, this remains a desire for further research. Furthermore, it shall be noted that definitive statements about the benefits for retrieval processes can only be made on real document collections after implementation of appropriate functionalities and tests.

In the next section we will no longer consider only individual information systems. Rather, we want to expand the focus to the consideration of heterogeneous information environments.

10 Semantic Interoperability and Inferences

Problems of establishing conceptual interoperability between entities of different indexing languages or between entities and indexates have already been considered in Section 6.2. Within this context, first criteria were given for establishing forms of semantic interoperability that can be understood as conceptual exchangeability between entities and indexates. We will now enhance these considerations by the aspects of inference and typed relations as introduced in Chapters 8 and 9 and thereby look for conclusions that can be drawn for designing interoperability scenarios for heterogenous information environments. Once more, we will set the focus of our considerations to context-oriented issues and not to technical procedures.

10.1 Conditions for Entity-based Interoperability

A treatment of content understanding interoperability cannot ignore the issue, how to note that two entities have the same conceptual meaning. This was done extensively in Section 6.2.3. As important conclusion of the discussion we must accept that every real world concept has by definition its own meaning which cannot be shared by any other concept identically. An understanding of true conceptual exchangeability can therefore not be derived from real world observations but only within the special settings of benefits expected of task-oriented tools. We can carry out our analysis of content-related equality only for entities that are used as representatives of concepts contained in knowledge representations.

Therefore we cannot do otherwise, but to focus all our discussion on the entities as elements of knowledge representations. A treatment of built indexates may suffer from their clarity of their syntactical structure. If constructed by using explicit syntactical connectors, interoperability statements can be based on an analysis of the entities and connectors. We have already discussed this approach in Section 6.2.4. If constructed with hidden syntax elements, especially if containing pre-combined parts, a treatment is out of scope of the present discussion.

With respect to our former discussion and with additionally regard to typed relations and inferences, we can specify the following criteria for determining the conceptual identity of different entities to be used for indexing and retrieval:

- the entities have the same conceptual content and constituent features
- the entities have the same conceptual extent
- the entities have the same relationships to other concepts
- the entities include the same near synonyms
- the entities are used identically

Determining the equality of conceptual entities requires an appreciation of the context and the conceptual analysis of possible aspect views, usually derived from the modeled structure of a knowledge representation. When speaking about the possible benefit of typed relations for retrieval processes in Chapter 8, we already mentioned this aspect and gave examples.

The most extensive constraint for interoperability would be to require conceptual identity of various entities in fulfilling all the above criteria. The more criteria are omitted or used in diluted form, the less the resulting interoperability determination will support the intended benefits of a wishful enhancement of building result sets with tolerable accuracy. This is most evident if only the last criterion is used, a criterion, on which most often the preparation of concordances is based.

At first glance, it is not easy to imagine a connection between the extreme positions. However, a consistent description of the different positions must be found as part of the modeling process if conceptual knowledge representation should support search processes by machine inferences. In any case, one expects a contribution to the heterogeneity treatment of inhomogeneously indexed document collections from measures for the production of interoperability.

It is common practice to start with multiple representations of knowledge, whose entities are considered from the point of interchangeability or common processability. For justification of this point of view, we will give a quote from *ISO 25964-2* (2013, 6):

> Mapping is the key step in the usual mechanism for achieving interoperability. If each of the concepts in Vocabulary A has been mapped to the corresponding concept(s) in Vocabulary B, it becomes possible to interchange (or augment) the terms or identifiers representing the concept in each of the vocabularies.

For a better understanding of the mapping problem, it is useful to remember that there is already a form of interoperability between the entities of *one* indexing language: the problem of *near synonyms*. We already discussed this problem in Section 8.1.3 and refer to the previously given arguments, for the visualization especially to Figure 8.5. The different treatment of near synonymous terms has consequences for building retrieval results:

If near synonyms are treated as synonyms, the result set may contain ballast in the form of unprecise hits with respect to the search interest. The reason for this phenomenon is the merging of the conceptual differences of each near synonym for the purpose of representing the sum of meanings by one preferred term of the indexing language. The search process consists of one single step.

In the case of treatment of associative relationships, the result sets have less ballast. Each related term can represent the semantic variety more precisely and has more discriminative power. The search process involves several steps.

We refer to an example given in Section 6.1 for making interoperability statements, cf. Table 6.1 and Figure 6.1. This example can be seen as a prototype for problems to be solved in this context. Three concepts

- *Library*
- *Public library*
- *Documentation center*

were treated as near synonyms respectively as descriptors of two fictitious thesauri. The discussion of this example has shown that considering merely the context-independent meaning of entities is not sufficient in terms of interoperability. The relationships of entities within the structure of each knowledge representation must also be considered, since these relationships provide a major contribution to the meaning of the entities within the structure of their respective knowledge representation.

Let us now consider the problem of content-oriented semantic interoperability from a general perspective. This means, we are interested in solutions of how entities that are considered to be conceptually interoperable can be used for a combined search process without having to accept decrease for the precision of the results.

We want to distinguish between two *interoperability models* (Glossary E4) for content-oriented preparation of interoperability[80].

The first model – we call it the *reference model* of semantic interoperability – (Glossary E4.1) is oriented at the classical function of indexes and connects an access vocabulary to the structured representation of the terms within an indexing language. In this model the interoperability of entities of two different knowledge representations is established by reference from an entity of the first knowledge representation to an entity of the second knowledge representation. The entities are not postulated to be conceptually exchangeable. The access vocabulary can be sorted alphabetically or based on a content structure. We have indicated this in Figure 10.1.

80 ISO 25964-2 speaks additionally of a third model. Meant by this are translations of vocabularies without any concern to their structure (ISO 25964-2 (2013), 7).

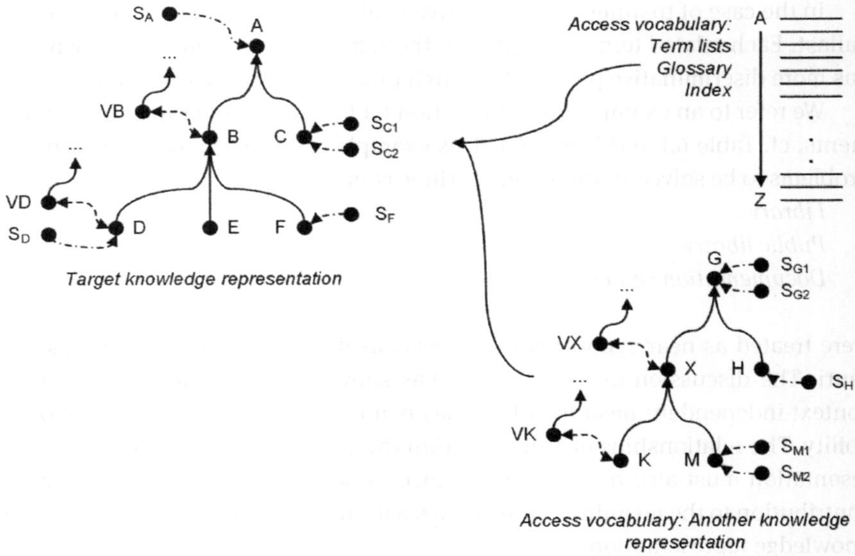

Fig. 10.1: The reference model of semantic interoperability.

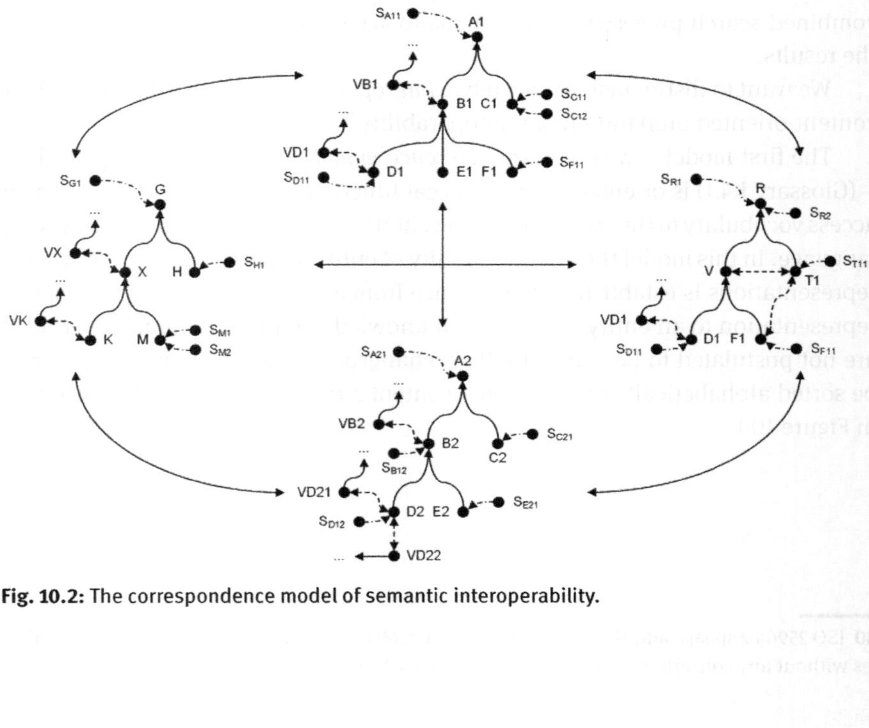

Fig. 10.2: The correspondence model of semantic interoperability.

It is characteristic for this model that no claim is raised, the elements of the access vocabulary would be semantically equivalent to the entities which they refer to. The access vocabulary has only uni-directional reference character.

In contrast, the second model – we call it the *correspondence model* – postulates a bi-directional interchangeability of various entities of indexing languages considered to be interoperable (Glossary E4.2). We illustrate this concept in Figure 10.2.

Presumption of the model is the task of formation of a hit for a search query. In this case the concept of a bi-directional interoperability is based on the idea to be able to automatically pass from one entity to the others considered as interoperable or to be able to use them together for a query formulation.

We will give once more a quote from *ISO 25964-2* (2013, 7):

> The non-equivalent pairs model addresses linkages between two vocabularies that do not share the same structure. [...] Direct mappings should be established between some or all of the concepts of one vocabulary and those of the other. The objective of the mappings is to help users to find information in a collection that has been indexed with one of the vocabularies, starting from a search statement that uses terms or notations from a different vocabulary.

In the context of our discussions we want to regard interoperability as an inference process. The formation of a result set by connecting entities of different knowledge representations should be seen as a reasoning process. This process not only takes the entities into account, but also includes the respective knowledge structures. It must be emphasized once more that we understand semantic interoperability as content-oriented and not only as presumptions for a technical process. The aim is to generate document sets by means of inference processes not just to enlarge the set of search results, but to improve the retrieval quality.

We want to search for content-oriented criteria for a semantic interchangeability of entities within the structural context of different indexing languages. In the following, we present some examples starting with a section of an indexing language as shown in Figure 10.3.

The entities $A, \dots, K$ are connected by hierarchical relationships. Some entities have synonymous terms (e.g. S_A -> A) or have associative relationships to other entities (e.g. VB <-> B, VD <-> D). Latter entities are linked to hierarchical connections for their part again. The conceptual context of an entity – i.e. the sum of their relationships to other entities – should be considered for their content-oriented understanding.

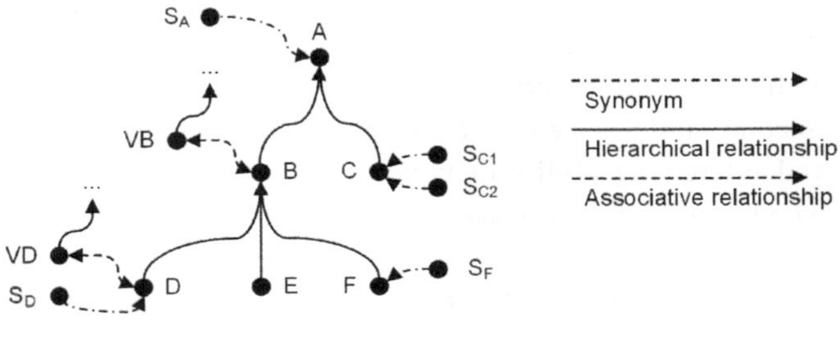

Fig. 10.3: Structural excerpt from an indexing language.

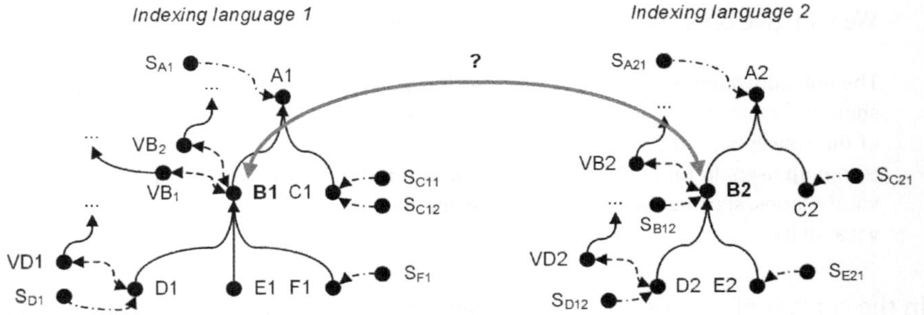

Fig. 10.4: Structural excerpt from two different indexing languages.

Starting from Figure 10.3 we want to consider two different structures for the included entities, as shown in Figure 10.4. All entities with a same letter should be named identically and are considered as context-independent and therefore not distinguishable.

Once more we have to find an answer to the question whether the entities *B1* and *B2* can be considered as semantically interoperable or not.

Formally speaking, we only know by our assumptions that *B1* and *B2* have the same name and cannot be distinguished context-independently. A more detailed answer to our question can therefore only be expected from a structural analysis. In doing so, we will try to identify maximal example-independent aspects. The following points can be specified:

- *B1* is hierarchically subordinate to *A1*, has three narrower concepts *D1, E1, F1* and two related concepts $VB1_1$, $VB1_2$;
- *B2* is hierarchically subordinate to *B1*, has two narrower concepts *D2, E2*, one related concept *VB2* and one synonym SB_2 as access term.

We get no direct evidence for a content-oriented identity of *B1* with *B2* from these observations. Rather, arguments can be seen that *B1* and *B2* are not equivalent by contents. The answer is left for an intellectual analysis and evaluation with subsequent decision that occurs possibly within the framework of a defaulted criterion catalog and can approve different types of an agreement.

We are in partial accordance with statements of *ISO 25964-2* (2013, 10–11):

> [...] establishing equivalence across vocabularies is far from straightforward. The mapping of concepts is complicated by the different languages that different people employ in discourse. [...] the following degrees of equivalence are often encountered: a) exact [...], b) inexact [...], c) partial [...], d) non-equivalence.

However, we must accept the objection that the criteria are not sufficiently clear-cut to describe different degrees of semantic interoperability and that they are not sufficiently oriented towards the structural preconditions.

Nevertheless, it can be seen that an *interconnection* of the two structures in terms of technical interoperability can bring benefits. We have already discussed such benefits in Chapter 5 by discussing different scenarios for heterogeneity treatment.

If it became evident that the determination of interoperability by aiming at semantic identity is difficult, one should look for other ways of interpreting semantic interoperability. This does not necessarily lead to the notion of functional interchangeability of entities in the sense that they are shared in the formation of result sets.

If, for example, both structures were organized at different depths, it may be desirable that a transition from one structure to the other opens new opportunities for conceptual navigation and making inferences about the hierarchical structure, as shown in Figure 10.5. The transition can be accomplished by a one-way connection and does not have to follow the paradigm of a bi-directional interchangeability.

In this sense, the interoperable connection from *B2* to *B1* would mean that

- the navigation within the *indexing language 2*, starting from the entity *B2*, can be extended to a navigation within the *indexing language 1* with the starting point *B1*,
- a query that leads firstly to the transitive closure of *B2* as a result – the set {*B2*, *D2*, *E2*} – can be extended to the transitive closure of *B1* – that is, the set {*B1*, *D1*, *E1*, *F1*, *G1*, *H1*, *K1*}, cf. Figure 9.6.

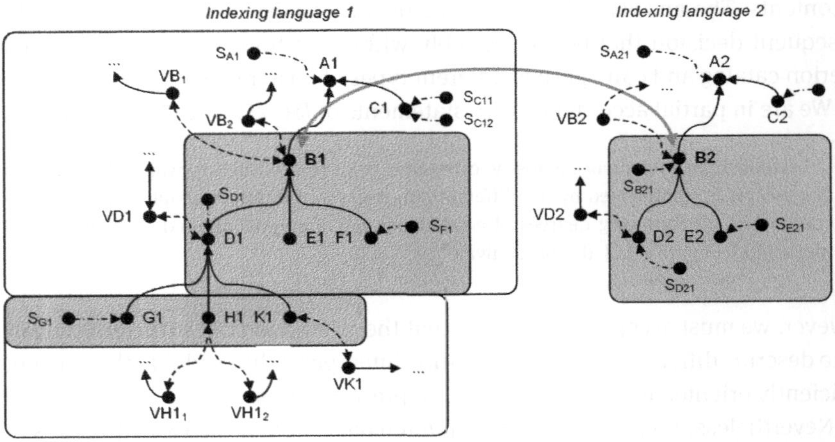

Fig. 10.5: Structural connection of indexing languages with access vocabulary and hierarchical expansion.

10.2 Models of Semantic Interoperability

Now we want to consider the question whether models of semantic interoperability can be formulated that ensure search processes with common use of entities of different knowledge representations. Aims should not be oriented at a trivial linked data interpretation. We want to consider the content-related correspondence with respect to both a context-independent interpretation and the existence of different contextual structures.

10.2.1 Ontological Spine and Satellite Ontologies

One possible approach consists of designing a core system surrounded by a number of satellite systems. This pathway has been proposed in different detailed forms in different places (Nicholson et al. 2006, Dunsire & Nicholson 2010)[81] and has been included in *ISO 25964-2*. We quote (2013, 8):

> When more than two vocabularies are required to interoperate, management of the possible combinations becomes complex. It is often convenient to designate one of the vocabularies as the backbone, or basic structure to which each of the subsidiary vocabularies is mapped.

81 Cf. also discussion in Section 5.3.3, especially the presentation of the *HILT* project.

> [...] Using this model, each concept in the backbone vocabulary should be mapped to the corresponding concept(s) in the other vocabularies.

Our proposal makes an extension to these ideas by additionally considering typed relations in compliance with localization[82] aspects (Gödert 2008, Gödert 2010a, Gödert 2010b). This approach is well-known from other contexts, such as software engineering, understood as an adaptation of computer software for non-native environments, especially other nations and cultures or the process of translating a product into different languages or adapting a language for a specific country or region. This understanding is insufficient for our purposes. Our idea of localization is not only translating a concept into different languages or adapting a language for a specific country or region but also the *representation of concepts and their semantic relations for their native environments, especially other cultures, history, or nations with their political and social structures*. We provide selected examples of such areas:

- *Historical evolutions and relationships*
- *Ethnic issues*
- *Religious topics*
- *Legal issues*
- *National organization forms and principles*
- *Social structures*
- *Political structures*
- *Education and educational system*
- *Cultural everyday topics (sports, household, hobby, customs, ...)*
- *Fauna and flora*

Let such issues now be included in indexing languages, however, usually without design intent and therefore usually not represented in explicit form.

We take up an example that has already been discussed in Section 6.1.2, but will consider it now from the viewpoint of localization. It compares the entries of *Legislation* and *Gesetzgebung* from the *Library of Congress Subject Headings (LCSH)* and the *Schlagwortnormdatei (SWD)* with their respective narrower terms in each of the controlled vocabularies. The hierarchical structure for each heading is reproduced in Figure 10.6.

82 We already introduced the concept *localization* in Section 5.2.

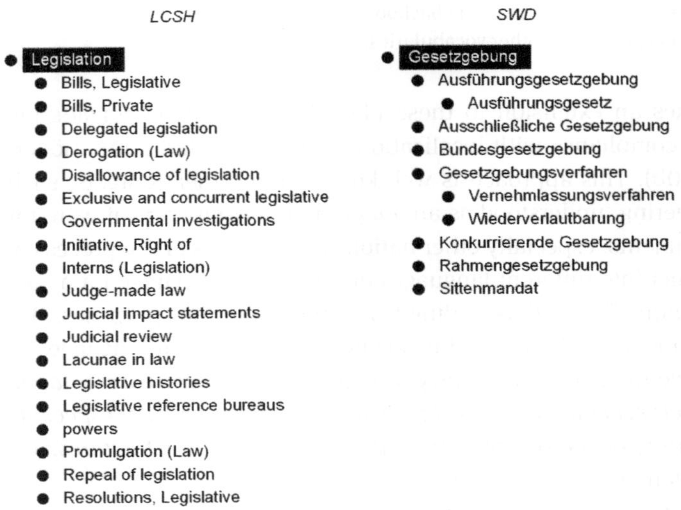

Fig. 10.6: The subject heading *legislation* (*Gesetzgebung*) in its hierarchical structure in the *SWD* and the *LCSH*.

Is it possible to make a determination whether *Legislation* and *Gesetzgebung* can be considered as semantically interoperable? Neither *SWD* nor *LCSH* provide comprehensive information about a contextual understanding of *Gesetzgebung* and *legislation* including a consideration of near synonyms. Once more, it must be emphasized that a contextual interpretation is undispensible, even more if aspects of localization have to be considered. Figure 6.2 has shown the respective environment for each heading, we will not repeat it here.

Even though the relational structure is poorly elaborated in both vocabularies, one can recognize significant differences originating from the respective procedures for establishing legal acts in both national environments. If on the one hand *Legislation* and *Legislative process* are seen as synonyms (*LCSH*), on the other hand *Gesetzgebung* and *Gesetzgebungsverfahren* are modeled as broader term / narrower term (*SWD*), the questions posed before emerge again: Does this form of structural difference imply semantic difference or is it justified to speak of *legislation* and *Gesetzgebung* as being semantically equivalent?

The example finds its parallel in another example of the headings for the constitutional system, the systems of government and public offices: *Prime ministers, Presidents, Heads of state* in the *LCSH*; *Regierungschef, Deutschland / Bundeskanzler, Präsident, Staatsoberhaupt, Staatspräsident* in the *SWD*. As the entries of Figure 10.7 show, influences for the conceptual structures can be seen that have their origin in the respective state constitutions, a typical characteristic for localization.

LCSH

Prime ministers
TT Public officers
Executive power
Statesmen
UF *Chancellors (Prime ministers)*
Premiers
BT Cabinet officers
Heads of state
NT Ex-prime ministers
Mothers of prime ministers
Women prime ministers
RAMEAU Chefs de gouvernement

Presidents
TT Executive power
Statesmen
CC JF255
UF *Presidency*
BT Heads of State
NT Children of presidents
Ex-presidents
Fathers of presidents
Generals as presidents
Grandchildren of presidents
Mothers of presidents
Women presidents
RT Executive power
RAMEAU Présidents

Presidents
TT Executive power
Statesmen
CC JF251
UF *Heads of government*
Rulers
State, Heads of
BT Executive power
Statesmen
NT Caliphs
Children of heads of state
Dictators
Emperors
Kings and rulers
Mothers of heads of state
Offenses against foreign heads of state
Offenses against heads of state
Presidents
Prime ministers
Prytanes
Regents
Women heads of state
RAMEAU Chefs d'État

SWD

Regierungschef
CC 8.2a
UF *Ministerpräsident*
Premierminister
NT Kabinettsprinzip
Kanzlersystem
Staatskanzlei
RT Regierungschefin

Deutschland / Regierungschef
USE Deutschland / Bundeskanzler

Deutschland / Bundeskanzler
CC 8.2a
UF *Bundeskanzler / Deutschland*
Deutschland / Regierungschef
CF Deutschland <Bundesrepublik>
Bundeskanzler

Präsident
CC 8.2a
NT Staatspräsident
Stadtpräsident
RT Expräsident
Präsidentin

Staatsoberhaupt
CC 8.2a
RT Staatspräsident

Staatspräsident
TT Präsident
CC 8.1
BT Präsident
RT Präsidiales Regierungssystem
Staatsoberhaupt

Fig. 10.7: Subject headings on the topic *Government* (*Regierungsformen*) in the *SWD* und the *LCSH.*

It is difficult to establish a complete conceptual correspondence between individual subject headings. However, it is conceivable that a change between both systems is desirable in order to access specialized facts represented by the respective localized structure. For fulfillment of this desire, the entities need not be semantically interoperable. They must only be linked in the sense of a reference and target vocabulary.

If indexing languages contain the issues we have summarized under localization aspects, they are worth not to fall victim to a crosswalk. Instead, they should be preserved and made available for dedicated forms of retrieval processes. Correspondingly, we are looking for a suitable way that permits to realize visions of semantic interoperability for knowledge representations expressing multi-lingual, multi-national, or multi-disciplinary contents.

One possible approach consists of a combination of a key system – we call it *ontological spine* – with localized systems where the local perspectives are decoupled from the key system and added back to the localized systems. Each of the localized systems can take the circumstances, aspects and structuring of their respective area-specific localization better into account than one system could do by considering localized issues randomly (Gödert 2008). A model of this idea is given by the illustration of Figure 10.8.

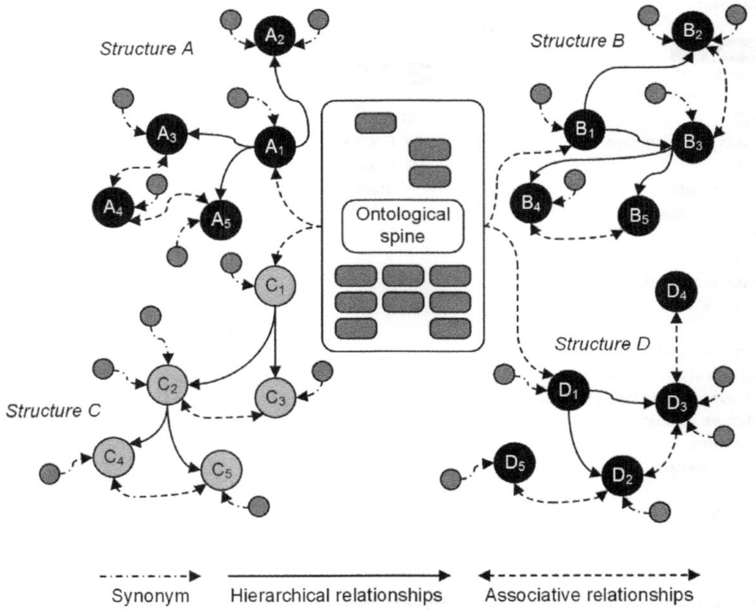

Fig. 10.8: Ontological spine with localized networks as semantic satellites.

Between the key system and the satellites mutual transitions are producible that provide access to the different perspectives of localization systems in a particular way for a particular question. This means that both differentiated contexts can specifically be queried and possibly unknown relationships can be explored. The above-mentioned facts on the legislative process in various countries can serve as an example. It is not necessary to be familiar with all the details of research in each localized structures. It only depends on the appropriate connections between entities of the core system and entities of localized systems. We illustrate in Figure 10.9 the junction between a key system without any localized issues and various localized satellite structures for the example *legislation*. An index-based access is possible to the ontological spine (2) or to one of the localized satellites (1). Each of these systems provides the transition to the spine. The spine likewise provides transition to all localized satellites. Thus, the distinctive structure of each of the satellites can be used for a search.

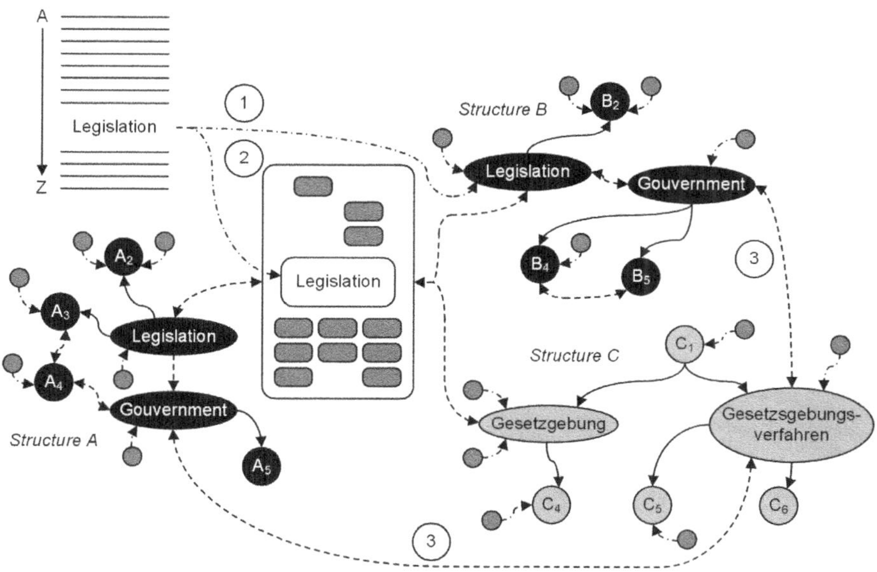

Fig. 10.9: Ontological spine with localized satellites for the example *Legislation* (*Gesetzgebung*) and *Government* (*Regierungsformen*).

In addition to the transitions between the localized satellites and the key system one can think of further connections between the satellites that are deemed necessary or useful, e.g. (3). The necessity or desirability of such connections should be tested in each case. The preceding discussion of content-oriented semantic interoperability taking into account the structural relationships has shown the problems of such an approach. In general, it can be said that uni-directional references offer better conditions for the production of semantically transparent structures than visions for the creation of bi-directional connections. It shall be mentioned again that content-oriented equivalence between the entities of two indexing languages is impossible if localization aspects are built-in parts of the structure. In existing indexing languages, especially the so-called pre-combined indexing languages, this is often the case. The separation into a key system as an ontological spine and a number of explicitly localized satellite systems would replace existing semantic equivalence by the definition of uni-directional transitions between the systems.

10.2.2 Degrees of Determinacy and Interoperability

From such uni-directional connections retrieval operations can be derived in many ways. In Section 7.3.3 we introduced the *degrees of determinacy* as a special form of uni-directional typed relations. This instrument is a result of methodological approaches that have been developed in the *CrissCross* project for the enrichment of the Relative Index of the German edition of the *DDC* by entries from the German *Schlagwortnormdatei (SWD)*. It shows how typed relations between entities of knowledge representations can be used for the production of a content-oriented semantic interoperability in heterogeneous information environments.

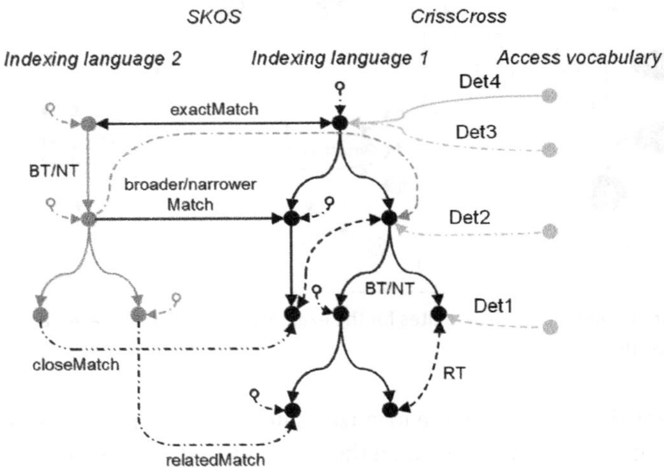

Fig. 10.10: Comparison of *SKOS* relations with *degrees of determinacy*.

We intend to take up the discussion again and first illustrate in Figure 10.10 the differences for connecting entities of an *indexing language 1* with entities of an *indexing language 2* in bi-directional manner using *SKOS* relations on the left hand side[83]. On the right hand side we illustrate the uni-directional connection of an access vocabulary with the entities of *indexing language 1* using the degrees of determinacy

We will generalize the interpretation of the degrees of determinacy (Glossary E3.2.5) to the general situation of connecting access vocabulary elements with entities of a knowledge representation. Thereby, we want to clarify the role of degrees of determinacy as design elements for interoperability issues. The apportionment of this differentiation process, which is applied into four stages in the following, can be adapted depending on the given modeling situation.

Degree of determinacy 4

The connotation scope of the term from the access vocabulary is identical to the connotation scope of the entity from the knowledge representation, i.e. it also has the same thematic context.

Degree of determinacy 3

The connotation scope of the term from the access vocabulary is identical or nearly identical to the connotation scope of the entity from the knowledge representation.

Degree of determinacy 2

The connotation scope of the term from the access vocabulary is identical or nearly identical to the connotation scope of a concept that can be seen logically as part of an entity from the knowledge representation but is less extensive in scope.

Degree of determinacy 1

The connotation scope of the term from the access vocabulary corresponds to a small part to the connotation scope of the entity from the knowledge representation.

---

83 For a short summary of *SKOS* essentials we refer to Section 3.2.2.

To select a degree of determinacy, contents considerations are required that take the context and the particular aspects of entities and reference terms into account. These considerations are similar to those for determining typed relations. However, these typological aspects are not explicitly expressed and therefore cannot be evaluated by machine processing. Benefit for a retrieval process can be derived by two ways. One way uses the degrees themselves as filters for generating result sets. As a second way, the user or the machine may use the numeric scale for a ranking of the document sets. Thus, the approach to use degrees of determinacy for representing semantic coupling by numerical figures, methodically takes an intermediate position in the spectrum of methods to enable machine-usability of content-oriented semantic statements. Even without going the elaborate way of using an inventory of typed relation expressing the semantic connections of entities, superficial equivalences can be avoided.

10.2.3 Entity-based Interoperability and Facets

We consider at last the ideal case of localized satellites that are connected with a faceted key system, in which the entities are organized hierarchically by different facets and associated with entities of other facets by typed relationships. We then obtain the generalization of the situation already discussed in Section 6.2.2. We give an illustration in Figure 10.11.

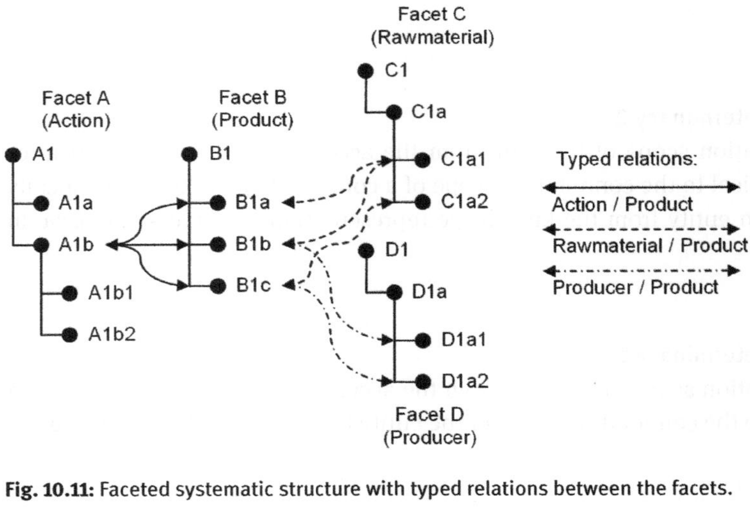

Fig. 10.11: Faceted systematic structure with typed relations between the facets.

The entities may be understood both as part of a vocabulary for performing searches as well as a means to restricting conditions regarding the relationships between them.

For a better comprehension of the abstract situation, we give an example with concrete contents:

Action = {baking}
Product = {baked goods, bread, cake, pie
Raw material = {flour, water, salt, leaven, butter, eggs, milk, cream}
Producer = {baker, confectioner}

It is easy to derive concrete statements from the abstract structures of the modeling, for example:

Baked goods that are created by the confectioner
Baked goods from flour, water and leaven that are created by the baker

Thinking of these two statements as search statements it becomes clear that the semantic differences between them must affect the particular search results.

In the following, we summarize the properties of our model of a faceted ontological spine and localized satellite systems with typed relationships:

- The structure of the ontological spine consists only of hierarchical relationships. To ensure the transitivity of reasoning, the entities are arranged in facets.
- Localization aspects are represented only in the respective satellites.
- The ontological spine can serve as an introduction to topics of a satellite system if language and localization are not familiar.
- The entities of the satellites function as an access vocabulary for the entities and the structure of the ontological spine.
- Typed relations can be established between the entities of the ontological spine and the localized satellites.
- Direct connections between the various entities of different localized satellites by typed relations are possible, but require more detailed design in terms of its formal properties. A direct content-oriented semantic correspondence is not implied.
- Further satellites (in other languages) can easily be connected to the ontological spine, without affecting existing localized satellites or the connection with the spine.
- The entities and the relationships between them can be interpreted both cognitive and by machine.

- The formal properties of the relationships between the entities are precisely determined, so that the spectrum of possible inferences along the edges of the network becomes transparent.
- By combining faceted structuring of entities, cross-faceted typed relations and inferences along suitable edges, retrieval conditions can be formulated which otherwise could be achieved only by using methods of syntactic indexing and their dedicated indexing languages. Thereby it is not necessary that all entities were assigned to the documents as indexing results.

10.3 Perspective: Ontology-based Indexing and Retrieval

We have just assembled all the requirements to give an appraisal of our model and to address the differences to the traditional model of indexing and information retrieval. The model we propose is called *ontology-based indexing and retrieval*. For an illustration we refer to Figure 7.1 at the beginning of the Chapter 7. As a matter of course this model is far from being completely developed and well matured. The proposal is rather an attempt to present first contours. It consists of a combination of different components. First of all, it is based on the usual idea which can be summarized as follows.

Generally speaking, indexing assigns certain features in the form of character strings to documents or data records. If indexing is done by an intellectual process, these features are commonly the entities of a knowledge representation. Meanwhile methods are well-known that assign entities of an indexing language by an automated process, generally with inferior content-oriented quality. Our main reference goes to methods of intellectual indexing. We assume that the differences of automated procedures do not need to be explained separately. Therefore the character strings are indexed entities from indexing languages or more generally from knowledge representations, the entities themselves represent objects or concepts which in turn are characterized by the properties and characteristics. The common presence of properties or characteristics makes it possible to establish different forms of relationships between the entities. These relationships can be used by machine inferences for the design of search operations, complementing the intellectual selection of entities.

A complementary description for information retrieval reads as follows. Retrieval processes use these assigned character strings as features for selection and for the formation of result sets for search queries. By linguistic manipulations word variants can be used successfully for a search query. If the character strings are indexed entities from indexing languages or more generally from knowledge representations, the entities can therefore be described as properties of documents that are used for the purpose of filtering by processing the query. The choice of the entities is usually based on the content-related search interests and is done via an intellectual process. As we have discussed, the search process can be supported by automated analyses of the conceptual structures of the knowledge representation for including more entities in the process of generating result sets, e.g.:

- Performing query expansion by including synonyms within a conceptual aspect.
- Inferences about the paths of hierarchical relationships (search-down / explosion / expand / drill-down).
- Boolean operations on two or more search terms with inferences from hierarchical structures to represent complex search queries.

Ambitious indexing approaches attempt to improve the findability of documents by assigning the representatives of a controlled vocabulary. But they also strive to represent different document topics separately by observing conditions of coextensive indexing. If aspect views are taken into account, they can be modeled within the structure of the indexing language or expressed explicitly via role operators. These ideas are known as coordinate respective syntactical indexing and can be summarized in tabular form as shown in Table 10.1:

Tab. 10.1: Properties of the classical indexing and retrieval model.

Indexing	Retrieval	Features
Coordinate indexing	Boolean retrieval	Retrieval categorization Linguistic normalization Relevance ranking
Syntactical indexing	Syntactical retrieval	Aspects by categories, facets Syntax operators between facets

In our model, we extend this well-known view by various components and speak of the extension as *ontology-based indexing and retrieval*. In tabular form, this looks as is shown in Table 10.2:

Tab. 10.2: Properties of the ontology-based indexing and retrieval model.

Indexing	Retrieval	Features
Ontology-based indexing	Ontology-based retrieval	Typed (aspect specified) relations Search for typed relations Inferences about typed relations

First, we extend the understanding of concept ordering in indexing languages to structuring of entities in knowledge representations with faceted structures and typed relations between the entities. Then we are interested in a particular connection between the typed relations and the syntactic features of a citation order in order to achieve best possible forms of a coextensive and consistent formulation of complex topics.

We model syntactic features of a citation order by cross-faceted typed relations and inferences along their edges. Thus, retrieval conditions can be formulated which otherwise can only be achieved by using methods of syntactic indexing and their dedicated indexing languages.

The cross-faceted typed relations which serve as selection criteria for creating document sets, are supported by inferences about the relation paths. The following factors give a more detailed description of the approach and justify it to speak of *ontology-based indexing*:

- The knowledge representation arranges the entities in facets with hierarchical relations and synonyms as *a priori* relationships. This structure is used for conceptual navigation (by hierarchy and internal facets association) and query expansion by synonyms within a conceptual aspect
- An inventory of typed relations is used which allows the combination of entities from different facets considering aspect orientation
- In this model indexing means that document-specific topics are represented by entities and the relationships between the various entities

The selection of entities for the search process is carried out by a navigation task in the knowledge representation. It is supported by analysis and selection of the relationships that were modeled by typed relations between the entities. Speaking of an *ontology-based retrieval* may be justified by fulfilling the following issues. This list is an enhancement of the list consisting of the three features given above:

- Performing query expansion by synonyms within a conceptual aspect
- Inferences about the paths of hierarchical relationships (search-down / explosion / expand / drill-down)

- Boolean operations on two or more entities including their inferred entities from hierarchical relationships within a facet to represent complex search queries
- Boolean operations on two or more different entities of aspect-oriented facets including their inferred entities from hierarchical relationships within a facet to represent more complex search queries
- Boolean operations on two or more different entities that need not be indexed individually under conditions of the presence of typed relations as expanded selection criteria
- As the case may be, consideration of syntax indicators, several networks or ontologies and specialized inferences

The introduced model does clearly not solve every problem of indexing and retrieval discussed in previous sections. In particular, the consequences for an indexing of complex document issues need to be laid down in a more precise way. The topics of documents can arise with the aid of relations which are not included in the *a priori* inventory of language documentation. It is particularly difficult to make general statements when the boundary between the *a priori* and the *a posteriori* character of relationships is not clearly pronounced. For example, an action – product relationship can be seen as a typed relation or an *a posteriori* aspect and consequently lead to different indexing results. Advanced methods of syntactic indexing use role operators to specify directional relationships. This produces particular good results if the indexing language is adapted to the particular method, as we have seen with *PRECIS*. This situation cannot readily be generalized, especially not for heterogeneous information environments. Our approach therefore developed a proposal to replace certain types of syntactic indexing with the combination of cross-faceted typed relations and inferences about the edges. It is not possible to already present all achievable goals.

Evidently, the sum of issues present more a program for future elaboration than a description of the state-of-the-art. The final stage may be characterized as *ontology-based indexing and retrieval* with respect to semantic interoperability in the Web context. Combining the methodological approaches to the semantic representation methods of the Semantic Web provides the opportunity to separate from proprietary application contexts. Already developed knowledge structures can be used for or shared with other applications in the sense of a content-oriented semantic interoperability.

11 Remaining Research Questions

In the previous chapter we have made a number of suggestions of how the strength of semantic knowledge representation could be combined with well-known indexing methods. We demonstrated by means of examples the potential of this combination, which we see in the generation of ontological, logically valid indexing data that is both cognitively and machine-interpretable. As already outlined in our introduction in Chapter 1, the conception of an information system unifying these functionalities is a visionary one.

Finally, we would like to spotlight the most relevant remaining research questions, which were raised in Part C. We believe that these research questions are essential for further concretions of the visionary approach and for promoting the development of semantic information spaces. The question that we deem to be worth asking can be separated into three categories of modeling, procedure and technology, and implementation.

11.1 Questions of Modeling

The open research questions of modeling are concerning methodical aspects of developing a general inventory of typed relations and logical aspects of transitivity properties within those inventories, as well as aspects of time-related changes of conceptualizations.

The development of inventories of typed relations is an issue, which clearly has a methodological deficit. Part C provided an overview of several attempts for analyzing resp. constructing inventories of typed relations (cf. Chapter 8), which showed rather heterogeneous ways of an approach and no established method of construction. Beyond that, it has not succeeded yet to develop a general inventory, which would be adequate for a consistent representation of cross-domain knowledge. Further research should take on this issue and work out a solid methodical basis for typification processes and for the consistent representation of domain-independent knowledge.

In Chapter 9 we introduced an understanding of inferences in the sense of logically defined "walk-throughs" between entities of knowledge structures, with the goal of creating extended access points to relevant documents in an information retrieval process. In this context, we also addressed the question, if those "walk-throughs" could also be reasonably implemented between entities that are connected by various types of relations. In other words: can transitive statements be derived from a set of entities, even if these entities built a network with not just one single type of relation, but with different types of relations?

Related to different types of associative relations, we noted that the derivation of transitive statements could be possible, provided that the relations are of the type “abstraction”, “part-whole”, or “chronology” (cf. Chapter 9). However, we had to qualify this assumption, as we have pointed out that even here some exceptional cases can appear, which may lead to inferred results that deemed to be invalid. Testing this assumption and bringing more certainty in this modeling task seems to be a relevant open question.

Regardless of specificity and extent, all knowledge structures represent a particular part of knowledge according to a certain point in time. So these representations remain static, while the world’s knowledge is subject to constant change, which is reflected in changes of conceptualizations. Consequently, a given knowledge structure needs occasional adaptation to these changes for remaining its validity and relevance. Further research in this field should focus on these time-related adaptations and the associated effects on interoperability between two or more knowledge representations. One of the core questions in this context could be, if there is a trade-off between the degree of time-related validity and relevance of a knowledge representation and its degree of interoperability?

11.2 Questions of Procedure

Questions of procedure emerge from engineering tasks of knowledge representations, notably of ontologies as the most complex representations. Typical engineering tasks could be the development of a new ontology, the modification of an existing ontology for application purposes, the merging of two or more ontologies into a single one or merely the harmonization of two or more ontologies for making them interoperable. All these engineering tasks pose questions about the adequate procedures.

In this context we consider methods of automatic indexing to be of relevance. It seems likely to use these established automation instruments for identifying meaningful terms from a given document collection and use them as a vocabulary from which a new ontology could be built up and used for indexing purposes.[84] Beyond that, one could think of not only using the entities of an ontology as descriptors in an indexing process, but also the existing semantic relations between the entities. Methods of automatic indexing could make this possible in a rather simple way, e.g. by adding to each entity that was allocated as a descriptor to a document, its outgoing semantic relations in an encoded form. In doing

84 A broad introduction into methods of automatic indexing is provided by Moens (2002).

so, a more extensive part of the knowledge structure would be added to the documents during the indexing process.

It also seems to be worth thinking about adding the entities from the other end of the semantic relations to the indexed documents – this could generate document-specific word clusters, which in turn could be used as a basis for more elaborated clustering techniques. It is of course questionable whether these ideas might actually bring concrete benefits for the descriptive power of indexing, the usefulness of ontologies in indexing processes or in the quality of information retrieval. Nevertheless, these research questions should be investigated.

Merging or harmonizing tasks of two or more knowledge structures, and particularly ontologies, are performed by numerous matching techniques. Euzenat and Shvaiko (2010) provide an overview on these techniques, which are mainly based upon algorithmically driven statistical, linguistic or structural comparisons. Also in this area many open research questions have to be investigated to find better solutions. These research questions may lead to new matching techniques, e.g. techniques that are able to discover and exploit the specific knowledge of the ontology's particular background domain or an approach for dealing automatically with multilingual knowledge structures (ibid., 269–272). Besides the advances in matching techniques, Euzenat and Shvaiko indicate some more trends, in the fields of matching strategies (e.g. how can various matching techniques be combined?) and matching systems (e.g. the ability of handling multiple input forms of knowledge representation resp. ontologies) (ibid., 272–273). We limit ourselves to stress the importance of these developments in informatics for the further dissemination and acceptance of semantic knowledge representation.

Another question of procedure accompanies with methods of syntactic indexing, to which we referred to repeatedly in this book. As we pointed out in Part C, there seems to be a trade-off between the benefits of syntactic indexing, which lies – as we have seen – in the high degree of document-specific, descriptive power and the ideal conception of semantic interoperability in heterogeneous information spaces. From this assumption we derive our preliminary conclusion that ideas of semantic interoperability and syntactic indexing are hard to combine. However, our suggestion of realizing a syntactic indexing-like functionality by establishing a combination of cross-faceted relationships and inference mechanisms needs to be tested and evaluated within further research. Until these testing and evaluation tasks are carried out, the suggestion of Part C must be seen as a rather vague idea.

This leads us to our third and last category of remaining research questions, which addresses aspects of technology and implementation to provide adequate search environments for testing and evaluating.

11.3 Questions of Technology and Implementation

Questions of technology and implementation arise from the necessity of providing search environments for testing and evaluating purposes, as well as for the development of prototype knowledge organization systems.

In the context of knowledge representation, technology driven questions mainly concerning decision problems on choosing adequate representational standards. In Chapter 3 we have discussed the established web-based representation languages *RDF* and *OWL*, and the application-based languages *XTM* and *SKOS*. As we pointed out, these languages differ not only in application purposes, but also in terms of complexity and representational power. Further research should focus on how to choose the adequate representation language for a given knowledge modeling. Obviously, there are interdependencies between these issues and the questions of modeling described in Section 11.1. Systematic investigation could lead to a framework for technology assessment for the design of ontology-based information retrieval systems or – in a broader sense – semantic information spaces.

After all, the design of those search environments is essential, when it comes to testing and evaluating the practical use of all modeling considerations we made in the previous chapters. In summary, we see need for further research in the field of modeling for gaining methodical consistency in the development of knowledge structures, in the field of procedure and implementation for handling various engineering tasks in the context of knowledge representation, and in field of technology and implementation for choosing and implementing adequate technologies and designing the "right" information systems. It becomes clear, that there is still much work to do until our vision of a productive use of semantic knowledge representation in information retrieval becomes reality. Finally, we hope that this book can be a modest contribution to this work and that it is read and understood as an encouragement and invitation to keep on the work on this fascinating and forward-looking issue.

Part D
Appendices

Systematic Glossary

This glossary contains primarily the terms which have been specifically introduced for our presentation, or are used at least in a different meaning. Its primary goal is to enable a rapid access to this concepts within their systematic context. An additional alphabetic access has been provided by integrating the terms into the alphabetical back-of-the-book index.

Some of the entries may look rather artificial. They were introduced to distinguish conceptual units more precisely giving reference to their occurrence as real world elements, as elements of indexing languages or knowledge representations, as elements of indexing results or as elements of search formulations. For a visualization of the different planes, we refer to Figure 7.4 in Section 7.3. If necessary, the kind of relationships between the respective elements should also be expressed by specific terminological elements.

It is necessary to give a comment for not considering the terms *indexing language* and *knowledge representation* in this glossary. Both terms are assumed to be generally known and will not specifically be defined. They have originated from different subject fields but are frequently used without respecting a sufficiently sharp conceptual shape. At present, there is no clear distinction between their meaning and use in the literature. Sometimes it is necessary to make a substantial difference between them, especially if regarding the characteristics of formal knowledge representations (e.g. expert systems) for drawing inferences. But sometimes it is justified to regard them as conceptually exchangeable (e.g. if speaking generally of all elements representing concepts in a knowledge structure). Therefore, in one context of our discussion we have to use the terms in their narrower and specific meaning, and in another context we will regard them as exchangeable, sometimes we will mention them both.

A Conceptual reference objects

Used for conceptual or terminological units on the real world stage.
For conceptual units on the stage of search processes, see terms under B.
For conceptual units on the stage of indexing languages or knowledge representations, *see* terms under C.
For conceptual units on the stage of indexing results, *see* terms under D.

A1 Concepts
Representations of concrete or abstract, real-life or fictive things or aspects of things.

A2 Terms
Linguistic representations of concepts, strings respectively.

A3 Semantic relations
Connections between concepts based on their semantic content.

A4 Topics
Topics refer to things in the world that are described via concepts and semantic relations.

B Query types

Used for conceptual or terminological units on the stage of search processes.
For conceptual units on the stage of real world phenomena, *see* terms under A.
For conceptual units on the stage of indexing languages or knowledge representations, *see* terms under C.
For conceptual units on the stage of indexing results, *see* terms under D.
For query types and conceptual exploration expressed by entities of an indexing language or knowledge representation, *see* C4.

B1 String-based query
Strings are used in query formulation that do not necessarily match terms of any concepts or topics.

B2 Conceptual query
Terms used in query formulation represent concepts.

B3 Topical query
Terms used in query formulation represent topics.

B4 Exploration
Semantic relations are utilized for query-reformulation or query modification (Knowledge exploration).

C Elements modeled in indexing languages or knowledge representations

Used for conceptual or terminological units on the stage of indexing languages or knowledge representations.
For conceptual units on the stage of real world phenomena, *see* terms under A.
For conceptual units on the stage of search processes, *see* terms under B.
For conceptual units on the stage of indexing results, *see* terms under D.

C1 Entities
Representations of concepts in indexing languages or knowledge representations.

C1.1 Simple entities
Entity that represents exactly one concept and is represented by a term that consist of exactly one string.

C1.2 Complex entities
Entity that can be characterized by a form of complexity either in denomination or its conceptual components.

C1.2.1 Terminologically complex entities
Entity that is represented by a term that consists of more than one string.

C1.2.2 Conceptually complex entities
Entity represents a complex concept with a multifaceted character.

C1.3 Core meaning of entities
In their core meaning, entities refer to concrete or abstract, real-life or fictive things in the world. Their core meaning is independent of the information resources to which the entities are assigned.

C1.4 Contextual meaning of entities
In their contextual meaning, entities refer to aspects of concrete or abstract, real-life or fictive things in the world, putting things in relation to other. Their contextual meaning can be dependent of the information resources to which the entities terms are assigned.

C1.5 Pre-combined entities
Entities with more than one conceptual component without making them explicit by formal or syntactical devices.

C1.5.1 Built entities
Entities with more than one conceptual component without making them explicit by formal or syntactical devices.

C1.5.2 Syntactic entities
Entities with more than one conceptual component with making them explicit by formal or syntactical devices.

C2 Indexing language terms
Linguistic representations of entities.

C3 Intrasystem relations
Semantic a priori relations between entities of one indexing language based on the semantic relationships between the concepts modeled by the entities.

C3.1 Typed relations
Semantic relations between entities of one indexing language with formal characterization of type and properties.

C3.2 Inference
Drawing machine-supported conclusions on the basis of modeled relationships in a knowledge representation.

C3.3 Induced inference
Deriving result sets by use of retrieval tools.

C3.4 Transitive closure
Set of all documents that can be generated formally by inference processes along the edges of the relation specified and by including the induced inferences for the assigned nodes.

C4 Entity-based searches
Searches for subject topics using entities of an indexing language or knowledge representation.

C4.1 Entity-based queries
Terms used in query formulation to represent entities of an indexing language or knowledge representation.

C4.2 Entity-based exploration
Query enhancement by user-machine feedback on the basis of the conceptual structure underlying the indexing language or knowledge representation.

D Elements specific for subject indexing data

Used for conceptual or terminological units on the stage of indexing languages or knowledge representations.
For conceptual units on the real world stage, *see* terms under A.
For conceptual units on the stage of search processes, *see* terms under B.
For conceptual units on the stage of indexing languages or knowledge representations, *see* terms under C.

D1 Indexates
Results of a subject indexing process. Representations of topics of concrete information resources with recourse to the modeled entities of an indexing language or knowledge representation.

D1.1 Elementary indexates
Indexates that consist of exactly one entity and are represented by the respective term of an indexing language or knowledge representation.

D1.2 Built indexates
Indexates that are constructed with recourse to two or more entities.

D1.2.1 Compound indexates
Built indexates that are represented by terms that formally do not reveal all their conceptual components.

D1.2.2 Composed indexates
Built indexates that are represented by different terms for the conceptual components they contain.

D1.2.3 Syntactic indexates
Built indexates that are represented by terms for the conceptual components they contain as well as by syntactic connectors that make explicit their constituting a posteriori relations.

E Elements specific for semantic interoperability

E1 Semantic interoperability
Interoperability between entities based on their linguistic representation or their semantic content regarding intersystem relationships.

E1.1 Term-based interoperability / String-based interoperability
Semantic interoperability between entities based on their linguistic representation viz. their IL terms. Considered only for reasons of completeness, not object of discussion.

E1.2 Entity-based interoperability / Conceptual interoperability
Semantic interoperability between entities based on their semantic content.

E1.3 Semantic congruence
Entities can be regarded as conceptual interoperable to a comparatively high degree for search interests.

E2 Entity-based mapping approaches
Methods for establishing entity-based interoperability.

E2.1 Focused mapping
Entity-based interoperability is determined by the core meaning of entities.

E2.2 Comprehensive mapping
Entity-based interoperability is determined by the contextual meaning of entities.

E3 Equivalent intersystem relationship
A priori relations holding between entities of different indexing languages that are either truly semantically equivalent or at least deemed as semantically equivalent for retrieval purposes.

E3.1 Undifferentiated interoperability
Semantic interoperability on the basis of equivalent intersystem relations with unclear (semantic) characteristics.

E3.2 Differentiated interoperability
Different types of semantic interoperability between entities on the basis of equivalent intersystem relations with exposed semantic characteristics are made explicit.

E3.2.1 Specified intersystem relationship
Equivalent intersystem relations exhibit specific information being valid exclusively in one direction. The type of specification may refer either to the conceptual or to the applicational level of entities.

E3.2.2 Identical intersystem relationship
Equivalent intersystem relations holding between conceptually identical entities.

E3.2.3 Containment intersystem relationship
Equivalent intersystem relations holding between entities whereat the concept one entity represents is contained in the concept the other entity represents. Inclusion intersystem relations consist of two inverse transitive relations.

E3.2.4 Perspective intersystem relationship
Equivalent intersystem relations holding between entities with strongly overlapping meaning that mainly differ in respect to their perspective.

E3.2.5 Degrees of determinacy
Method for typing intersystem relationships by numerical figures that add application-oriented content to the established equivalent intersystem relations.

E3.3 Uni-directional interoperability
Entities seen as access and a target vocabulary.

E3.4 Bi-directional interoperability
Exchangeable entities.

E.4 Interoperability models
Models of semantic interoperability with respect to conceptual exchangeability of entities.

E4.1 Reference model of semantic interoperability
Interoperability of entities of two different knowledge representations is established by reference from an entity of the first knowledge representation to an entity of the second knowledge representation.

E4.2 **Correspondence model of semantic interoperability**
Interoperability of entities is seen as a bi-directional interchangeability of various entities of knowledge representations.

Abbreviations

AACR	Anglo-American Cataloging Rules
ALCTS	Association for Library Collections and Technical Services
ANSI/NISO	American National Standards Institute / National Information Standards Organization
ASIST	American Society for Information Science and Technology
BC	Bliss Classification
BC2	Bliss Classification, 2nd ed.
BMBF	Bundesministerium für Bildung und Forschung
BNF	Bibliothèque Nationale de France
BS	British Standard
CAS	Chemical Abstracts Service
CC	Colon Classification
CDLR	Center for Digital Library Research
CENL	Conference of European National Libraries
COMPASS	COMPuter Aided Subject System
CRG	Classification Research Group
DDC	Dewey Decimal Classification
DFG	Deutsche Forschungsgemeinschaft
DNB	Deutsche Nationalbibliothek
DOPE	Drug Ontology Project for Elsevier
DTD	Document Type Definitions
EDINA	Jisc-designated national data centre at the University of Edinburgh
GND	Gemeinsame Normdatei / Integrated Authority File
FRBR	Functional Requirements for Bibliographic Records
FRSAD	Functional Requirements for Subject Authority Data
GESIS	Leibniz-Institut für Sozialwissenschaften
HILT	High-Level Thesaurus
IAEA	International Atomic Energy Agency
IFLA	International Federation of Library Associations and Institutions
INIS	International Nuclear Information System
INIS/ETDE	International Nuclear Information System / Energy Technology Data Exchange
IR	Information Retrieval
ISO	International Standardization Organization
JISC	Joint Information Systems Committee
KoMoHe	Competence Center Modeling and Treatment of Semantic Heterogeneity
KOS	Knowledge Organization System
LCSH	Library of Congress Subject Headings
LMI	Link Management Interface
MACS	Multilingual ACcess to Subjects
MADS	Metadata Description Schema
MODS	Metadata Object Description Schema
OCLC	Online Computer Library Center
OWA	Open World Assumption

OWL	Web Ontoloy Language
OWL DL	OWL Description Logic
PRECIS	PREserved Context Index System
Rameau	Répertoire d'autorité-matière encyclopédique et alphabétique unifié
RDF	Resource Description Framework
RDFS	Resource Description Framework Schema
RIF	Rule Interchange Format
SGML	Standard Generalized Markup Language
SKOS	Simple Knowledge Organization System
SKOS Core MVS	SKOS Core Mapping Vocabulary Specification
SNL	Swiss National Library
SPARQL	Protocol and RDF Query Language
SWD	Schlagwortnormdatei
TAO	Topics, Associations, Occurrences (of Topic Maps)
ThesSoz	Thesaurus for Social Sciences
TREC	Text REtrieval Conference
UDC	Universal Decimal Classification
UML	Unified Modeling Language
URI	Unified Resource Identifier
URL	Unified Resource Locator
W3C	World Wide Web Consortium
WWW	World Wide Web
XML	Extensible Markup Language
XTM	XML Topic Maps

List of figures

All figures were created by the authors. Some of them are screen shots of software applications or Web pages.

Chapter 4

Chapter 5

Chapter 6

Chapter 7

Chapter 8

Chapter 9

Chapter 10

List of tables

Chapter 10

References

Additional references that were not cited in the context of our presentation can be found at: http://ixtrieve.fh-koeln.de/LitIE/.

Almeida, M.B. (2013). Revisiting ontologies: a necessary clarification. *Journal of the American Society for Information Science and Technology*, 64(8), 1682–1693.

American Library Association / Subcommittee on Subject Relationships/Reference Structures (1997). Final Report to the ALCTS/CCS Subject Analysis Committee. June 1997. Retrieved from http://web2.ala.org/ala/alctscontent/CCS/committees/subjectanalysis/subjectrelations/finalreport.cfm.

ANSI/NISO (2005). Guidelines for the construction, format and management of monolingual controlled vocabularies. Bethesda, MD: NISO Press.

Antoniou, G., & Harmelen, F. v. (2008). A Semantic Web primer (2nd ed.). Cambridge, Mass.: MIT Press.

ASIS&T Thesaurus of Information Science, Technology and Librarianship (3rd ed.). (2005). Medford, NJ: Information Today.

Assem, M. v., Malaisé, V., Miles, A., & Schreiber, G. (2006). A method to convert thesauri to SKOS. In Domingue, J et al. (eds.), *The Semantic Web: research and applications, 3rd European Semantic Web conference (ESWC 2006)*, 95–109. Berlin: Springer.

Austin, D. (1969a). Prospects for a new general classification. *Journal of librarianship*, 1, 149–169.

Austin, D. (1969b). The new general faceted classification: an outline of the CRG scheme. *Catalogue and index*, 14, 11–13.

Austin, D. (1976a). The CRG research into a freely faceted scheme. In Maltby, A. (ed.), *Classification in the 1970s*. (rev. ed.), 158–194. London: Bingley.

Austin, D. (1976b). Citation order and linguistic structure. In Boyd Rayward, W. (ed.), *The variety of librarianship. Essays in honor of J. W. Metcalfe*, 19–46. Sydney: Library Association of Australia.

Austin, D. (1984). PRECIS: a manual of concept analysis and subject indexing. (2nd ed.). London: British Library.

Austin, D. (1987). PRECIS: Introduction. In *Encyclopedia of library and information science*, 42, Suppl.7, 375–422. New York, NY: Dekker.

Austin, D. (2009). PRECIS. ELIS Classic, from 1987. *Encyclopedia of library and information science*. (3rd ed.), 4251–4271. London: Taylor and Francis.

Bates, M.J. (1989). The design of browsing and berrypicking techniques for the online search interface. *Online Review*, 13(5), 407–424.

Bayer, O., Höhfeld, S., Josbächer, F., Kimm, N., Kradepohl, I., Kwiatkowski, M., Puschmann, C., Sabbagh, M., Werner, N., & Vollmer, U. (2005). Evaluation of an ontology-based knowledge-management-system. A case study of Convera Retrieval Ware 8.0. *Information Services & Use*, 25(3/4), 181–195.

Bean, C.A. (ed.) (2001). Relationships in the organization of knowledge. Boston: Kluwer Academic.

Beckett, D. (2004). RDF/XML syntax specification (revised). W3C recommendation. Retrieved from http://www.w3.org/TR/REC-rdf-syntax.

Beckett, D., & Berners-Lee, T. (2011). Turtle – terse RDF triple language. W3C team submission. Retrieved from http://www.w3.org/TeamSubmission/turtle.

Begthol, C. (1986). Semantic validity: concepts of warrant in bibliographic classification systems. *Library resources and technical services*, 30(2), 109–125.
Berners-Lee, T., & Connolly, D. (2011). Notation3 (N3): A readable RDF syntax. W3C team submission. Retrieved from http://www.w3.org/TeamSubmission/n3.
Berners-Lee, T., Hendler, J., & Lassila, O. (2001). The Semantic Web. A new form of web content that is meaningful to computers will unleash a revolution of new possibilities. *Scientific American*, 284(5), 35–43.
Bibel, W., Hölldobler, S., & Schaub, T. (1993). Wissensrepräsentation und Inferenz: eine grundlegende Einführung. Wiesbaden: Vieweg.
Bizer, C., Heath, T., & Berners-Lee, T. (2009). Linked data – the story so far. *International Journal of semantic web and information systems*, 5(3), 1–22.
Bliss Bibliographic Classification - BC2: introduction and auxiliary schedules (2nd ed.). (1992). Mills, J. (ed.) London: Butterworths.
Boteram, F. (2008). Semantische Relationen in Dokumentationssprachen: vom Thesaurus zum semantischen Netz. Köln, Fachhochschule, Institut für Informationswissenschaft. Retrieved from http://www.fbi.fh-koeln.de/institut/papers/kabi/volltexte/band054.pdf.
Boteram, F, Gödert, W., & Hubrich, J. (2009). Thematische Recherche und Interoperabilität: Wege zur Optimierung des Zugriffs auf heterogen erschlossene Bestände. Retrieved from http://www.opus-bayern.de/bib-info/volltexte//2009/782/ [urn:nbn:de:0290-opus-7828].
Boteram, F., & Hubrich, J. (2010). Specifying intersystem relations: requirements, strategies, and issues. *Knowledge organization*, 37(3), 216–222.
Boteram, F. (ed.) (2011) Concepts in Context: Proceedings of the Cologne Conference on Interoperability and Semantics in Knowledge Organization, July 19th - 20th, 2010. Würzburg: Ergon.
Boteram, F. (2011). Integrating Semantic Interoperability into FRSAD. In Boteram, F. (ed.), *Concepts in Context. Proceedings of the Cologne Conference on Interoperability and Semantics in Knowledge Organization, July 19–20, 2010*, 169–180. Würzburg: Ergon.
Bray, T., Hollander, D., Layman, A., Tobin, R., & Thompson, H. S. (2009). Namespaces in XML 1.0. W3C recommendation (3rd ed.). Retrieved from http://www.w3.org/TR/REC-xml-names.
Bray, T., Paoli, J., Sperberg-McQueen, C. M., Maler, E., & Yergeau, F. (2008). Extensible markup language (XML) 1.0. W3C recommendation (5th ed.). Retrieved from http://www.w3.org/TR/2008/REC-xml-20081126.
Broughton, V. (2001). Faceted classification as a basis for knowledge organization in a digital environment: the Bliss Bibliographic Classification as a model for vocabulary management and the creation of multi-dimensional knowledge structures. *New review of hypermedia and multimedia*, 7(7), 67–102.
Bruijn, J. de (2003). Using ontologies. Enabling knowledge sharing and reuse on the Semantic Web. DERI technical report DERI-2003-10-29. Retrieved from http://www.deri.org/fileadmin/documents/DERI-TR-2003-10-29.pdf.
BS 8723-2 (2005). Structured vocabularies for information retrieval – Guide – Thesauri. London: British Standards Institution.
Buchanan, B. (1979). Theory of library classification. London: Bingley.
Buckland, M., & Gey, F. (1994). The relationship between recall and precision. *Journal of the American Society for Information Science*, 45(1), 12–19.

Castells, P., Fernández, M., & Vallet, D. (2007). An adaption of the vector-space model for ontology-based information retrieval. IEEE Transactions on knowledge and data engineering, 19(2), 261–272.

Chan, L. M., & Zeng, M. L. (2004). Trends and issues in establishing interoperability among knowledge organization systems. *Journal of the American Society for Information Science and Technology*, 55(5), 377–395.

Chaplan, M. A. (1995). Mapping laborline thesaurus terms to Library of Congress subject headings: implications for vocabulary switching. *Library Quarterly*, 65(1), 39–61.

Classification Research Group (1969). Classification and information control: Papers representing the work of the Classification Research Group during 1960–1968. London: Library Association.

Classification Research Group (1985). The need for a faceted classification as the basis of all methods of information retrieval. In Chan, L. M. (ed.), *Theory of subject analysis: a sourcebook*, 154–167. Littleton, CO: Libraries Unlimited.

Clavel-Merrin, G., Žumer, M., & Landry, P. (2006). Report on cross-language subject access options (deliverable 3.4). Retrieved from http://www.nuk.uni-lj.si/telmemor/docs/D3.4-Cross-language-access.pdf.

Coates, E. J. (1969). CRG proposals for a new general classification. In *Classification and information control. Papers representing the work of the Classification Research Group during 1960–1968*, 19–22. London: Library Association.

Connolly, D. W. (2006). Web naming and addressing overview. Retrieved from http://www.w3.org/Addressing.

Cool, C., & Belkin, N. J. (2011). Interactive information retrieval: history and background. In Ruthven, I. et al. (eds.), *Interactive information seeking, behavior and retrieval*, 1–14. London: Facet Publishing.

Cruse, D. A. (2002). Hyponymy and its varieties.In Green, R. (ed.), *The semantics of relationships: an interdisciplinary perspective*, 3–21. Dordrecht: Kluwer.

Deerwester, S. C., Dumais, S. T., Landauer, T. K., Furnas, G. W., & Harshman, R. A. (1990). Indexing by latent semantic analysis. *Journal of the American Society for Information Science*, 41(6), 391–407.

Denton, W.: How to make a faceted classification and put it on the Web. Retrieved from http://www.miskatonic.org/library/facet-web-howto.html.

Dextre-Clarke, S. (2011). In pursuit of interoperability: Can we standardize mapping types? In Boteram, F. (ed.), *Concepts in context. Proceedings of the Cologne conference on interoperability and semantics in knowledge organization, July 19–20, 2010*, 91–110. Würzburg: Ergon.

Dextre Clarke, S. G. (2011). Knowledge Organization System Standards. In *Encyclopedia of library and information science*. (3rd ed.), 3164–3175. London: Taylor and Francis.

Dunsire, G., & Nicholson, D. (2010). Signposting the crossroads: terminology Web services and classification-based interoperability. *Knowledge organization*, 37(4), 280–286.

Efthimiadis, E. (1996). Query expansion. In Williams, M. E. (ed.), *Annual review of information systems and technology*, 31, 121–187.

Ellis, D. (1996). Progress and problems in information retrieval. London: Library Assoc. Publ.

Euzenat, J., & Shvaiko, P. (2010). Ontology matching. Berlin: Springer.

Fellbaum, C. (1998). WordNet. An electronic lexical database. Cambridge, Mass.: MIT Press.

Foskett, D. J. (1970). Classification for a general index language: a review of recent research by the Classification Research Group. London: Library Association.

Fuhr, N., & Nottelmann, H. (2003). Evaluating different methods of estimating retrieval quality for resource selection. In *Proceedings of the 26th annual international ACM SIGIR conference on research and development in information retrieval*, 290–297. New York, NY: ACM.

Functional Requirements for Subject Authority Data (FRSAD) : a conceptual model. (2011). Zeng, M. L. (ed.). Berlin: De Gruyter Saur. Retrieved from http://www.ifla.org/files/classification-and-indexing/functional-requirements-for-subject-authority-data/frsad-final-report.pdf.

Garshol, L. M.: Tolog: a Topic Map query language. Retried from http://www.ontopia.net/topicmaps/materials/tolog.html.

Garshol, L. M. (2005). Metadata? Thesauri? Taxonomies? Topic Maps!: making sense of it all. *Journal of information science*, 30(4), 378–391. Retrieved from http://www.ontopia.net/topicmaps/materials/tm-vs-thesauri.html.

Garshol, L. M. (2002). What are Topic Maps? Retrieved from http://www.xml.com/pub/a/2002/09/11/topicmaps.html.

Geroimenko, V. (2003). Dictionary of XML technologies and the Semantic Web. London: Springer.

Gödert, W. (1987). Zum Problem der Äquivalenzrelation in Dokumentationssprachen. *Nachrichten für Dokumentation*, 38 (2), 91–94.

Gödert, W. (2007). Multilingualität und Lokalisierung zur Wissenserkundung: oder vom Nutzen semantischer Netze für das Information Retrieval. In Weigel, H. (ed.), *Wa(h)re Information. 29. Österreichischer Bibliothekartag Bregenz, 19.–23.09.2006*, 233–242. Graz-Feldkirch: Neugebauer.

Gödert, W. (2008). Ontological spine, localization and multilingual access: some reflections and a proposal. In Knull-Schlomann, K. (ed.), *New perspectives on subject indexing and classification: essays in honour of Magda Heiner-Freiling,*. 233–240. Leipzig: Deutsche Nationalbibliothek.

Gödert, W. (2010a). Semantische Wissensrepräsentation und Interoperabilität: Teil 1: Interoperabilität als Weg zur Wissensexploration, *Information - Wissenschaft und Praxis*, 61(1), 5–18.

Gödert, W. (2010b). Semantische Wissensrepräsentation und Interoperabilität: Teil 2: Ein formales Modell semantischer Interoperabilität. *Information - Wissenschaft und Praxis*, 61(1), 19–28.

Gödert, W., Lepsky, K. & Nagelschmidt, M. (2011). Informationserschließung und Automatisches Indexieren: ein Lehr- und Arbeitsbuch. Berlin: Springer.

Green, R., & Bean, C. A. (2006). Aligning systems of relationships. In Raghavan, K. S. (ed.), *Knowledge organization, information systems and other essays: Professor A.Neelameghan Festschrift*, 111–128. New Delhi: Ess Ess.

Green, R. (2008). Making visible hidden relationships in the Dewey Decimal Classification: how relative index terms relate to DDC classes. In Arsenault, C. (ed.), *Culture and identity in knowledge organization: Proceedings of the Tenth International ISKO Conference 5–8 August 2008, Montreal, Canada*, 8–14. Würzburg: Ergon.

Green, R., & Panzer, M. (2011). Relations in the notational hierarchy of the Dewey Decimal Classification. In Slavic, A. (ed.), *Classification and ontology: formal approaches and access to knowledge: proceedings of the International UDC Seminar, 19–20 September 2011, The Hague, The Netherlands*, 161–176. Würzburg: Ergon.

Grossman, D. A., & Frieder, O. (2004). Information retrieval: algorithms and heuristics (2nd ed.). Dordrecht: Springer.

Gruber, T. R. (1993). A translation approach to portable ontology specifications. *Knowledge acquisition*, 5(2), 199–220.

Harken, S. E., et al. (2006). Subject semantic interoperability. Report of the Subcommittee on Semantic Interoperability to the ALCTS Subject Analysis Committee : Final report. University of North Dakota, approved by SAC June 2006. Retrieved from http://www.ala.org/alcts/sites/ala.org.alcts/files/content/mgrps/camms/cmtes/sac/inact/semantic/sacsem_rpt.pdf.

Harman, D. (1992). Relevance feedback revisited. In Belkin, N. (ed.), *Proceedings of the 15th annual international ACM SIGIR conference on research and development in information retrieval*, 1–10. New York, NY: ACM.

Hodge, G. (2000). Systems of knowledge organization for digital libraries: beyond traditional authority files. Wasginton, DC: Digital Library Federation.

Hoppenbrouwers, J. (2001). MACS. Multilingual access to subjects. Architecture of the MACS system. Tilburg: Tilburg University. Retrieved from http://infolab.uvt.nl/pub/hoppenbrouwersj-2001-23.pdf.

Horridge, M., & Patel-Schneider, P. (2012). OWL 2 Web Ontology Language Manchester syntax. W3C working group note 11 december 2012 (2nd ed.). Retrieved from http://www.w3.org/TR/owl2-manchester-syntax.

Hubrich, J. (2010). Thematische Suche in heterogenen Informationsräumen. In Bergner, U. (ed.), *The Ne(x)t generation: das Angebot der Bibliotheken; 30. Österreichischer Bibliothekartag, Graz, 15.–18.9.2009*, 234–242. Graz-Feldkirch: Neugebauer.

Hubrich, J. (2011). Intersystem relations: Characteristics and functionalities. In Boteram, F. (ed.), *Concepts in context: Proceedings of the Cologne Conference on Interoperability and Semantics in Knowledge Organization July 19th – 20th, 2010*, 69–89. Würzburg, Ergon.

Hubrich, J. (2013). Vom Stringmatching zur Begriffsexploration: das Potential integrierter begrifflicher Interoperabilität. In Ohly, H. P. (ed.), *Wissen - Wissenschaft - Organisation: Proceedings der 12. Tagung der Deutschen Sektion der Internationalen Gesellschaft für Wissensorganisation Bonn, 19. bis 21. Oktober 2009*, 161–172 Würzburg: Ergon.

Hunting, S. (2003). How to start topic mapping right away with the XML specification. In Park, J. (ed.), *XML Topic Maps. Creating and using Topic Maps for the web*, 81–101. Boston, MA: Addison-Wesley.

IFLA Study Group on the Functional Requirements for Bibliographic Records. (2009). Functional requirements for bibliographic records (FRBR). Final report.. Retrieved from http://www.ifla.org/files/cataloguing/frbr/frbr_2008.pdf.

IFLA Study Group on the Functional Requirements for Bibliographic Records (1998). Functional requirements for bibliographic records (FRBR). München: Saur.

INFODATA Thesaurus (2000). INFODATA Thesaurus, Version: Oct. 2000. Potsdam: Informationszentrum für Informationswissenschaft und -praxis.

Ingwersen, P. (1992). Information retrieval interaction. London: Taylor Graham.

Isaac, A., Summers, E. (2009). SKOS simple knowledge organization system primer. W3C working group note. Retrieved from http://www.w3.org/TR/skos-primer.

ISO 2788 (1974). Guidelines for the establishment and development of monolingual thesauri (1st ed.). Geneva: ISO.

ISO 5963 (1985). Methods for examining documents, determining their subjects, and selecting indexing terms. Geneva: ISO.

ISO 5964 (1985). Guidelines for the establishment and development of multilingual thesauri. Geneva: ISO.

ISO 13250 (1999). Topic Maps. Information technology. Geneva: ISO.

ISO 13250-2 (2006). Topic Maps – Part 2: data model. Retrieved from http://www.isotopicmaps.org/sam/sam-model.

ISO 25964-1 (2011). Thesauri and interoperability with other vocabularies. Part1: Thesauri for information retrieval. (1st ed.), 2011-08-08. Geneva: ISO.

ISO 25964-2 (2013). Thesauri and interoperability with other vocabularies: Part 2: Interoperability with other vocabularies. (1st ed.), 2013-03-15. Geneva: ISO.

Jacobs, J. H., Mengel, T, & Müller, K. (2010). Benefits of the CrissCross project for conceptual interoperability and retrieval. In Gnoli, C. (ed.), *Paradigms and conceptual systems in knowledge organization. Proceedings of the eleventh international ISKO conference, 23–26 February, Rome, Italy*, 236–241. Würzburg: Ergon.

Jacobs, J. H., Mengel, T., & Müller, K. (2011). Insights and outlooks: a retrospective view on the CrissCross project. In Boteram, F. (ed.), *Concepts in context. Proceedings of the Cologne conference on interoperability and semantics in knowledge organization, July 19–20, 2010*, 37–49. Würzburg: Ergon.

Jahns, Y., & Karg, H. (2011). Translingual retrieval: moving between vocabularies – MACS 2010. In Boteram, F. (ed.), *Concepts in context. Proceedings of the Cologne conference on interoperability and semantics in knowledge organization, July 19–20, 2010*, 51–68. Würzburg: Ergon.

Jouis, C. (2002). Logic of relationships. In Green, R., Bean, C. A. & Myaeng, S. H. (eds.), The semantics of relationships. An interdisciplinary perspective, 127–140. Dordrecht: Kluwer Academic Publ.

Kekäläinen, J., & Järvelin, K. (1998). The impact of query structure and query expansion on retrieval performance. In *Proceedings of the 21st annual international ACM SIGIR conference on research and development in information retrieval*, 130–137. New York, NY: ACM Press.

Köhler, J., et al. (2006). Ontology based text indexing and querying for the semantic web. *Knowledge-based systems*, 19(8), 744–754.

Kowalski, G. (2011). Information retrieval architecture and algorithms. New York, NY: Springer.

Landry, P. (200). Providing multilingual access through linking of subject heading languages: the MACS approach. In Bernardi, R. (ed.), *Proceedings of the workshop on advanced technologies for digital libraries*, 34–37. Bozen: Univ.-Press.

Langville, A., & Meyer, C. (2006). Google's PageRank and beyond. The science of search engine rankings. Princeton: Princeton Univ. Press.

Lenat, D. B. (1995). CYC: A large scale investment in knowledge infrastructure. *Communications of the Association for Computing Machinery*, 38(11), 32–38.

Lenat, D. B., & Guha, R. V. (1990). Building large knowledge-based systems representation and inference in the CYC project. Wokingham: Addison-Wesley.

Lepsky, K., & Vorhauer, J. (2006). Lingo - ein Open source System für die Automatische Indexierung deutschsprachiger Dokumente. *ABI-Technik*, 26(1), 18–28.

Macgregor, G., & McCulloch, E. (2008). Analysis of equivalence mapping for terminology services. *Journal of Information Science*. 34(1), 70–92.

MADS/RDF (2012). MADS/RDF primer (updated: 10th may 2012). Retrieved from http://www.loc.gov/standards/mads/rdf.

Mandala, R., Tokunaga, T., & Hozumi, T. (1998). The use of WordNet in information retrieval. In *COLING/ACL workshop on usage of WordNet in natural language processing systems*, 31–37. Retrieved from http://acl.ldc.upenn.edu/W/W98/W98-0704.pdf.

Marchionini, G. (2006). Exploratory search: From finding to understanding. *Communications of the ACM*, 49(4), 41–46.

Matuszek, C., Cabral, J., & Witbrock, M. (2006). An introduction to the syntax and content of Cyc. In Chitta, B (ed.), *Formalizing and compiling background knowledge and its applications to knowledge representation and question answering. Papers from AAAI spring symposium*, 44–49. Menlo Park, CA: AAAI Press.

Meyer, A. (2013). wiki2rdf: Automatische Extraktion von RDF-Tripeln aus Artikelvolltexten der Wikipedia. *Information - Wissenschaft und Praxis*, 64(2/3), 115–126.

Michel, D. (1997). Taxonomy of Subject Relationships. Retrieved from http://web2.ala.org/ala/alctscontent/CCS/committees/subjectanalysis/subjectrelations/msrscu2.pdf. [Part of: Final Report to the ALCTS/CCS Subject Analysis Committee. June 1997; Retrieved from http://web2.ala.org/ala/alctscontent/CCS/committees/subjectanalysis/subjectrelations/finalreport.cfm].

Miles, A., & Bechhofer, S. (2009a). SKOS Simple Knowledge Organization System. W3C recommendation. Retrieved from http://www.w3.org/TR/skos-reference.

Miles, A., & Bechhofer, S. (2009b). SKOS Simple Knowledge Organization System eXtension for labels (SKOS-XL) namespace document – HTML variant. Retrieved from http://www.w3.org/TR/skos-reference/skos-xl.html.

Miles, A., & Brickley, D. (2004). SKOS mapping vocabulary specification. Retrieved from http://www.w3.org/2004/02/skos/mapping/spec/2004-11-11.html.

Mitchell, J. S. (2001). Relationships in the Dewey Decimal Classification system. In Bean, C. A. (ed.), *Relationships in the organization of knowledge*, 211–226. Boston, MA: Kluwer.

Mitchell, J. S., Zeng, M. L., & Žumer, M. (2011). Extending models for controlled vocabularies to classification systems: modelling DDC with FRSAD. In Slavic, A. (ed.), *Classification and ontology: formal approaches and access to knowledge: proceedings of the International UDC Seminar, 19–20 September 2011, The Hague, The Netherlands*, 241–250. Würzburg: Ergon.

Moens, M.-F. (2002). Automatic indexing and abstracting of document texts. Boston, MA: Kluwer Acad. Publ.

Mooers, C. (1951). Zatocoding applied to meachanical organization of knowledge. *American Documentation*, 2(1), 20–32.

Motik, B., Patel-Schneider, P., & Parsia, B. (2012). OWL 2 Web Ontology Language structural specification and functional style syntax. W3C recommendation (2nd ed.). Retrieved from http://www.w3.org/TR/owl2-syntax.

Murphy, M. L. (2008). Semantic relations and the lexicon: antonymy, synonymy and other paradigms. Cambridge: Cambridge Univ. Press.

Nicholson, D. M., Dawson, A., & Shiri, A. (2006). HILT: a pilot terminology mapping service with a DDC spine. *Cataloging and classification quarterly*, 42(3/4), 187–200.

Nicholson, D., & Neill, S. (2001). Interoperability in subject terminologies: the HILT project. *New Review of Information Networking*, 7(1), 147–158.

Nicholson, D. (2003). Subject-based interoperability: issues from the high-level thesaurus (HILT) project. *International Cataloguing and Bibliographic Control*, 32(1), 14–16.

Nicholson, D., Dawson, A., & Shiri, A. (2006). HILT: a terminology mapping service with a DDC spine. *Cataloguing and Classification Quarterly*, 42(3/4), 187–200.

Odgen, C. K., & Richards, I. A. (1923). The meaning of meaning: a study of the influence of language upon thought and of the science of symbolism. London: Routledge & Kegan Paul.

Panzer, M. (2011). Two tales of a concept: aligning FRSAD with SKOS. In Boteram, F. (ed.), *Concepts in Context. Proceedings of the Cologne Conference on Interoperability and Semantics in Knowledge Organization, July 19–20, 2010*, 157–168. Würzburg: Ergon.

Paralic, J., & Kostial, I. (2003). Ontology-based information retrieval. In *Proceedings of the 14th international conference on information and intelligent systems ILS 2003*, 23–28. Varadzin: FOI.

Park, J. (ed.) (2003). XML topic maps: creating and using topic maps for the Web. Boston: Addison-Wesley.

Pepper, S., Moore, G., & TopicMaps.Org Authoring Group (2001). XML Topic Maps (XTM) 1.0: TopicMaps.Org Specification. Retrieved from http://www.topicmaps.org/xtm/1.0/xtm1-20010806.html.

Pepper, S. (2002). The TAO of topic maps: finding the way in the age of infoglut. Retrieved from http://www.ontopia.net/topicmaps/materials/tao.html.

Pepper, S., Vitali, F., Garshol, L. M., Gessa, N., & Presutti, V. (2006a). A survey of RDF/Topic Maps interoperability proposals. W3C working group note. Retrieved from http://www.w3.org/TR/rdftm-survey.

Pepper, S., Presutti, V., Garshol, L. M., & Vitali, F. (2006b). Guidelines for RDF/Topic Maps interoperability. W3C editor's draft. Retrieved from http://www.w3.org/2001/sw/BestPractices/RDFTM/guidelines-20060630.html.

Pepper, S. (2010). Topic Maps. In *Encyclopedia of library and information science*. (3rd ed.), 5247–5259. New York, NY: Taylor & Francis.

Perreault, J. (1994). Categories and relators: a new schema. *Knowledge organization*, 21(4), 189–198.

Peterson, D., Shudi, G., Ashok, M., Sperberg-McQueen, C. M., & Thompson, H. S. (2012). XML schema definition language (XSD) 1.1. Part 2: Datatypes. Retrieved from http://www.w3.org/TR/xmlschema11-2.

Petras, V., & Mayr, P. (2009). Cross-concordances: terminology mapping and its effectiveness for information retrieval. *International Cataloguing and Bibliographic Control*, 38(3), 43–52.

Pribbenow, S. (2002). Meronymic relationships: from classical mereology to complex part-whole relations. In Green, R. (ed.), *The semantics of relationships: an interdisciplinary perspective*, 35–50. Dordrecht: Kluwer.

Probets, S., O'Brien, A., & Si, L. E. (2010). Integration of distributed terminology resources to facilitate subject cross-browsing for library portal systems. *Aslib Proceedings*, 62(4/5), 70–92.

Putkey, T. (2011). Using SKOS to express faceted classification on the Semantic Web. In *Library Philosophy and Practice*, september(2011). Retrieved from http://unllib.unl.edu/LPP/.

Ranganathan, S. R., et al. (1987). Colon Classification: basic and depth version. (7th ed.). Vol.1: Schedules for classification. Bangalore: Sarada Ranganathan Endowment for Library Science.

Rasmussen, E. (2011). Access models. In Ruthven, I. et al. (eds.), *Interactive information seeking, behavior and retrieval*, 95–111. London: Facet Publishing.

Rath, H. (2003). Topic Map fundamentals for knowledge representation. In Park, J. (ed), *XML Topic Maps. Creating and using Topic Maps for the web*, 357–381. Boston, MA: Addison-Wesley.

Reiner, U. (2008a): Automatic analysis of Dewey Decimal Classification notations. In Preisach, C. (ed.), *Data analysis, machine learning and applications. Proceedings of the 31st Annual Conference of the Gesellschaft für Klassifikation e.V., Albert-Ludwigs-Universität Freiburg, March 7–9, 2007*, 697–704. Berlin: Springer.

Reiner, U. (2008b). DDC-based search in the data of the German National Bibliography. In Knull-Schlomann, K. (ed.), *New pespectives on subject indexing and classification: essays in honour of Magda Heiner-Freiling*, 121–129. Leipzig: Deutsche Nationalbibliothek.

Riesthuis, G. J. A. (2008). Subject searching in merged catalogues: a plea for redundancy. In Knull-Schlomann, K. (ed.), *New perspectives on subject indexing and classification: essays in honour of Magda Heiner-Freiling*, 257–260. Leipzig: Deutsche Nationalbibliothek.

Riesthuis, G. J. A., Landry, P., Chan, L. M., Furner, J., Kunz, M., Leth, P., McGarry, D., McIlwaine, I., Naudi, M., & Zeng, M. L. (2009). Guidelines for multilingual thesauri (IFLA professional reports ; 115. The Hague: IFLA Classification and Indexing Section. Retrieved from http://ifap.ru/library/book411.pdf.

Rijsbergen, C. J. v. (1979). Information retrieval (2nd ed.). London: Butterworths.

Robertson, S. (1997). The probability ranking principle in IR. In Sparck-Jones, K. et al. (eds.), *Readings in information retrieval*, 281–286. San Francisco, Cal.: Morgan Kaufmann.

Robertson, S., & Sparck-Jones, K. (1976). Relevance weighting of search terms. *Journal of the American Society for Information Science and Technology*, 27(3), 129–146.

Salton, G., Yang, C. S., & Wong, A. (1975). A vector-space model for automatic indexing. *Communications of the ACM*, 18(11), 613–620.

Shiri, A., Crawford, R., & Chowdhury, G. (2002). Thesaurus-enhanced search interfaces. *Journal of Information Science*, 28(2), 111–122.

Shudi, G., Sperberg-McQueen, C. M., & Thompson, H. S. (2012). XML schema definition language (XSD) 1.1. Part 1: Structures. Retrieved from http://www.w3.org/TR/xmlschema11-1.

Smiraglia, R., Heuvel, C. van den, & Dousa, D. (2011). Interactions between elementary structures in universes of knowledge. In Slavic, A. (ed.), *Classification and ontology: formal approaches and access to knowledge: proceedings of the International UDC Seminar, 19–20 September 2011, The Hague, The Netherlands*, 25–40. Würzburg: Ergon.

Stock, W. G. (2010). Concepts and semantic relations in information science. *Journal of the American Society for Information Science and Technology*, 61(10), 1951–1969.

Stock, W. G., & Stock, M. (2013). Handbook of Information Science. Berlin: De Gruyter Saur.

Stojanovic, N. (2005). Ontology-based information retrieval: methods and tools for cooperative query answering. Ph.D. thesis: Univ. of Karlsruhe.

Stuckenschmidt, H., Harmelen, F. van, & Waard, A. de (2004). Exploring large document repositories with RDF technology: the DOPE project. *IEEE intelligent systems*, 19(3), 34–40.

Summers, E., Isaac, A., Redding, C., & Krech, D. (2008). LCSH, SKOS and Linked Data. In Greenberg, J. et al. (eds.), *Metadata for semantic and social applications. Proceedings of the international conference on Dublin Core and metadata applications* (DC 2008), 25–33. Göttingen, Univ.-Verl.

Svenonius, E. (2000). The intellectual foundation of information organization. Cambridge, MA: MIT Press.

Tolog language tutorial (2007). Ver. 3.4. Retrieved from http://www.ontopia.net/omnigator/docs/query/tutorial.html.

Tudhope, D., Alani, H., & Jones, C. (2001). Augmenting thesaurus relationships: possibilities for retrieval. *Journal of digital information*, 1(8). Retrieved from http://jodi.ecs.soton.ac.uk/Articles/v01/i08/Tudhope/.

Ullrich, M., Maier, J., & Angele, J. (2003). *T*axonomie, Thesaurus, Topic Map, Ontologie – ein Vergleich. Ontoprise Whitepaper Series. Karlsruhe, Deutschland. Retrieved from http://www.ontoprise.de/content/e1276/e1358/e1362/TaxonomieThesaurusTopicMapOntologiev13_ger.pdf.

Vizine-Goetz, D., Hickey, C., Houghton, A., & Thompson, R. (2004). Vocabulary mapping for terminology services. Journal of Digital Information, 4(4). Retrieved from http://journals.tdl.org/jodi/index.php/jodi/article/view/114/113.

Vatant, B. (2003). Topic Maps from representation to identity. Conversation, names, and published subject indicators. In Park, J. (ed), *XML Topic Maps. Creating and using Topic Maps for the web*, 67–79. Boston, MA: Addison-Wesley.

Weller, K., Peters, I. (2008). *Reconsidering relationships for knowledge representation*. Retrieved from http://i-know.tugraz.at/wp-content/uploads/2008/11/62_reconsidering-relationships-for-knowledge-representation.pdf.

White, R. W., & Roth, R. A. (2009). Exploratory search. Beyond the query-response paradigm. San Rafael: Morgan & Claypool.

World Wide Web Consortium (2007). Semantic layer cake. Retrieved from http://www.w3.org/2007/03/layerCake.png.

World Wide Web Consortium OWL Working Group (2009). OWL 2 Web Ontology Language document overview. W3C recommendation. Retrieved from http://www.w3.org/TR/owl2-overview.

Zapilko, B., & Sure, Y. (2009). Converting the TheSoz to SKOS. Technical reports 2009/7. Bonn: GESIS. Retrieved from http://www.gesis.org/fileadmin/upload/forschung/publikationen/gesis_reihen/gesis_methodenberichte/2009/TechnicalReport_09_07.pdf

Zeng, M., & Panzer, M. (2009). Modeling classification systems in SKOS: Some challenges and best practices. In *Semantic interoperability for Linked Data. Proceedings of the international conference on Dublin Core and metadata applications* (DC 2009), 3–14. Seoul: Corean Library Assoc.

Zeng, M. L. & Žumer, M. (2011). Modeling knowledge organization systems and structures: a discussion in the context of conceptual and data models. In *Proceedings of ISKO UK biennial conference, 4th and 5th July 2011, London*. Preprint. Retrieved from http://www.iskouk.org/conf2011/papers/zumer.pdf.

Zeng, M. L., Žumer, M., Salaba, A., Furner, J., Chan, L. M., O'Neill, E., & Vizine-Goetz, D. (2011). Functinal requirements for subject authority data (FRSAD). A conceptual model. Berlin: De Gruyter Saur.

Žumer, M. (2011). FRSAD: Challenges of modelling the Aboutness. In Boteram, F. (ed.), *Concepts in Context. Proceedings of the Cologne Conference on Interoperability and Semantics in Knowledge Organization, July 19–20, 2010*, 149–156. Würzburg: Ergon.

Index

Printed and bound by CPI Group (UK) Ltd, Croydon, CR0 4YY
13/09/2026
14960850-0001